WEARY OF WAR

LIFE ON THE CONFEDERATE HOME FRONT

JOE A. MOBLEY

Reflections on the Civil War Era
John David Smith, Series Editor

PRAEGER

Westport, Connecticut
London

Library of Congress Cataloging-in-Publication Data

Mobley, Joe A.
Weary of war : life on the Confederate home front / Joe A. Mobley.
    p.   cm. — (Reflections on the Civil War era, ISSN 1939–649X)
    Includes bibliographical references and index.
    ISBN 978–0–275–99202–6 (alk. paper)
    1. Confederate States of America—Social conditions.
2. Confederate States of America—Social life and customs.   3. United
States—History—Civil War, 1861–1865—Social aspects.   I. Title.
    E487.M63   2008
    973.7'13—dc22   2007044132

British Library Cataloguing in Publication Data is available.

Library of Congress Catalog Card Number: 2007044132
ISBN: 978–0–275–99202–6
ISSN: 1939–649X

First published in 2008

Praeger Publishers, 88 Post Road West, Westport, CT 06881
An imprint of Greenwood Publishing Group, Inc.
www.praeger.com

Printed in the United States of America

For Kay

CONTENTS

Series Foreword   vii

Acknowledgments   ix

Introduction   xi

Chapter One: Death, Sickness, and Despair   1

Chapter Two: Agriculture, Industry, and Transportation   19

Chapter Three: Destitution, Poor Relief, and Ersatz   33

Chapter Four: Conscription, Desertion, and Internal Conflict   49

Chapter Five: Slaves, Free Blacks, and Foreigners   65

Chapter Six: Refugees, Cities, and Towns   83

Chapter Seven: Religion, Education, and Cultural Life   103

Chapter Eight: Courtship, Marriage, and Family Life   125

Epilogue   141

Notes   145

Bibliographical Essay   165

Index   169

SERIES FOREWORD

"Like Ol' Man River," the distinguished Civil War historian Peter J. Parish wrote in 1998, "Civil War historiography just keeps rolling along. It changes course occasionally, leaving behind bayous of stagnant argument, while it carves out new lines of inquiry and debate."

Since Confederate general Robert E. Lee's men stacked their guns at Appomattox Court House in April 1865, historians and partisans have been fighting a war of words over the causes, battles, results, and broad meaning of the internecine conflict that cost more than 620,000 American lives. Writers have contributed between 50,000 and 60,000 books and pamphlets on the topic. Viewed in terms of defining American freedom and nationalism, western expansion and economic development, the Civil War quite literally launched modern America. "The Civil War," Kentucky poet, novelist, and literary critic Robert Penn Warren explained, "is for the American imagination, the great single event of our history. Without too much wrenching, it may, in fact, be said to *be* American history."

The books in Praeger's *Reflections on the Civil War Era* series examine pivotal aspects of the American Civil War. Topics range from examinations of military campaigns and local conditions to analyses of institutional, intellectual, and social history. Questions of class, gender, and race run through each volume in the series. Authors, veteran experts in their respective fields, provide concise, informed, and readable syntheses—fresh looks at familiar topics with new source material and original arguments.

"Like all great conflicts," Parish noted in 1999, "the American Civil War reflected the society and the age in which it was fought." Books in *Reflections on the Civil War Era* series interpret the war as a salient event in the hammering out and understanding of American identity before, during, and after the secession crisis of 1860–1861. Readers will find the volumes valuable guides as they chart the troubled waters of mid-nineteenth-century American life.

John David Smith
Charles H. Stone Distinguished Professor of American History
The University of North Carolina at Charlotte

ACKNOWLEDGMENTS

I wish to express my appreciation to several individuals for their assistance in the completion of this work. Many thanks must go to John David Smith, editor of this series, who gave me the opportunity to write the book and encouraged and guided me through the process. I owe a note of thanks to my mentor and friend William C. Harris for lending an interested ear and providing sound advice. I am grateful to Paulette Mitchell for her photograph of the Horton Grove slave quarters and to Elizabeth Wyche for access to Dr. Cyril Granville Wyche's account book. For their assistance in obtaining photographs, thanks are also due to Cindy VanHorn at the Lincoln Museum in Fort Wayne, Indiana; Kim Cumber at the North Carolina State Archives, Raleigh; Eric N. Blevins at the North Carolina Museum of History, Raleigh; J. Dean Knight at Tryon Palace Historic Sites and Gardens, New Bern, North Carolina; Teresa Burke at the Emory University Library, Atlanta, Georgia; and Heather W. Milne at the Museum of the Confederacy, Richmond, Virginia. Most of all, I am indebted to my wife, Kathleen B. (Kay) Wyche. She proofread and corrected the draft; and, as always, her editorial skill, patience, and encouragement proved invaluable. She is a true partner, and this book is dedicated to her.

INTRODUCTION

After almost a century and a half, the Civil War continues to fascinate Americans as perhaps no other event in our history. Like some great family ghost, it prowls through the national psyche and haunts the American imagination.

The Civil War was a pivotal event in the history of the United States. In a crucial sense, it constituted both an end and a beginning in our national experience. Because of the war, the nation that emerged from a baptism of blood and fire in 1865 had been changed. It was radically different from the one that had existed four years earlier. By ending slavery the war transformed social, economic, and political conditions in the country. The conflict confirmed that the nation was indivisible and that the democratic experiment, which much of the Old World viewed with skepticism in the nineteenth century, was still intact. The Civil War also marked the beginning of the end of a national economy based primarily on agriculture. The demands of a wartime economy added an impetus to the Industrial Revolution, which would speed the country away from its simple, agrarian beginnings and rush it pell-mell into the complicated, industrializing twentieth century.

Since the surrender of the Confederate States of America in 1865, thousands of books, pamphlets, and articles have been written about the great sectional conflict. New titles—both history and fiction—appear every year. The motion picture, television, and electronic industries seize on the popularity of the subject for their media presentations and products. Amid this large and constant interest in the Civil War, each generation of historians and enthusiasts has interpreted the causes, events, and significance of the war from various perspectives.

No story of the Civil War is complete without the saga of life on the Confederate home front. For most of the general public, the war's generals, battles, and politics remain the major interests. But in the sectional conflict, as in all wars, there were two major stories—one about soldiers and their leaders on the battlefront, and the other about civilians at home.

In the Confederacy the two "fronts" were not always separate. Fighting took place throughout the South, and the folk at home felt the hard hand of war directly. Their plight has been described as a struggle "behind the lines." But that description is not entirely accurate. For the inhabitants of the Confederacy, there were no fixed battle lines from which they remained distanced. Their war was not fought in some faraway land while they remained safely at home. Instead, it raged in their midst and permeated every aspect of their daily lives. It swept through their farms, into their cities and towns, and along their rivers and highways. As Federal troops invaded the South, death and destruction prevailed all around the native inhabitants, caught in the cross fire of two huge armies wrestling back and forth across the countryside. Not completely unlike their kinsmen and friends in army ranks, civilians in the Confederate states endured their own hardships of sickness, despair, shortages of life's necessities, and a failing morale. Many fled their homes and wandered throughout the South in an attempt to escape the invasion. A large number found themselves unwillingly caught in the maelstrom of vicious fighting for a cause—Confederate nationalism—in which they did not believe. Conversely, for thousands of African American Southerners, the arrival of Union armies brought good news and led to their liberation from the bonds of slavery and their first taste of such advantages as education and legal marriage and family life.

The first historians to stress the crucial part that conditions on the home front played in the Confederacy's ultimate downfall were Charles H. Wesley and Charles W. Ramsdell. In his book *The Collapse of the Confederacy*, published in 1937, Wesley maintained that military and economic factors alone did not explain Confederate defeat. He insisted that in large measure the Confederacy collapsed because of "disintegrating internal factors."[1] In the Walter Lynwood Fleming Lectures, also in 1937, and his posthumous 1944 book *Behind the Lines in the Southern Confederacy*, Ramsdell argued that in the end the Confederate war effort failed primarily because of internal problems. Those two scholars drew attention to such difficulties as poor industrial capacity, undiversified agriculture, a weak fiscal system, inefficient and demoralizing governmental policies, pervasive shortages, and the inability and unwillingness of the civilian population to sustain support for the government in the capital at Richmond.

Following Wesley's and Ramsdell's lead in the first two decades after World War II, a number of historians began to write in depth about various aspects of the Confederate home front. In monographs, articles, and compiled works, they carefully explored many topics related to the day-to-day circumstances of wartime Southerners. Those historians of the 1940s and 1950s wrote about agriculture, industry, and transportation. They noted the pain, deprivation, and dislocation that the war inflicted on the home-front population and examined public relief programs and ersatz (substitute) remedies for shortages of necessities and luxuries. They described religion, education, and social and cultural life. They measured the depth of the public's loyalty to the Confederate cause and the people's response to the policies of the Confederate and state governments. And they elaborated on the important roles that Southern white women and African Americans of both genders played in the Civil War.

Continuing to turn the furrows plowed by those writers, a new generation of scholars in the 1960s and 1970s applied additional insight and analysis to the study of the Civil War South. This new class of historians placed an even larger emphasis than their predecessors on social history and the plight of the ordinary people. They were strongly influenced by the Civil Rights and feminist movements of their era. From that time to the present, historians have continued to expand on such issues as the roles of women and African Americans, social and economic changes caused by the war, and the nature of Confederate nationalism. They have studied life in the Confederacy from new and varied perspectives, such as class and gender. As historian James L. Roark concludes, "In recent years, the Confederate home front has come into its own."[2] This growing interest continues to prompt debate among scholars about Southern wartime conditions at home, the reasons for the collapse of the Confederacy, and the willingness of the people of the South to support a long and violent struggle for independence.

Having the benefit of this vast store of scholarship, I offer this book as a fresh look at life on the Confederate home front for the general reader and the new student of the American Civil War. I strive to address the important issues that Wesley and Ramsdell highlighted decades ago, and I hope that the reader will derive from the following pages a concise understanding of life for people "behind the lines" in the Confederacy.

ONE

❧❧❧

DEATH, SICKNESS, AND DESPAIR

Virtually no one in the South escaped witnessing—either directly or indirectly—the horrors of battlefield deaths, wounds, and sickness. The brutality and butchery of Civil War battles were probably the greatest of any war in U.S. history, and civilians at home received letters from soldiers graphically describing the carnage, pain, and suffering that they endured. After one battle a Confederate soldier wrote of seeing "the top of a man's Skull Hanging by the Hair to a limb some 8 or 9 feet from the ground." Another described "a man Siting behind a large oak tree his head . . . shot off." The field where the battle had taken place was "strewn with nude figures blackened and mutilated by fire that swept across the dry foliage in the wake of the fighting." Another Confederate soldier, assigned to a burial detail at Gettysburg, wrote home that "the sights and smells that assailed us were simply indescribable." The "corpses [were] swollen to twice their original size, some of them actually burst asunder with the pressure of foul gases. . . . The odors were nauseating and so deadly that in a short time we all sickened and were lying with our mouths close to the ground, most of us vomiting profusely."[1] Amid the many amputations of arms and legs taking place around him after one battle, Confederate soldier Richard Slade actually considered himself fortunate to have received only a mangled hand. He wrote home that "my fingers are getting better I did not have but one of them taken off the second one was broken & the Doctors insisted on taking it off but I would not let them & I saved my finger by this means. It looks rather hard to see them take off legs & arms & fingers

& cut the men all into pieces but thank God they have not got [but] only a small part of me."[2]

Soldiers also wrote to their families about being lonely and homesick. In late 1861 Lt. Warren Magee confessed to his wife that "I had thought I would not write to [you] for a few days as I have just written to you, but some how or other I studdy about Home to day i feel like I must write you afew lines. I have been studdying about you and the children all day. oh how I wish I was at home with you this day. it seems as if there is nothing else in this world would please me better than to be with my family."[3] In 1862 D. Hunter wrote to his wife, "I want to see the children very bad[.] their [*sic*] is several men in the same fix that I am in that hav young babs at home that they never saw."[4] Descriptions of the horrors of war and cries of loneliness from husbands, fathers, brothers, and sons at the front weighed upon the hearts and minds of families at home and weakened their support for the war.

The number of men who served in the Confederate army has never been exactly determined. Estimates range from 600,000 to 1,500,000, with the best estimate probably lying somewhere between those two figures. Regardless of the exact total, the significant number who left home for camps and battlefields represented a huge loss of labor, protection, and support for wives and children on the home front. Confederate military deaths totaled approximately 258,000. Of that number an estimated 94,000 men died in battle or of mortal wounds.[5] Those soldiers who fell victim to the horrors of war but managed to return home permanently during the conflict were not always able to contribute to the welfare and sustenance of their families. Even though they had survived the war, some of those men remained scarred physically and psychologically by the violence. Their wounds and despair also left their marks on loved ones. One such veteran, William Core of Guilford County, North Carolina, wrote the following to his state's governor on January 12, 1863.

> Dear sir
>   i seet my self to let you know that i am a poor wounded soldier i have but uon arm and but uon finger and thumb on it i was in service to a day in the 2 regement i have binn home ever sence the 2[8] of August Dear Sir you know that i cant mentain my fam[ily] long with uon thumb and finger while i was in the army there was the sum of 4 dollars allow to my wife and 2 children a mounth and sence i have got home tore up my family is [al]lowed nothing i think the government ought to mentain me and my family i have no way in the wourld [to] earn 5 cents i think it verry hard to go to the army and get ruined and now suffer for some thing to eat i hope you will take this under consideration and provide some way for me i live near hipoint [High Point] please sen me a few lynes what i must doo.

In response to Core's request, Gov. Zebulon B. Vance could merely instruct one of his aides to "ansr. this the best you can."[6]

Although they might not have been on the front lines, people on the home front were never far from the physical reality of the disaster and cruelty of war. Many saw with their own eyes the gruesome results of modern warfare as makeshift hospitals were thrown up hastily all over the South. Various structures—barns, sheds, stores, schools, warehouses, factories, churches, and private houses—became temporary wards for the care of wounded and sick soldiers. From the outset of the war, Southern soldiers received emergency care at field hospitals or dressing stations near the battlefield. But the Confederate Medical Department did not establish general hospitals until late 1861. In the interim general hospital care was provided exclusively by a number of private groups and institutions, using civilian caretakers and nurses. By late 1862, however, the Confederate government had taken over or closed most of those private facilities.

Before the war cities such as Richmond, New Orleans, Charleston, and Mobile operated public hospitals for civilians—usually for the treatment of indigents and transients. Some of these facilities treated both black and white patients but in separate wards. Others provided separate hospitals for slaves.[7] The strain of the war and the demands by the military for medical personnel made the operation of city hospitals difficult and forced most of them to close. Those that remained in operation, however, sometimes treated soldiers. In January 1863, for example, the Richmond City Council billed the Confederate government $7,470 for soldiers treated in the city hospital.[8] In Memphis in June and July 1861, the Mother's Home Association, under the supervision of "the efficient and attentive physician" G. W. Curry, administered to 209 patients.[9] Most civilians in the Confederacy were not treated at hospitals. Instead, they were usually treated at home, where they were cared for by family members and attended by a visiting physician. Residents in the countryside especially had to rely on local doctors and home remedies. Federal military hospitals in occupied areas including Louisiana, eastern North Carolina, eastern Tennessee, and Arkansas treated local civilians—native whites, recently arrived Northerners, fugitive slaves, refugees—during epidemics such as yellow fever or smallpox.[10]

State medical departments established general hospitals for the troops from their states. In October 1861, for example, North Carolina opened the First North Carolina Hospital in Petersburg, Virginia. The state opened a second hospital in Petersburg in early 1862 and founded Moore Hospital in a former tobacco factory in Richmond in May of that year. The Confederate government gradually assumed control over the state-sponsored hospitals also. Virginia probably had the most military hospitals. The Charlottesville General Hospital treated more than 22,700 wounded during the war. Over time, thirty-two general hospitals administered to Southern soldiers in Richmond. The two largest military hospitals in the Confederacy were the Chimborazo Hospital and the Winder Hospital, both located in the Confederate capital. The Winder facility included ninety-eight buildings and could treat 4,300 patients at a time. Chimborazo treated more than 77,800 soldiers before the war ended.

A number of private hospitals also tended to wounded soldiers in Richmond. The most famous of these was the small hospital operated by twenty-seven-year-old Sally Tompkins and her female volunteers. Miss Tompkins opened the facility in 1862 at her own expense and cared for about 1,333 wounded soldiers. When the Confederate authorities attempted to close the hospital, President Jefferson Davis commissioned her a captain in the army so that she could continue to operate.[11]

By 1862 another type of hospital, known as the "wayside" or "way" hospital, had appeared, usually near railroad depots or along major rail lines. These small medical stations cared for injured or infirm soldiers traveling between the front and their homes. Convalescent troops could find overnight accommodation at these places as they waited for train connections. Soldiers' conditions often worsened while aboard the trains. Many men found respite from a long journey at the wayside hospitals, and occasionally some died there and were buried nearby. Civilian volunteers, including physicians and nurses, staffed the wayside hospitals until they were taken over by the Confederate government.

Despite shortages at home, civilians made sizable donations of supplies to military hospitals in the Confederacy. They contributed—especially early in the conflict when shortages were not so extreme—such foodstuffs as bacon, flour, potatoes, lard, eggs, butter, rice, poultry, vegetables, and dried fruit. They also donated clothing, bedding, towels, bandages, cutlery, and cooking utensils. Local committees, usually led by women, took up the task of collecting supplies and shipping them to the hospitals. The Georgia Hospital Relief Association and the South Carolina Hospital Aid Association collected money, supplies, and medicines for hospitals in Richmond, dispatched surgeons to field hospitals, and helped establish wayside facilities.[12]

The need for nurses to staff Confederate hospitals led many Southern white women to volunteer their services. Such action represented a departure from accepted social custom for upper-class women in the South. It was not considered proper or respectable for women to work in "an army hospital which presented sights that no lady should see." Originally most army hospitals were staffed with soldiers who were male nurses. Slaves served as cooks, laundresses, janitors, and orderlies. Nevertheless, "numerous southern women of good families braved the frowns of father or brother to volunteer as nurses." One volunteer nurse, Kate Cumming, who traveled from her home in Mobile, Alabama, to Corinth, Mississippi, to help the Confederate wounded at an impromptu hospital, remarked: "As to the plea of its being no place for a refined lady, I wondered what Miss Nightingale and the hundreds of refined ladies of Great Britain who went to the Crimea, would say to that." In September 1862 the Confederate Congress authorized the employment of civilian matrons and nurses in army hospitals, and a significant number of women then became part of the army medical service.[13]

With hospitals of various capacities appearing throughout the towns, cities, and way stations of the Confederacy, the folk on the home front were not shielded from or immune to the horrors of the battlefield. They witnessed firsthand the wounds, sickness, and death that befell Confederate soldiers. They saw with their own eyes the awful conditions under which the sons of the South suffered and died. Young Alice Ready, who visited an army hospital in Murfreesboro, Tennessee, departed shaken and appalled at the poor care and wretched circumstances under which many of the men were dying, with "no more notice taken of them than if they had been dogs."[14] When Kate Cumming arrived at the Corinth hospital, "Nothing that I had ever heard or read had given me the faintest idea of the horrors witnessed here.... The men are lying all over the house, on their blankets, just as they were brought in from the battlefield.... The foul air from this mass of human beings at first made me giddy and sick, but I soon got over it. We have to walk, and when we give the men anything kneel, in blood and water."[15]

In Columbia, South Carolina, Mary Boykin Chesnut forced herself to continue her work as a volunteer nurse at a soldiers' hospital despite her revulsion at the horror that she witnessed there. No matter how revolting she found the experience, she had "to be a hospital nurse." Otherwise, "at heart I felt a coward and skulker." Nevertheless, "That fearful hospital haunts me all day long—worse at night. So much suffering, loathsome wounds, distortion, stumps of limbs exhibited to all and not half cured."[16]

The people of the South also experienced firsthand the violence of war as Union columns invaded their region, bringing devastation to their plantations and farms, their villages and towns. Civilians frequently found themselves caught in the cross fire of battling armies. Such was the case of fourteen-year-old Sue Chancellor and her family when Union and Confederate forces clashed at Chancellorsville, Virginia, in May 1862. As the battle began, Union general Joseph Hooker commandeered the Chancellor house for his headquarters, and it soon came under Confederate bombardment. Hooker ordered Sue, her mother, an aunt, a "half-grown" brother, and a young black servant into the basement for safety. "The house was full of the wounded," Sue later recalled. "They had taken our sitting room as an operating table." In the basement the terrified family crouched in water over the tops of their shoes. The Chancellors spent the night huddled in an upstairs room. But "early in the morning they came for us to go [back] to the cellar, and in passing through the upper porch I saw the chairs riddled with bullets and the shattered columns which had fallen on General Hooker. Oh, the Horror of that day! There were piles of legs and arms outside the sitting room window and rows of dead bodies covered with canvas. The fighting was awful, and the frightened men crowded into the basement for protection from the deadly fire of the Confederates, but an officer came and ordered them out, commanding them not to intrude upon the terror-stricken women." As the Confederate fire intensified, Hooker's men and the Chancellor family were forced to flee the house and yard. Sue remembered that when they emerged from the basement, "the woods around the house were a sheet of fire; the air was filled with shot and shell;

horses were running, rearing, and screaming; the men were amass with confusion, moaning, cursing, and praying. They were bringing the wounded out of the house, for it was on fire in several places." As she left the scene, clinging to her mother, she looked back and saw that "our old home was completely enveloped in flames."[17]

The war produced much psychological distress for both soldiers and their families. Even though they might have cheated death and survived the war, some combatants carried the mental anguish of their experiences to their graves. The loss of loved ones on the battlefield resulted in depression and heartbreak for family members who remained at home. In Warren County, North Carolina, Edward and Rebecca Davis, of Lake O'Woods Plantation, lost two sons in Virginia battles. The boys' deaths left their mother almost destroyed by grief. "I just can't bear it," she wrote, "to think, speak, or write about, and when I lie down at night and it comes to mind, I soar aloft in my imagination, and leave all earthly things behind. I just know that if I reflect much upon it, . . . it would be more than my mental or physical powers could stand."[18]

A lawyer in South Carolina remarked on his wife's growing anxiety about her two sons in the army: "My wife, strong & active, full of energy, with the will to accomplish all she desires, is showing failing symptoms. Her only two boys are in field . . . on their way to Virginia. She would not have them stay, & yet in the still night I can hear her deep sighs & sometimes suppressed moans, I know she is thinking of them."[19]

Even without war casualties, child mortality was high and left many parents despondent over the deaths of their children. In April 1864 President Jefferson Davis and his wife, Varina, suffered the heartbreak of losing a child. While playing on the piazza of the Confederate White House, their five-year-old son fell to the pavement below. With both legs broken and his skull fractured, "Joe" lived only a short time. Away from the executive mansion when the accident occurred, both Davis and his wife rushed home to cradle their child in the last throes of his young life. When he died, Mrs. Davis immediately lapsed into a "flood of tears and wild lamentations." The usually restrained and unemotional president displayed "unutterable anguish" and "seemed ready to burst with unspeakable grief" before growing rigid in manner. "Not mine, oh, Lord, but thine," he cried, and dismissed a government messenger with the words "I must have this day with my little child." He spent the night pacing in his bedroom with "heavy sorrow."[20] Childhood diseases claimed the lives of many Southern children, and infant mortality was high throughout the Confederacy. In June 1862 Lt. Col. John S. Preston, commandant of prison and conscript camps in South Carolina, instructed the childless diarist Mary Boykin Chesnut to "thank God on your knees that you have no children to break your heart. Mrs. Preston and I spent the first ten years of our married life in mortal agony over ill and dying children."[21]

Refugees too were prone to depression and sadness, as a result of their displacement. Uprooted from familiar surroundings by wartime violence and destruction, they often suffered feelings of anxiety, detachment, homesickness, and helplessness. In large numbers refugee families endured "their own peculiar type of battle fatigue" as they left behind their homes, possessions, and acquaintances to travel and wander in search of living space away from Union attack and the ravages of warfare.[22] Without the aid of modern psychotherapy, drugs, and other treatment to deal with trauma, anxiety, and depression, Southerners were largely left on their own to cope with their grief and psychological wounds.

Along with psychological stress, drunkenness and alcoholism became serious problems on the home front as well as in the army. To combat these ills, state legislatures passed laws prohibiting the making of whiskey, and at times various local authorities throughout the South banned the production and sale of alcoholic beverages. Virginia, Georgia, Alabama, Florida, and North Carolina prohibited the distilling of grain in 1862. Louisiana approved such a law in January 1863, and Texas provided for a county-option law in December 1863. State laws prohibited only the distilling, and not the consumption, of liquor. Legislatures gave as their reason for the laws shortages and rising prices for grain but did not address the social problems resulting from overindulgence.

The Medical Department of the Confederate army, however, consistently used large quantities of whiskey and brandy, and the Confederate government operated distilleries throughout the South to supply the needs of its military hospitals. But Govs. Joseph E. Brown of Georgia and Zebulon B. Vance of North Carolina demanded that the War Department close its distilleries within their states. They denied that the Confederacy had the authority to operate such facilities in the face of state laws prohibiting all manufacturing of spirits.[23]

Despite statutes prohibiting the distillation of corn and other grain, many Southerners continued to manufacture large quantities of spirits to sell and turn a profit. Large amounts of whiskey and brandy came into the Confederacy aboard blockade-runners until February 6, 1864, when the Davis government forbade the importation of alcoholic beverages. As the conflict wore on, public drunkenness became a major difficulty in towns and cities. Conflict often developed between the civilian residents and Confederate soldiers stationed in and near urban areas. After the Confederate Congress authorized the suspension of the writ of habeas corpus in 1862, "prohibition of liquor became an objective of martial law." Military commanders recognized that rampant drunkenness among both soldiers and civilians was a severe hindrance to keeping good order and discipline in a society under military jurisdiction.[24]

The Confederate capital of Richmond, for example, had many drinking establishments that served the large numbers of soldiers and their officers who passed through the city or took leave there. According to historian E. Merton Coulter, "The hope of every soldier was to visit Richmond as often as possible, there to get drunk. . . . Soldiers drank and fought one another and others on the street, broke open saloons on Sundays," and engaged in all types of raucous behavior associated with drunkenness.[25] After Jefferson Davis proclaimed martial law in Richmond in

February 1862, Gen. John H. Winder, commanding the Department of Henrico, issued a general order forbidding the sale of liquor in the city. In the fall he limited the importation of liquor into the city to 150 barrels (6,000 gallons) and ordered that none of it could be sold to soldiers.[26]

Conflict frequently developed between town residents and Confederate soldiers as a result of the latter's frequent patronage of local barrooms. In July 1864 residents of Mobile were demanding that the barrooms be closed because the drunkenness of soldiers was becoming a major obstacle to maintaining civil order and discipline. With the beginning of the Battle of Mobile Bay in early August, the town fathers passed an ordinance that prohibited the dispensing of liquor, but the mayor shortly revoked the order because, once the battle was over, "there is no longer any military necessity for closing the drinking saloons and barrooms." The mayor's action enraged some of Mobile's inhabitants. One critic wrote to the Mobile *Register* that "blockade runners, speculators, and extortioners have been continuously and unsparingly denounced as enemies to their country, while the vendors of poison in the shape of vile whiskey, at the most extravagant prices have not only escaped [censure] justly merited, but have been actually puffed in public journals for their ostentatious liberality in spreading a free lunch—a baked opossum or a catfish stew or some other concoction." Many town dwellers shared the opinion that the permanent closing of drinking establishments should be declared a "military necessity" and steps should be taken by civil and military authorities to rid the streets of drunk and disorderly soldiers.[27]

Confederate soldiers felt that attempts to restrict the sale of liquor were unjustly aimed at them. The troops interpreted municipal efforts to restrict the distribution of alcoholic spirits as another example of the injustice of having to serve in the ranks while civilians and officers indulged themselves in privileges and comforts denied to the common soldiers. To them the hoarding of liquor was unfair in view of the tasks they were expected to perform in defense of the South.

In Mobile enlisted men guilty of overindulgence in alcoholic spirits were brought before the mayor's court for trial and sentencing, and almost every session included several cases of drunken and disorderly conduct, sometimes among the local inhabitants as well as the soldiers. On one such occasion, a soldier was charged with assault by the proprietor of a drinking house, who had demanded $5.00 per drink when the usual price was $3.50. Upon being served, the soldier protested the injustice of the price and gave the bar owner "a popped skull," for which the soldier received a $50.00 fine.[28]

In February 1865 the governor of Alabama directed that the barrooms in Mobile be closed. The governor's mandate was frequently ignored. Even where the dispensing of individual drinks was prohibited, wholesale quantities of liquors were still legally available. "Notwithstanding the closing of the barrooms in the city," remarked the

Register, "men somehow manage to get plenty of the ardent. The only difference now is between 3 to 5 dollars a drink and thirty dollars a quart. To sell a drink is penal, but to sell a quart, a gallon, or barrel is respectable. Heigh-hi hi-ho, the more you put down the less you pick up."[29] Because there was no consistent local enforcement of the governor's order forbidding the sale of whiskey in barrooms, and because merchants dealing in spirits had considerable influence in town government, liquor continued to flow in Mobile. That situation, however, ended on April 1, 1865, when, with Union attack on the town of Mobile imminent, all drinking establishments were closed by the Confederate military commander.[30]

Southern militia musters were often marked by drunkenness. In Bladen County, North Carolina, one resident wrote about a militia muster: "Dr. McDaniel was examining the militia last Saturday and everybody in Elizabeth[town] was drunk. And he was so drunk he could not set up. So he discharged all of them. When he started to go home he went to walk down the steps drunk. Kelly fell on him and like to have broke his neck. He got up and said, 'Boys that is not the way to serve President Davis.'"[31] Other episodes throughout the countryside and towns of the Confederacy were not so humorous, merely sad. As the war worsened for the South and the strain of the conflict grew among the homefolk, so did the public's resort to alcohol for temporary escape and comfort.

Along with the mental stress of wartime, disease and sickness took their toll on the people of the Southern Confederacy. Having been a source of public fear before the war, yellow fever remained a serious threat in the port cities of the South during the conflict. Apparently, blockade-runners—with someone aboard infected with the yellow fever virus—brought the deadly disease spread by the *Aedes aegypti* mosquito. When the vessel *Kate* arrived in Wilmington, North Carolina, in the first week in September 1862, port officials waived the standard period of quarantine in order to disperse the much-needed food and supplies brought by the ship. Within a few days, yellow fever broke out in the city. Mrs. C. P. Bolles, a resident of Wilmington who contracted the disease but survived, described the epidemic that raged through the streets and neighborhoods.

> The disease spread rapidly, after the first two weeks our physicians had more than they could contend with, and Charleston was quick in responding to the call for assistance, sending her physicians, and nurses, as many as needed, a dozen or more "Sisters of Mercy." As I made my way over to the window one day about the middle of October to see if the weather cock across the street, on the pinnacle of the Cape Fear Bank Building, indicated any change in the weather, feeling so desperately hopeless, with no one near me but my husband who was too ill to realize the situation. As I looked out I saw all windows closed with no sign of life save the "Little Sisters of Mercy" darting across the streets—flitting from door to door, entering to administer to the sick and dying. Then as I gazed on, I saw a shabby old hearse coming across the corner, drawn by a lean horse,

looking as if he had the fever and a young colored man leaning over, too sick to hold the reins, and before the setting of another sun he was laid by the side of many of his fellow men, white and colored in a deep trench that had been provided for the dead in Oakdale Cemetery.

Before the arrival of cold weather in November finally ended the epidemic by killing the mosquitoes that transported the infection, 1,000 to 1,100 people in Wilmington had died from the virus, "leaving a pall of sorrow over the entire community."[32]

The dreaded disease also struck Charleston in July 1864, and then the Federal-occupied town of New Bern, North Carolina. Before the epidemic ended in New Bern with the onset of cold weather, between 650 and 750 civilians had died, and 303 Union soldiers had succumbed to the disease. Those residents of the coastal areas who could afford to do so fled inland to escape the ravages of the deadly "yellow jack." During the antebellum era, yellow fever had been one of the most feared scourges to attack the port cities of the South, including Charleston, Mobile, and New Orleans. The most susceptible cities were the ports of the Gulf Coast.[33]

At the time of the Civil War, physicians had not yet determined that yellow fever was transferred from one person to another through the bite of the mosquito. Most considered the disease not contagious. Until the 1840s the common belief was that the illness originated from a gas, or "miasma," resulting from the impact of heat and humidity on rotting organic material or other unsanitary substances. In the 1850s, however, medical authorities theorized that the disease was "transportable," frequently by ships arriving in U.S. harbors. They concluded that such items as bedding, clothing, and dishes used by infected persons contained the virus and resulted in its spread. Quarantine of vessels and proper sanitation were the recommended methods of preventing an outbreak of the malady.

Once "yellow jack" struck, the standard response to preventing its spread was to burn tar, turpentine, and rosin throughout the streets. The resulting smoke theoretically would prevent the virus from traveling through the air. Doctors also ordered "lime storms," in which clouds of chloride of lime were released into the atmosphere to prevent the spread of airborne infection. Daily doses of whiskey and quinine were also prescribed as preventatives.

The severity of the disease varied from victim to victim. Some suffered only a mild form consisting of flu-like symptoms lasting a few days. With the remission of the symptoms, the patient had immunity to the disease. But more commonly the stricken person would be seized with fever, chills, and muscle aches and within a short time would suffer liver failure and jaundice, a condition that gave the disease its name—yellow fever. That development would be followed by hemorrhaging from the mouth, nose, and stomach lining. The digested blood would be expelled from the stomach in a horrifying black vomit. In the final stage, the patient endured violent convulsions and died of kidney failure.[34]

Also spread by mosquitoes, malaria struck both the army and civilian population. Characterized by chills and fever, this disease thrived in the warm, wet climate prevalent in much of the South. It commonly occurred in the low country, which had much water and many mosquitoes. Unlike with yellow fever, according to one authority, "The cold winter months were not free of the disease because of chronic cases, relapses, and the first clinical appearance of some infections previously suppressed by quinine used prophylactically."[35] Also unlike yellow fever, whose mosquito carriers thrived in the various water containers of towns and cities, malaria was spread by the *Anopheles* mosquito, which flourished in marshes and swamps. But as they had with yellow fever, physicians believed that malaria was derived from vapors, or "miasmas," from ponds or swamps. Preventive measures included the burning of tar and turpentine to prevent the spread of the illness through the air. Quinine was the only effective drug for treating the symptoms of the disease. Often in short supply, it remained much in demand throughout the South.[36]

In fact, "of all the major shortages appearing during the Civil War that of medicine received greater study and more widespread concentrated effort designed to remedy the situation than did any other."[37] To a large extent, the Confederate states had relied on the Northern states for drugs and medical supplies prior to the war. With the outbreak of the conflict, the U.S. government immediately labeled medicine contraband and prohibited its export into the rebellious Southern states. Those restrictions remained in effect until the war's conclusion. As a result only three sources of medical supplies remained open to the South. Confederate regiments might capture the medical stores of the enemy. Or drugs might be smuggled through the blockade. Or the Confederacy might manufacture its own medicines. All three tactics were attempted. But civilians benefited little from the capture of Union supplies, as most materials obtained through that means went to the army. Running the blockade proved more helpful for the home-front populace. Almost all blockade-runners brought in a shipment of medicines. Those designated for civilian use were sold at auction at the port of arrival for high prices. Coastal residents at or near the port had an advantage over the residents of the interior in obtaining the imported drugs. Medicines were also smuggled through the land blockade, usually concealed in the clothing of persons passing through Union lines or by others, including speculators, traveling interior rivers.[38] But most civilians, particularly those in the hinterland of the South, attempted to get medicines by manufacturing their own.

The Confederate government exerted some effort to procure medicine for the civilian population, as well as for the army. It established agents in Europe to obtain needed medical supplies. But this attempt had little success, and most of the supplies received from abroad went to the military. As an alternative to importation, the Medical Department of the army created chemical laboratories in almost every Southern state. The mission of those facilities was to carry out research on indigenous plants that could be used in the manufacture of drugs. The laboratories employed some of the South's leading scientists and received the strong support of Samuel Preston Moore, surgeon general of the Confederacy. He collected information on medicinal plants at his headquarters in Richmond, and he dispatched pamphlets throughout the South encouraging the use of "medicinal substances of the vegetable kingdom." Moore also enlisted Charleston physician Francis Peyre Porcher to study native plants and publish a guide to their composition and use as medicine. Porcher published *Resources of Southern Fields and Forests, Medical, Economical, and Agricultural* in 1863, and it was widely consulted in Southern households.

Next to quinine, morphine and chloroform were the drugs most needed and sought by the civilian population. Those drugs had no viable substitutes. Most supplies of them came through the blockade, and such shipments always proved inadequate. The largest shares went to the army. But narcotic painkillers were also desperately needed for surgery among civilians. As a result Surgeon General Moore sought to secure opium through the growing of poppies. At his request Porcher investigated and concluded that opium of an "excellent quality" could be derived from poppies cultivated in the Confederacy. Moore prepared and distributed a circular encouraging "medical purveyors over the South" to provide poppy seed and to publish in local newspapers requests for civilians to grow the flowers for the production of opium. Many Southerners began growing the crop, but few actually collected the gum from the poppies and delivered it to medical authorities. The homegrown-opium effort therefore met with little success.

Because medicines were in such short supply, substitute remedies increasingly became standard treatment in Southern homes. But many of these "medicines" did little to improve the health of the patient. A proposed cure for diarrhea—a common malady behind the lines as well as among Confederate soldiers—might be a brew of blackberry roots, persimmons, and water or a mixture of salt, vinegar, and water. Jimsonweed and other roots might be combined in the hope of relieving pain. A remedy concocted from poplar trees supposedly relieved gout and rheumatism. Southerners commonly associated the use of laxatives with good health, and they preferred castor oil for this purpose. However, that substance—usually imported through the blockade—was scarce and expensive. So some folk began cultivating the castor-oil plant and manufacturing small quantities of the laxative for home use and even for sale. Others tried various leaves and roots boiled in water. Calomel (mercurous chloride) was also administered as a purgative and in the hope of destroying intestinal worms.[39]

Quinine became the drug for which Southerners sought the most substitutes. When the drug itself, derived from the South American cinchona tree, could be obtained, it sold for $400 to $600 an ounce. The most common substitute for quinine was a mixture that included the bark from dogwood, cherry, or willow trees.

Home manufacturers of the ersatz drug sometimes boiled all three barks together and frequently added whiskey to the brew, which was known as "Old Indig." Other substitutes included cottonseed tea, horehound tea, and other plants mixed with water or whiskey. Despite the best efforts of civilians to make do with home remedies, their attempts proved less than adequate. As one historian of the home front has written, "Imaginary ills were about all that could have been cured with Confederate medicines."

Surgery was primitive both in the army and behind the lines. Anesthesia—including chloroform, ether, and nitrous oxide—had been discovered before the war. But few physicians were properly trained in its use, and shortages of those anesthetics meant that whiskey was often substituted to deaden pain. Because most of the surgical instruments, which were scarce, went to army surgeons, doctors on the home front had to derive substitutes for those items as well. Penknives, forks, and knitting needles often had to serve. There was a shortage of bandages and sponges, for which bedsheets, pillowcases, and various other cloth items had to suffice.[40]

A shortage of physicians also prevailed, as many of them were conscripted into the army. A visit to a physician or dentist could be expensive, especially in the final months of the war, when landslide inflation prevailed. A doctor's charge of $30.00 for an office visit was not unusual. When Anna Long Thomas Fuller and her daughter of Louisburg, North Carolina, visited a dentist in Raleigh in December 1864, the total charge came to $90.00 for filling a tooth for Mrs. Fuller and extracting one for her daughter.[41] The account book of Dr. Cyril Granville Wyche of Columbus County, North Carolina, reveals that he administered various treatments and drugs throughout the war. In July 1862 he charged Arch Barefoot $5.00 for "1 dose of quinine"; in August 1863 he collected from Lucy Smith $15.00 for quinine and spirits of niter, and on a subsequent visit another $15.00 for quinine and brandy. Dr. Wyche's standard fee for a house call during the war was $5.00, and he treated both whites and their slaves. His fee for "6 grs. tartar emetic" was 50 cents, for a dose of salts 25 cents, for one package of Epsom salts $1.00, for a bottle of laudanum (an opiate) $1.00, for a package of magnesia $1.00, and for a tooth extraction $1.00. In January 1863 he vaccinated a family (presumably for smallpox) for $2.50. For "attending" a woman in labor he collected $10.00.[42]

Wartime conditions made it difficult to provide for the formal education of physicians. With the onset of the conflict, the medical schools in the South began closing. Only the Medical College of Virginia in Richmond remained open until the end of the war. That institution trained about 400 students, but most of them served in the military hospitals in the Richmond area or as medical officers in the Army of Northern Virginia. When the Medical College of South Carolina closed its doors, the entire faculty joined the Confederate service. In an effort to maintain a sufficient number of medical doctors for the home front, the Confederate Congress in October

1862 amended the Conscription Act of 1862 to exempt from the draft "physicians who had practiced for five years."[43]

Even trained physicians, however, had only limited success in treating illness and disease. The chief reason was that "the existence and importance of the pathogenic microbes was still unknown. The concept of living, subvisible, self-multiplying, invasive organisms, some of them widely disseminated and even ubiquitous, as the cause of disease had not yet been accepted." According to one authority, "Most of the common infectious diseases were clinically recognized, but their causation, transmission, and control were not." Quinine was effective in treating malaria, but the drug frequently failed as a suppressant, apparently because it was not administered in sufficient dosage.

Once they appeared, virtually all communicable diseases flourished and spread unchecked among both the military and civilian populations. The only exception was smallpox, for which there was an effective vaccine. That disease did not produce any large epidemics among soldiers, primarily because most had been vaccinated.[44] But outbreaks did occur in the South, particularly among the unvaccinated African American population. On December 13, 1863, John A. Hedrick, U.S. Treasury collector in Union-held eastern North Carolina, reported from the port of Beaufort that "small pox is quite prevalent in Newbern, especially among the negroes. There were 18 cases black, and 8 white reported on Sunday. The Physician in charge of the small-pox camp, told Dr. Page that there were 250 cases in said camp." About two weeks later, Hedrick observed that the scourge had reached Beaufort. But he soon noted that the spread of the disease apparently had been checked. He wrote to his brother that "the small-pox, I think, has some what abated, as there are fewer cases reported than there were about three weeks ago. It has prevailed mostly among the contrabands [escaped slaves]." As was the case in Beaufort on a later occasion, smallpox sometimes arrived in Southern ports aboard ships carrying passengers or crews who had not been vaccinated. Hedrick reported on March 25, 1865, that "the Steamer Carolina arrived in Port yesterday with a case of Smallpox on board." On April 11 he recorded: "I was walking around the borders of the town this morning and was hailed by a white woman with a child in her arms, who seemed very much frightened, and told me that a negroe man lying on the other side of the road had been there for the last two days sick, and was now broken out with smallpox. I did not take the trouble to examine into his case but reported the facts to the Post Surgeon, who promised to have him removed to the Small Pox hospital. There have been quite a number of cases of Small Pox in this place lately and I have been informed that it was very prevalent in New York and Brooklyn during the last winter. Two cases have been brought to this place on vessels from New York."[45]

In the winter of 1863–1864, black women and children particularly suffered when smallpox swept through the Mississippi Valley.[46] During the winter of 1862–1863, an epidemic of smallpox broke out in the crowded poor neighborhoods of Richmond.

The spread of the disease, however, was quickly checked when the city enacted a quarantine and provided free immunization to those residents who could not pay for it. Some Confederates accused Federal commanders of attempting a type of biological warfare by spreading smallpox. On one occasion, Surgeon General Moore reportedly accused the Yankees of dispatching a contaminated black man through Confederate lines to spread the virus. But no evidence exists that either side used disease as a biological weapon against the opposing army or civilians.[47]

A variety of other communicable diseases afflicted both the Southern military and civilian populations. Typhus ("ship fever" or "jail fever")—marked by high fever, rash, headache, and delirium—was spread by body lice. It was more common in army regiments and aboard ships than among civilians. The largest epidemic in the Confederacy occurred in Wilmington, North Carolina, in 1865, where the infection was transported by Union soldiers released from the Confederate prison at Salisbury. About 300 soldiers, including nine medical officers, died, but it is uncertain how many local folk might have succumbed to the disease.

Typhoid fever, which resulted from a bacterial infection often acquired from fecal contamination of food or drinking water, caused high fever, diarrhea, headache, and intestinal inflammation. It produced a "relatively high" mortality, had a "protracted course" and "numerous sources of infection," and was easily communicated from person to person. No precise figures exist for the number of people who became ill or were carriers during the Civil War, but the disease was certainly "common," in both North and South, and was "one of the most deadly."[48]

Pneumonia was a widespread and serious respiratory infection, "but chiefly as a secondary complication in other diseases and not as a primary epidemic disease."[49] Before the war the standard treatments had been bloodletting and the administering of antimony and the tartar emetic. Apparently those procedures continued among civilian physicians during the conflict, although in the army they frequently "were dispensed with in favor of a carefully regulated diet, brandy or whiskey, opium, and quinine," as well as various other herbal and questionable treatments. Pulmonary and respiratory maladies such as bronchitis and catarrh afflicted both civilians and soldiers. The highly communicable tuberculosis (or consumption), which affected primarily the lungs, was debilitating and often fatal. Doctors' standard prescriptions included nourishing food, various tonics, and healthy "open air."[50]

Because prostitution was a common practice in urban areas throughout the Confederacy, venereal diseases—gonorrhea and syphilis—became a significant health problem. Prostitutes had thrived in antebellum Richmond, and when Confederate soldiers appeared in large numbers in the city, the world's oldest profession boomed. As a result venereal disease was epidemic in the Confederate capital, especially, but not exclusively, among the soldiers.[51] In December 1862 the Richmond *Examiner* declared that "if the Mayor of Richmond lacks any incentive [for] breaking up the resorts of ill-fame in the city, let him visit military hospitals, where the sick and disabled soldiers are received for treatment and look upon the human forms lying there, wrecked upon the treacherous shoals of vice and passion which encounters the soldier at the corner of every street, lane, and alley of the city."[52]

In 1860 prostitution, which included white and black prostitutes, thrived in Nashville, Tennessee, and it became more widespread during the war. After the Federal army captured the city, U.S. authorities implemented measures to control the scourge of venereal disease that accompanied the trade in illicit sex. They established a system of inspecting, treating, and licensing prostitutes. According to physician and medical historian Thomas Lowry, "This first American exercise in legalized prostitution seems to have had some benefit. As of April 30, 1864, 352 women were licensed and 92 infected women had been treated in the new facility created for this purpose." Soon "the licensing and examination procedures were extended to cover 'colored prostitutes.'" The Federals implemented a similar program in Memphis when they captured that citadel.[53]

When Union troops occupied Mobile immediately after the war, Federal medical officers found prostitution and the accompanying problem of venereal disease to be rampant. The army established a hospital for the care and treatment of "abandoned women." According to an order by the district headquarters, such a facility was necessary in the port city "in order to mitigate the evils of prostitution, to prevent the increase of disease, and to provide for proper medical attendance for such women as may be infected." Every "public woman" was required to report to the hospital, register her name and address, and submit to an examination. If she was free of disease, she would receive a certificate stating that this was the case. After the first examination, each woman was required to report for reexamination every week, and those with disease were to receive medical treatment. "All women," the order went on, "who come under the provisions of this order, whether living in public houses or otherwise carrying on an illicit trade, who do not comply with its requirements, will be severely punished, and if living in public houses these houses will be closed and broken up."[54]

Without the aid of modern antibiotics, the treatment for venereal disease was primitive and largely ineffective. Proposed medical cures included doses of mercury, silver nitrate, zinc sulfate, and copaiba, derived from South American trees and described as a "thick, yellowish-brown, spicy-smelling liquid—with an ungodly taste—used for everything under the sun, most especially gonorrhea." Other treatments included administering various plant and herbal concoctions, sometimes along with whiskey, and cauterization.[55] According to one authority, "the late serious complications of gonorrhea were largely ignored and the delayed tertiary stage cardiovascular and central nervous system manifestations of syphilis were either unknown or not related to that disease." Nevertheless, although the impact of venereal diseases cannot be

accurately determined, the large number of prostitutes in the South and the procliv-
ity of soldiers to acquire the maladies and convey them to the civilian population
upon their return home must have had a significant impact on contemporary and
subsequent generations.[56] The effects of venereal disease in the civilian population
often appeared many years after the war. Men infected with gonorrhea endured "ure-
thral strictures," while their womenfolk suffered "pelvic inflammatory diseases and
the gonococcal arthritis seen in the late phases of the disease, as well as having infer-
tility problems or tubal pregnancies." Syphilis was even worse, ultimately resulting in
destruction of the brain, staggering and psychotic behavior, and death. One estimate
concludes that one-third of Confederate and Union veterans died of the late stages of
venereal disease. "No one knows," writes Lowry, "how many wives and widows went
to their graves, rotted and ravaged by the pox that their men brought home, or how
many veterans' children were blinded by gonorrhea or stunted by syphilis."[57]

A plethora of other epidemic illnesses and diseases existed among the folk of the
Confederacy, although most were more prevalent in the ranks of the army than on the
home front. The numbers and crowding of soldiers living in unhygienic conditions
facilitated the communicability of sickness. Measles proved epidemic among the
troops at times but less serious among civilians. Although not usually fatal in itself, the
disease could lead to acute or chronic bronchitis and pneumonia and a predisposition
to tuberculosis. Mumps, another highly contagious disease, also frequently swept
through army camps. Scurvy, the result of dietary deficiency, probably was more
common among soldiers and sailors than civilians, who generally had greater access
to fresh vegetables and fruits. Physicians of the era recognized that a well-rounded
diet prevented the disease. Arthritis was not known, and physicians usually diagnosed
any chronic inflammation of muscles and joints as rheumatism. Prescribed remedies
were mostly ineffective. The bowel ailments dysentery and diarrhea, produced by
bacteria from unsanitary water and food, prevailed throughout the South, but civilians
probably suffered less from the more serious of the two, dysentery, than did the troops.
On the other hand, scarlet fever struck Richmond in 1862 and Atlanta the following
year, though there is little evidence of outbreaks among Confederate troops. Diseases
that might have existed among the civilian population but for which no figures survive
include diphtheria, hepatitis, jaundice, "congestion of the brain," and various other
"fevers" and maladies. Influenza was not diagnosed as such in the Civil War era.
Because the need for antiseptic practices in surgery had not been fully recognized,
infection, even after minor surgery, commonly occurred. But given the relatively
primitive nature of medical knowledge and training of the period as compared to
present-day practice, frequent misdiagnosis, as well as misunderstanding of the causes
and treatment of disease, is not surprising.[58]

What is surprising to modern students of the Civil War is how the people of the
Confederacy managed to endure, cope, and even at times overcome the physical and

psychological ravages inflicted upon them by four long years of fighting and suffering. Although not soldiers in the ranks, they nevertheless were affected by the upheaval and pain of war; and their plight was not made any easier by a Confederate government that had recklessly committed to a colossal conflict that it was ill prepared to fight.

TWO

❧

AGRICULTURE, INDUSTRY, AND TRANSPORTATION

The welfare of the home-front population depended in large measure on the wartime South's ability to grow, manufacture, and distribute food and supplies. An effective Federal coastal blockade and the disappearance of imports from the North forced the Confederate States of America to produce more at home. The farms and plantations had to yield more foodstuffs, and new or expanded industries had the difficult task of manufacturing products that theretofore had been imported.

The *Charleston Mercury* accurately portrayed the Southern economy when it proclaimed in February 1861: "We are eminently an agricultural people; yet distinguished from other tillers of the soil by this, that the larger part of our labor is directed to production of commodities intended for consumption abroad, and paid for by the importation of foreign production from all the nations of the world." The newspaper maintained that the fledgling Confederate government should have only "limited power" in imposing duties or taxes or interfering with such a system.[1] But what the *Mercury* and those who agreed with it could not see was that the South's devotion to an agricultural system based on slave labor and the export of staple crops, especially cotton, made it difficult for the region to transform itself into a wartime producer of grain and livestock. Such a transformation was never completely successful. As a result foodstuffs were frequently in short supply, and shortages for both soldiers and civilians contributed to the Confederate defeat.[2]

In order for the Confederacy to survive, it would have to feed and clothe its people both in the army and on the home front. To ensure adequate supplies and prevent widespread hunger and possible starvation, the Southern states needed to concentrate on growing food crops. But the chief economic staple for planters and farmers before the war had been cotton, and many growers wanted to continue to devote their acreage to what had been the South's largest agricultural moneymaker. Governmental policies contributed to the concept of cotton as an economic necessity, for initially that commodity was considered a vital part of the Confederacy's financial and foreign policy. Both the Confederate and state governments viewed cotton as an essential element in securing foreign loans and credit for needed supplies slipped through the blockade. The Davis government also hoped that a shortage of the staple, brought on by the war, would induce Britain and France to aid the Confederacy in its bid for independence. But as the war continued and the blockade tightened, "cotton diplomacy" failed, and cotton's value as a source of national revenue and as a diplomatic device declined. Nevertheless, the price of cotton continued to climb, and planters persisted in growing large quantities of it.[3]

Before the war other cash crops had included rice, grown in the largest quantities in the tidewater of South Carolina and Georgia; sugar from the cane fields of Louisiana; and tobacco, hemp, and wheat from the Upper South states of Maryland, Virginia, North Carolina, Kentucky, Tennessee, and Missouri. Farmers and planters grew more corn than any other crop, but it was not a cash commodity. Instead, it served to feed the South's people and livestock. Planters raised the temperamental long-staple cotton in coastal South Carolina and Georgia. But far and away the South's most abundant cash crop was short-staple cotton, which grew from the Carolinas to Texas.[4]

Committed to the concept of unrestrained individual rights, many cotton producers opposed any attempts by the government to dictate what crops they could grow. In some states planters voluntarily agreed to limited cotton acreage and appointed committees of safety or vigilance to enforce restrictions. State governments also passed laws limiting the amount of cotton that could be grown. Their actions, however, came late. Because the 1861 crop had already been planted when the war broke out, efforts to limit production did not begin until 1862. In March of that year, Arkansas enacted a law restricting cotton production to two bales per hand. Other states failed to pass laws until after the 1862 crop had been picked and baled. The limits placed on production by state governments varied from three acres per hand in Georgia to one acre per hand in South Carolina. Alabama levied a 10-cent-per-pound tax on any amount above 2,500 pounds per hand. Louisiana and Texas never enacted restrictive laws.

The Confederate Congress discussed limiting cotton production but in the end decided that passing a law to that effect would intrude on the rights of the states. Only a nonbinding resolution urging Southerners to plant food crops instead of cotton and tobacco was forthcoming from the lawmakers in Richmond. During the planting season of 1863, President Davis issued a proclamation asking Southerners to refrain voluntarily from planting cotton and tobacco. The largest producer of tobacco was Virginia, and the state legislature approved a limitation of 2,500 plants per hand. Tobacco planters, however, largely ignored the ordinance.[5]

Some scholars have challenged historians' often-held notion that many patriotic planters voluntarily decreased cotton production in favor of food crops to feed the populace. Stanley Lebergott, for example, has convincingly argued that planters in general put their own interests ahead of the immediate needs of the army and the homefolk and continued to grow large quantities of cotton for their own profit. He points out that during the war the Confederate states exported more than 900,000 bales of cotton to the North and 500,000 bales overseas. James L. Roark has concluded that "under Confederate policy, the production of cotton became unpleasant, unpatriotic, and even unprofitable. However, when the needs of the plantation clashed with the demands of the Confederacy, planters usually chose the homestead over the homeland."[6]

Planters throughout the Confederacy evaded requests, proclamations, and laws to restrict cotton production and grow such crops as corn, wheat, potatoes, beans, and peas. Some grew edible crops near main roads but raised cotton farther away. A number of planters openly defied government requests and laws. Even though President Davis and Gov. Joseph E. Brown of Georgia appealed late in the war for Georgia to plant more corn and less cotton, "not an acre in fifty in the best corn district of Georgia was planted in corn." The irascible Georgian Robert Toombs, former Confederate secretary of war, army general, and an antagonist to Davis, planted a full cotton crop and defiantly bragged that he "would plant as much cotton as he pleased regardless of laws and vigilance committees."[7]

Cotton growers who continued production of the staple sold much of it to brokers for shipment overseas through the blockade. In some areas businessmen, brokers, and speculators carried on a sizable illegal overland cotton trade with Northern buyers through army lines. In Alabama, for example, a large cotton trade flourished with agents or branch houses in Union-occupied New Orleans, who paid for the cotton in gold or greenbacks. Confederate authorities could do little to check such illicit commerce. Citizens in threatened areas retained and stored cotton, hoping for more lucrative times, and refused to surrender it to Confederate military authorities for destruction to prevent it from falling into the hands of the Union army and bolstering the enemy's coffers. When, in the final month of the war, Confederate officers ordered that all cotton, along with resin and turpentine, be collected and burned to keep it from falling into the hands of the enemy, the inhabitants of Mobile, Alabama, refused to cooperate. When Federal troops occupied the town on April 12, 1865, more than 20,000 bales of cotton and 25,000 barrels of resin and turpentine were found unscathed.[8]

Planter James Lusk Alcorn—whose Mississippi plantation Mound Place was valued at a quarter of a million dollars and worked by nearly one hundred slaves in 1860— secured large wartime profits by carrying on a successful "smuggling business" in cotton. At first he was ostracized by his planter neighbors, but by late 1862 most had joined him in the lucrative cotton trade that thrived as Federal forces occupied the Mississippi area. Roark writes that "up and down the Mississippi River, in fact, in Natchez, Memphis, Vicksburg, wherever Federal troops opened up the cotton market, local planters, after some hesitation perhaps, flocked to the market place."[9]

Overall cotton production did decline during the war. The number of bales grown in 1861 totaled 4,500,000. That dropped to 1,500,000 in the following year, to fewer than 500,000 in 1863, and to 300,000 in 1864. In the final weeks of the war, though, more planters with an eye to the future and a conviction that the war would soon end began planting cotton on a larger scale, and they produced 1,500,000 bales in the fall of 1865. They correctly anticipated that prices would rise significantly after the war. During the conflict New York prices for cotton rose from 13 cents per pound in 1861 to 31 cents in 1862, 67 cents in 1863, $1.01 in 1864, and a high of $1.90 in 1865.[10]

Still, with the overall drop in cotton production, more land could be used for growing food crops. Before the war, in order to devote as much land as possible to cotton, the South had imported from the northwest many of its foodstuffs. Now that the conflict had cut off those imports, the region had to produce more of its own corn, wheat, and other grains, as well as flour, pork, and beef. The fields devoted to corn particularly increased in number and expanded in size.

The largest grain-growing and meat-producing areas were in the Upper South. Supplies from the states there, however, were inhibited as Federal troops invaded and occupied the region, and both sides confiscated or impressed local crops and other supplies. As wheat became scarce, folk at home came to rely more and more on cornmeal, and flour went to the troops in bulk or as hardtack. A drought in 1862 devastated the grain crops in Virginia and the Deep South. But the following year brought a bumper crop of corn.[11]

Throughout the Confederacy planters and farmers raised hogs for local consumption. In 1860 the South had 20,637,000 hogs slated for eventual slaughter. In central Georgia alone in 1863, locals slaughtered 10,897 hogs, which produced 1,569,750 pounds of pork.[12] But many planters in the Deep South objected to raising swine on a large scale as undignified. "Planters had rather raise a pound of cotton at three cents than a pound of bacon at a dollar," cried one Georgia newspaper. Texas reigned as the largest producer of beef cattle, which were herded to market east of the Mississippi River. Texas beef was also packed as salt beef for the army at an Alexandria, Louisiana, slaughterhouse. After the Union army gained control of the Mississippi in 1863, the flow of Texas beef east of the river nearly ceased. Florida then became the major supplier for the east. But, like Texas, it had no railroad ties to other regions of the South.[13]

Slave labor remained the mainstay of large-scale agriculture. But the efficiency of the system was hindered by the disruptive circumstances of the war. With masters and overseers away serving in the army, supervision of workers became more difficult and the slaves less efficient. Field hands impressed to work on Confederate fortifications were not available for the cultivation of crops or care of livestock. Emboldened by less control and news of emancipation, slaves became more defiant and less cooperative. At times they refused to work or ran away. The loss of their labor had an adverse impact on agricultural production, and that effect worsened as the war continued.[14] The African American abolitionist Frederick Douglass accurately predicted the important result of the diminution or withdrawal of slave labor for Southern agriculture and the Confederate war effort. "The very stomach of this rebellion," he proclaimed, "is the negro in the condition of a slave. Arrest that hoe in the hands of the negro and you smite rebellion in the very seat of its life."[15]

Just as the people of the Civil War South witnessed a change in their region's agricultural production, they also saw an unfamiliar surge in the growth and development of industry. Unable to import many necessary items from the North or through the blockade, the South was forced to establish and expand its own industries. Historian Emory M. Thomas has written that "in terms of industrial strength the Confederacy was born with little and died with less." Yet in order to wage war and maintain its population at home, the Confederacy had to industrialize to an extent that was unpredicted in the agricultural South before the war. "At the prod of the War Department and the wartime market," contends Thomas, "Confederate manufactures accomplished little short of an industrial revolution."[16] Whether or not the rise of wartime Southern industry approached the scale of a true industrial revolution is open to debate. But one can conclude with certainty that the Confederacy underwent considerable industrial growth and that such an economic transformation had a measurable impact on the home-front population.

The Federal blockade hampered the importation from overseas of essential armaments and other war materials. Thus, out of necessity the Confederate government became directly involved in industrial production. The relative success of the South's weapons and munitions industries was attributable in large part to the leadership of Gen. Josiah Gorgas, chief of the Confederate Ordnance Bureau. War industries were scattered throughout the South. The government owned a number of them; private companies holding government contracts owned others. Locations of arsenals included Richmond, Virginia; Fayetteville, North Carolina; Charleston, South Carolina; Atlanta, Macon, Augusta, and Columbus, Georgia; Montgomery and Selma, Alabama; Jackson, Mississippi; Little Rock, Arkansas; and San Antonio, Texas. Cook and Brother Armory of Athens, Georgia, for example, had the capacity to manufacture 600 rifles per month, and the Confederate government contracted with the Rudisell Gold Mine Company of North Carolina for sulfur. In addition to its Confederate arsenal, Selma had the Naval Iron Foundry, five ironworks, and a gunpowder factory.

Richmond ranked as the Confederacy's largest industrial center. There the Tredegar Iron Works functioned as the most prolific producer of war materials. A private firm owned and operated since 1843 by Joseph R. Anderson, a graduate of West Point and a strong supporter of secession, Tredegar had produced cannon and gun carriages for the U.S. government before the war. During the conflict the company forged over 50 percent of the artillery manufactured domestically for the Confederate military. It also manufactured iron plates for ironclad vessels, propeller shafts, and torpedoes. The Richmond facility included two rolling mills, a foundry, machine shops, and forges. In addition Anderson expanded his operations in Virginia to include a tannery, shoemaking shops, a firebrick kiln, a sawmill, coal mines, a farm, nine canal boats, and a blockade-runner. At the outbreak of the war, Tredegar employed 700 workers. By January 1863 the number had grown to 2,500.[17]

New industries popped up throughout the South to supply the needs of soldiers and civilians. A shortage of shoes prevailed and was never completely eliminated. Leather remained scarce, but a number of private factories struggled to fill the shortage of footwear. The Quartermaster Department operated a factory in Richmond that was turning out 800 pairs of shoes daily in June 1864. A shoe factory in Columbus, Georgia, was making 5,000 pairs per week in November 1863. In one month in 1863, a shoe manufactory in Atlanta produced 40,000 pairs. Textile mills also began to dot the countryside to meet the demand for cloth for uniforms and clothing. North Carolina had the greatest number of mills. Of the South's eighty textile factories in operation in 1864, half were in the Tar Heel State. Conflict developed between the Confederate government and the states that supplied their own troops about the distribution of the cloth coming from those mills. The War Department claimed that states such as North Carolina were appropriating cloth that should go to the Confederate military at large.[18]

Agricultural Mississippi saw a remarkable birth of industry once the war began. Its industries became major suppliers for the Confederate army in the west. The towns of Jackson, Bankston, Columbus, Enterprise, Natchez, and Woodville all had clothing factories that employed local workers and turned out a total of 10,000 garments per week. Shoemakers in the state, working under government contracts, produced 8,000 pairs of shoes weekly. Companies in the towns of Enterprise and Canton built about sixty wagons and ambulances each week. A Magnolia tannery provided a large quantity of hides, and other facilities manufactured blankets and tents. According to a Jackson newspaper, such industries had "sprung up almost like magic."[19]

Factories in Columbus and Savannah, Georgia, and Richmond labored to satisfy the major demand for essential glassware items such as bottles, vials, windowpanes, and lamp chimneys. Hospitals especially needed glass containers. The manufacture of tobacco, for both smoking and chewing, continued to thrive. The major production sites for tobacco were at Richmond and Lynchburg, Virginia. Plants in Columbus began making grain sacks, socks, and wooden buttons. One in Montgomery, Alabama, produced blankets. Textile mills such as William Gregg's in South Carolina and the Eagle Manufacturing Company in Georgia increased their production in an effort to meet military and civilian needs. The state prison in Jackson, Mississippi, operated a textile mill. Soap factories appeared in Dalton and Augusta, Georgia, and Little Rock, Arkansas. A new ice-making machine developed by Capt. Camille Girardy in Augusta even began producing ice in 1864. Every Confederate state encouraged the establishment of factories to produce cotton and wool cards, cloth, and iron.

Industrialization was not limited to large war factories. The majority of industries were small operations with a limited output. They appeared in towns and villages throughout the South, especially in those where artisans, mechanics, and crafts-men had worked before the war. Small industries everywhere provided all sorts of items, many for domestic use. For example, one in Greensboro, Alabama, made pen-cils. Knives and forks came from Macon, Georgia, and Raleigh, North Carolina. A company in the village of Davidson College, North Carolina, made brooms. Black-smiths in Macon, Georgia, forged household furniture. Charleston workers turned out lampblack, umbrellas, and mirrors. One operation in Augusta County, Virginia, took advantage of nearby kaolin deposits to make chinaware. Some small industries attempted to meet the demand for cotton and wool cards, which was never satisfied. Others manufactured "soap, candles, wool and cotton materials, thread, matches, looms and spinning jennies, boxes, envelopes, writing paper, shoes, shoe pegs, various simple machines, utensils, lace, wagons, baskets, barrels, buckets, knitting needles, rope, furniture, cigars, glass, raincoats, ploughs, starch, hats, cutlery, buttons, and sewing machines."

Several newspapers and political and military leaders urged Southern folk to turn to manufacturing necessities. They emphasized that to be employed in mechanical or industrial work did not imply an inferior social status, which was a common view in an agrarian society that revered the planter ideal. "Let no one," declared the *Southern Cultivator*, "in whatever sphere he may have been reared, whether rich or poor educated or illiterate ... look down on manufacturing pursuits as beneath his dignity." Georgia became the most industrialized state in the Confederacy. It was followed by North Carolina, Alabama, and Virginia, in that order. Virtually every city or town of any size had one or more industries, no matter how small.[20]

The new emphasis on industrialization led to the publication of the *Merchants and Manufacturers Journal* in the fall of 1861 to encourage industrial development. The Direct Trade and Cotton Spinners Convention of Georgia, which had convened in Atlanta in 1860 to promote foreign trade, met again in April and changed its name to the Manufacturing and Direct Trade Association of the Confederate States. It sought to trade more goods with Europe and to influence Congress to import more duty-free cotton machinery. Four hundred delegates from nine states came together at another industrial convention in Macon, Georgia, in October 1861 to support manufacturing and the expansion of trade. The Planters Convention of the South, a promoter of agriculture, even began to encourage commercial and industrial development. In 1863 the Confederate Congress mandated that, until the end of the war, all machinery for the production of cotton and wool cloth could be imported without payment of any duty.

The inability to import or manufacture machinery, however, was a major deterrent to successful, large-scale industrialization in the Confederacy. Sustaining a viable labor supply was another obstacle to establishing a manufacturing economy. The army appropriated a large percentage of the white male workforce. Slaves, white women, and even sometimes children had to fill the void. At the Tredegar Iron Works, Anderson constantly faced the difficulty of keeping a sufficient number of workers as his labor force swelled to over three times the number of men employed at the start of the war. Some mechanics and iron foundry workers were detailed to Tredegar from the army. Anderson utilized hundreds of slaves but at one point was reduced to employing African American convicts from the state prisons. In order to feed the 2,500 laborers, he dispatched agents into several states to buy food. He purchased a large quantity of livestock, which was transported, slaughtered, and sold to his laborers at cost. In the winter of 1862–1863, the Tredegar employees consumed 1,000 hogs. To help clothe his workers Anderson utilized his tannery and shoe factory and sent cotton by blockade-runners to Bermuda to be traded for cloth.[21] Some larger towns and cities established associations to mobilize skilled and unskilled labor. In New Orleans in 1861, one such organization formed "to promote mechanical interests; to provide Southern mechanics and workmen; to establish an office where a register will be kept of all the members out of employment, so that employers will know where to find such as they want; and to establish a branch or branches of the association in every state of the Confederacy."[22]

To maintain themselves and their families, working-class women throughout the South whose menfolk were in the army sought jobs in the new industries established to produce war supplies and material. Many left their households and exclusive roles as wives and mothers for the first time. A significant number of single women also suddenly found themselves in the industrial workforce and away from home for the first time. For example, 400 "mill girls" worked in the cotton-cloth mill in Roswell, Georgia, that was destroyed by the troops of Gen. William T. Sherman in July 1864. To prevent the young female industrial workers from resuming manufacturing once his columns had departed, Sherman exiled them to Marietta, Georgia, by wagon and then to Louisville, Kentucky, by rail. A Northern newspaper correspondent described their initial journey: "Four hundred weeping and terrified Ellens, Susans, and Maggies transported, in the springless and seatless army wagons, away from their lovers and brothers and the sunny south, and all for the offense of weaving tent-cloth and spinning stocking yarns."[23]

Southern industrial workers frequently found wages low and working conditions dangerous. Faced with inflation and rising prices, they had difficulty supporting themselves and their families. In Georgia a "poor mechanic" complained to a local newspaper that his income was less than it had been before the war. Hazardous conditions and accidents were common in all operations. Perhaps the worst industrial accident was an explosion at the Confederate States Laboratory in Richmond, which killed between forty and fifty women. A similar event at a gunpowder plant in Jackson, Mississippi, resulted in the deaths of thirty-five men, women, and children. Still another devastating accident occurred at the Confederate States Laboratory in Augusta, Georgia. Nine employees were killed when 18,000 pounds of gunpowder exploded. The deceased were "blown to atoms. Hardly a vestige of them remaining. Portions of bodies were found hanging on the trees." Child laborers frequently became the victims of industrial accidents. When molten lead splashed on the face of Martin Reilly at a Savannah foundry, he became blind in one eye. The youth worked at the site to help support his widowed mother. Fifteen-year-old John Henry died when struck by a falling tree at Oglesby Mill near Augusta, Georgia. His father had been killed earlier at the mill. An exploding artillery shell mortally wounded two boys, ages twelve and fifteen, at the Naval Iron Works in Columbus.[24]

Poor working conditions and low wages led to labor strikes, which had been virtually unheard of in the prewar South. Irish workmen went on strike for higher wages in Richmond in 1861, and a series of strikes followed in other locales. In that same year, railroad machinists in Virginia and Tennessee went on strike, demanding $15.00 a day. Their request was denied. In the following year, employees in a harness factory stopped work in protest of unpaid wages. Men who went on strike suddenly became subject to conscription, even if they had previously received exemption from the draft to perform essential war work. When workers at the Mississippi Manufacturing Company in Bankston demonstrated publicly for better working conditions, they were dispersed by Confederate cavalry. In 1863 a group of soldiers detailed from the army to work in the Richmond Armory went on strike for wages higher than the $3.00 per hour they were making. The government dispatched them back to the army and a pay of $11.00 per month. Postal workers who went on strike for more pay had better luck when their salaries were adjusted. But a group of lithographers, who had been exempted from the draft, suddenly found themselves in military prison for withholding their labor. When Irish gravediggers went on strike in the Confederate capital, authorities substituted black laborers. The Irish attacked and drove away the African American diggers but still lost their employment when Virginia replaced them with prison inmates.

A large labor strike occurred in New Orleans in November 1861, when workers building the ironclad *Mississippi* took action to have their wages increased from $3.00 to $4.00 per day. To break the strike, the owner of the shipbuilding company, Asa F. Tift, brought in twenty laborers from Richmond. But the strikers kept them from working. To avoid further delays, the company gave in to the workers' demands.[25]

Struggling to feed and clothe their children and themselves, wives and mothers laboring in industries sometimes collectively demanded salary increases in the face of inflation and rising prices for necessities. In December 1863 female workers at the

Confederate States Laboratory in Richmond staged a strike for higher wages. They were being paid $2.40 per day and successfully negotiated for $3.00. At the same facility in October 1864, unmarried women, who were being paid $5.00 per day, demanded to be paid the same $7.00 that the married women received. When the single women went on strike, their married sisters supported them. But this time the management fired them all and hired 300 new workers.

For the most part, the strikes and protests by the South's industrial workers were spontaneous events and not part of a larger movement to form labor organizations or unions. The skilled newspaper typesetters of Richmond organized themselves into the Richmond Typographical Society, went on strike for higher wages, and attempted to enforce closed-shop practices among typesetters. A grand jury indicted them for conspiracy, but the case was dismissed on a technical point of law. In Augusta telegraph operators formed the Southern Telegraphic Association and went on strike for better pay, shorter working hours, and a closed shop. The telegraph companies, however, fired all the telegraphers who joined the union, and the War Department conscripted them into military service. Beyond these failed attempts by the two skilled groups, no substantial organized labor movement ever materialized.[26]

Despite the best efforts of many growers and workers, neither agricultural nor industrial production managed to fill the needs of the people of the Confederacy sufficiently. Shortages existed everywhere, though some areas at times suffered more than others, and the types of shortages varied from place to place. Historian Mary Elizabeth Massey described the situation well when she wrote:

> Shortages of supplies during the Civil War were so numerous and so prevalent that scarcely anyone escaped them. A North Carolina farmer, living in the Piedmont area, might have plenty to eat and a comfortable house in which to live, but he might have to do without shoes or to cut his farm acreage because an impressment officer had taken his last horse. A Richmond lady, heiress of great fortune, name, and prestige, might be able to purchase high-priced imported clothing or even stretch her extravagant prewar wardrobe over four years, but she might be unable to purchase quinine when she contracted malaria or to have brilliant illumination in her home. A Texas businessman might have plenty of meat straight from the nearby range, or he might obtain costly imported merchandise by way of Mexico, but at the same time he might have no salt for his meat and no newspaper to tell him the events of the day. Everyone in some way suffered from the shortages. Some effects were far-reaching, others were trifling, but all played a part in the drama of the war.[27]

There were a number of reasons why the Confederate states failed to provide adequately and consistently for the inhabitants of the Southern home front. The Federal blockade inhibited the importation of supplies. A large percentage of the products of farm and factory had to go for the support of a huge army. Hoarding and speculating also contributed to the problem of inequitable distribution. Inflation combined with rising prices placed desired items out of reach for many Southerners. Most of the new industries were small, their output was limited, and they often lacked "proper equipment, adequate raw materials, experienced workers, and managerial help." Federal troops invading the South frequently destroyed or took over for their own use factories, crops, and livestock.[28]

But perhaps the major cause of the failure to provide sufficiently and equitably for home-front folk was the Confederacy's wretched transportation system. When the Civil War began, the South had few interstate roads or highways. The Boston Post Road—called the Coastal Traffic Road—ran south of Washington through Savannah, Georgia, to St. Augustine, Florida. In Virginia the Great Valley Road connected with the Valley Turnpike from Hagerstown, Maryland, and with a route from Richmond at Lynchburg and then continued on to Knoxville, Tennessee. An additional route connected Knoxville and Nashville. Then General Jackson's Military Road tied Nashville to Madisonville, Louisiana, near New Orleans. Still another road, known as the Unicoy Road, ran from Nashville to Augusta, Georgia. One of the most famous of the Southern highways was the Old Natchez Road, once called the Natchez Trace. It ran from Natchez, Mississippi, to Nashville and had been an important path for keelboat men returning northward after selling their cargoes and boats at New Orleans or other sites on the lower Mississippi River. The Trace had also served as a wagon road, although the advent of the steamboat reduced traffic on the road.

Other long-distance highways included one running from Nashville to Memphis and then to Little Rock and Fort Smith, Arkansas. The Butterfield Overland Mail connected Washita and El Paso, Texas, and a Florida road ran from Pensacola to St. Augustine. The states, counties, and towns constructed various other roads, some of which charged tolls.

But the Southern roads had never been consistently maintained, and the ability of state and local governments to keep them in good repair diminished further during the war. Only a few highways, such as the Valley Turnpike, were paved. Others used gravel, where it was accessible. Some routes employed planks or "corduroy" (logs) to overcome muddy conditions. Streets in cities and towns might have stone blocks or cobblestones. But most public thoroughfares were dirt, and their condition and maintenance depended upon mandatory labor by local citizens. The roads were often filled with potholes and ruts. As the war wore on and available labor and funds declined, their condition worsened. Violent weather and traffic wore away the roadbeds. Bridges deteriorated or were destroyed by the armies, and ferries often operated erratically.[29] Union invasion and occupation severely curtailed the South's reliance on rivers for transporting agricultural and other supplies. When Federal troops seized control of the Mississippi River and its port towns in 1863, they gained control of virtually the entire Mississippi River Valley and cut off supplies from the Trans-Mississippi region to the eastern Confederacy.[30]

Railroads—the technological and transportation boon in nineteenth-century America—also left much to be desired in the Confederacy compared to the Northern states. According to historian Robert C. Black III, "it was possible in 1861 to trace through the South the outlines of two major railroad routes, one complete, the other unfinished. In general they followed a basic southwest-to-northeast pattern imposed by the Appalachian Mountains.... [T]he southwestern terminus of the system lay in Mississippi and Louisiana; the northeastern anchor was Richmond, Virginia. The first of these lines involved a northerly passage through Corinth, Chattanooga, and Bristol; the second, and unfinished, route ran via Montgomery, Atlanta, Augusta, Wilmington, and Petersburg." One hundred and thirteen railroad lines of various sizes ran throughout the Southern states.[31]

But there was no real railroad *system* in the Confederacy. Railway lines had never been evenly distributed. Because rivers, "often swift-running in their passage from the mountains to the sea, had never served as really satisfactory channels of trade," the Atlantic Seaboard states had a "relatively high degree of railway development."[32] In 1861 Virginia could claim the most miles of track, with 1,800 miles. Georgia had almost 1,400, and South Carolina nearly 1,000. North Carolina had around 900 miles. The Gulf states, however, had long enjoyed the natural advantages for trade and transportation of such rivers as the Mississippi, the Alabama, and the Tombigbee. Railroad development, consequently, was less extensive in the west than in the east. Alabama had only 643 miles of track, and Mississippi 797. Louisiana included a mere 328 miles of rail, and Florida had slightly less. Neither Arkansas nor Texas could boast of the number of its miles. In the western South, only Tennessee had a sizable system of completed track, with 1,284 miles.

When the war broke out, the Confederate states had few trunk lines. Separate companies owned much of the track, which customarily led to seaports and centers of trade. The average length of a main line was usually less than 200 miles. The longest line owned by one company was the Mobile and Ohio, which was 469 miles in length and connected Mobile, Alabama, to Columbus, Kentucky. It was completed soon after the conflict began. West of the Mississippi River, all the railroads were "scattered and local."[33]

At many points in the Confederacy, serious gaps existed in important routes. For example, a fifty-mile break divided the line between Danville, Virginia, and Greensboro, North Carolina. The tracks of Texas and Florida did not connect with those of other states, and those in central Alabama remained incomplete. A Virginia law prohibited any railroad from laying track within a city without the permission of local officials. Because Richmond officials did not grant such permission, none of the five railroads that ran toward the city intersected. Cargoes destined from one line to another had to be moved by wagon through the streets. In Petersburg crosstown supplies had to be moved in a similar manner. In Augusta, Georgia, railways from South Carolina and Georgia remained separated from the Augusta and Savannah line by a mere 600 yards. Varied track gauges further compounded the difficulty of shipping supplies by rail. The standard gauge for the width of track was 5 feet. But railroads in some states had a gauge of 4 feet 8 $\frac{1}{2}$ inches. The New Orleans, Opelousas, and Great Western; the Memphis and Little Rock; and the Vicksburg, Shreveport, and Texas all had a track gauge of 5 feet 6 inches. The Roanoke Valley Railroad actually built two segments of its own line with different gauges. The varied gauges of track slowed and disrupted long-distance traffic, because supplies on cars of one track width had to be unloaded and reloaded on cars of another gauge. The South's inability to manufacture sufficient iron to replace worn-out track, to build and repair locomotives and cars, to provide fuel and lubricants, and to keep an adequate labor force further inhibited rail transportation.[34]

The overall failure or success of agricultural and industrial production in the Confederacy is hard to measure. No wartime census data exist from which to draw precise conclusions. It is relatively certain, though, that a labor force diminished by a large number of white men serving in the military inhibited productivity in field and factory. The flight, impressment, and resistance of slaves adversely affected their involuntary contributions to an economic system that kept them in bondage. A substandard transportation network made it difficult to distribute those supplies that were available. The needs of the army usually took priority over those of the civilian population, and armies from both sides impressed or confiscated much that could have helped feed and clothe the Southern people. As never before, women stepped up on farms and plantations and in various jobs and industries to fill the void of workers created by the absence of husbands, fathers, sons, and brothers gone for soldiers. Their achievements in the face of adversity must have been sizable. But in the end, probably no amount of effort by the inhabitants of the Confederate home front could have saved them from the deprivations that war can inflict upon an agrarian society. Civilians everywhere did without necessities as well as customary luxuries. No one escaped wartime hardship entirely. But the Southern folk adapted as best they could. They found new and inventive ways to cope, and the most destitute among them looked to their local governments for relief.

THREE

❦

DESTITUTION, POOR RELIEF, AND ERSATZ

The reality of the pain and costs of war was visited directly on the people of the Confederacy by shortages of food, clothing, housing, medicine, and myriad other "necessities." To some extent everyone in the South endured the lack of essentials and luxuries, a situation exacerbated by the Union blockade of Confederate seaports. At first shortages of certain items were viewed as mere inconveniences. In June 1861 the *Charleston Mercury* trumpeted the worth of "Home Resources." The editor observed that "it is perfectly surprising how well we get on without Yankee notions. It is surprising how little we really needed, or should have bought of their jimcrackeries." The Southern states could produce everything they really needed, asserted the *Mercury*, both the weapons of war and the necessities of life.[1] But as the war wore on, genuine and widespread suffering developed, particularly—and not surprisingly—among the poor. "The prospect for the winter is gloomy indeed," wrote Anna Long Thomas Fuller of Louisburg, North Carolina, in November 1864. "Prices are exorbitant. The poor must suffer, I'm sure. I hear there are a number of families in our community who have been without meat for months."[2]

The shortage that Southerners felt most was limited food supplies. Much of the crop and livestock production on Confederate farms went to feed the army. With so many men away serving in the ranks, a diminished labor force existed. Poor transportation facilities made it difficult to ship supplies to areas in need, and an ever-tightening blockade restricted available quantities of various foodstuffs. A lack of salt hindered the preserving and shipping of beef and pork, significant components of the

Southern diet. Crews at salt-making stations—such as those at Saltville, Virginia, in Alabama and Louisiana, and along the coasts—labored to produce salt, but there never seemed to be enough of the valuable preservative, especially during the winter season, when livestock was slaughtered and the meat preserved. The blockade contributed to the problem of insufficient salt, which had largely been imported from Europe and the West Indies prior to the war. After meat and salt, sugar was probably the most-missed food item in the Confederacy. Most of the South depended on the cane fields of Louisiana for sugar. But when Union forces captured New Orleans and then gained complete control over the Mississippi River, thereby dividing the Confederacy, sugar nearly disappeared in the east. Housewives hoarded the precious commodity, some sugar arrived on blockade-runners, and a small amount came from the cane grown in Florida and Georgia.[3]

Although not as severe or as quick to appear as dwindling food supplies, a serious shortage of clothing and shoes developed before the war ended. The antebellum South had imported most of its clothing and shoes from the North and Europe. Its mills had produced largely a coarse material intended primarily for slave clothing. The few mills that manufactured a better grade of cloth had limited production. Similarly, little expertise existed in the making of shoes. The small number of cobblers in the region could not keep the Southern population properly shod, and the shortage of shoes exceeded that of clothing. Leather was never available in large supply, and the government requisitioned two-thirds of what was produced. The problem for folk on the home front was made worse when the Confederate and state governments took over many clothing factories and shoemaking operations in an effort to supply the army. Much-needed cloth and shoes usually made up a part of the cargoes of blockade-runners. But the supply remained insufficient.[4] In April 1862 Mrs. Margaret Preston of Lexington, Virginia, lamented the difficulty of obtaining cloth. "I actually dressed my baby all winter," she despaired, "in calico dresses made out of the lining of an old dressing gown."[5] In March 1863 women in Salisbury, North Carolina, complained that "many of us have been shoeless this whole winter except the cloth shoes we can make for ourselves which are not protection even against the cold."[6] Even members of the upper class sometimes went without shoes. Young Susan Bradford of Pine Hill Plantation in Leon County, Florida, noted in her diary in April 1864, "Today I have no shoes to put on. All my life I have never wanted to go bare-footed, as most Southern children do. The very touch of my naked feet to the bare ground made me shiver." Two days later she recorded that "today I have on railroad stockings and slippers. Guess what those slippers are made of? Whenever I go to Uncle Richard's I see an old black uncle, hard at work plaiting shucks and weaving the plaits together into door mats. It seemed to me a lighter braid might be sewed into something resembling shoes, so I picked out the softest shucks and soon had enough to make one slipper. So pleased was I that I soon had a pair of shoes ready to wear."[7]

Closely associated with the dearth of clothing was an insufficient number of cotton and wool cards, which were needed in households to convert cotton and wool into thread to be woven into cloth for family clothing. Attempts by the states to build machinery and manufacture the cards on a large scale proved largely unsuccessful. One machine manufacturer who inspected a card-making factory at Milledgeville, Georgia, found its machinery erratic and its output poor. He concluded that "our only resource for obtaining cards is in foreign importation & running the blockade." But the number of cards that arrived through the blockade was never enough to meet the demand.[8] Cotton was plentiful for both home spinning and textile mill production. Wool, however, did not exist in the same quantity, and authorities urged some farmers not to kill their sheep for mutton.

The unsettling nature of war produced a shortage in housing as well. Refugees fleeing from Federal attack particularly had problems finding adequate shelter. They migrated into cities and towns and were usually overcrowded in private residences, boardinghouses, and hotels. The housing shortage was worsened by a lack of new construction and the destruction spread by both armies. Lumber supplies were small.

Adequate stocks of household items and the "little things of life" disappeared during the war. Coal and wood for heating and cooking remained in short supply. Forests contained much wood, but limited labor and transportation hampered its distribution. Usually imported from New England, candles were few and much desired. "Lucifer" matches, which had been obtained from the North before the war, arrived through the blockade, but never in sufficient numbers. Substitute "Confederate" matches proved much less satisfactory for lighting fires, candles, and lamps. Kerosene, the customary fuel for lamps, virtually vanished from households. The cities that provided gaslight for streets, offices, and houses had to deal with sporadic and expensive service and supply. Northern lubricating oil for machinery and sperm oil for illumination were cut off. Broken and worn-out furniture could seldom be replaced. The military's demand for iron left little for manufacturing cookstoves, which were too heavy for import through the blockade. Beds and bedding, including springs, mattresses, blankets, sheets, and pillowcases, became ragged and torn and could not be replaced. Many bed linens were shredded into bandages for army hospitals. Cracked, broken, or lost cooking utensils, dishes, glassware, silverware, washbowls, pitchers, and other ceramic containers and fragile household items usually were not replaced. Broken farm tools, harnesses, and other equipment often fell to the same fate. Nails, screws, and locks became increasingly scarce, as did household implements such as sewing needles and thread, knitting needles, pins, buttons, buckles, and snaps. Most of these had to come through the blockade. Cleanliness suffered when soap supplies diminished. The imports coffee, tea, and ice became seldom-seen but desired luxuries. Hospitals in need of ice asked civilians to conserve and donate it. Because of a shortage of paper and ink, a number of newspapers and magazines ceased publication, and book printers closed their shops. The paper mills that managed to remain open labored with worn-out machinery and a lack of raw materials. Pencils, pens, stamps, envelopes, and stationery were hard to come by.

The Confederacy attempted to cope with such shortages in a variety of ways. As noted earlier, a number of factories sprang up or enlarged their capacities to replace many articles previously imported but now unavailable from the North and overseas. But for the home-front population—because of limited resources and labor as well as a need to put the military first—these efforts were never enough to provide adequate supplies in a would-be nation whose antebellum plantation economy lacked a strong industrial base.[9]

The ordinary folk's need and desire for the essentials of living led to the establishment of "cottage industries" in civilian homes, barns, and sheds. Cotton and wool cards, made from scarce wire and leather, ranked at the top of the list for home manufacture. The demand for them never declined, and the price of a pair rose from 40 cents before the war to the wartime price of $40.00. According to historian Mary Elizabeth Massey, "So critical was the situation that it caused real anxiety among those who had to produce their cloth or do without, for the poorer people, unlike the leaders of society, had no clothing stock from which to draw. . . . If a family had any cards, the chances were they possessed not more than one pair, and only the most trusted hands on the place were allowed to touch them."[10]

To alleviate or compensate for the vast shortages that seemed to grow daily, the people of the Confederacy began to resort to ersatz remedies for items that they so needed and desired. They proved persistent, if not always successful, in making do with what substitutes they could produce or scrounge. At times they showed amazing creativity in finding substitutes for the necessities and luxuries that they had enjoyed before the war. But of course there is no substitute for the calories and nutrients of food, and there never seemed to be enough, especially for the poor. The scarcest foodstuffs were generally items not produced in sufficient quantities locally, and the extent of shortages varied according to time and place.[11]

As a shortage of meat grew, more Southerners, especially in the towns and cities, began to raise and slaughter their own livestock. Where animals could be consumed immediately in this manner, without the need to salt and ship the meat, supplies tended to be larger than in areas that depended on preserved and shipped meat. In her diary in March 1864, Mary B. Chesnut commented on the large number of hogs in Mobile—"those horrid beasts from which delicious pork and sausages are made."[12] In the winter of 1865, livestock, particularly hogs, was so plentiful in the Alabama port as to create problems for the city's authorities. The animals were permitted to run unrestrained in the streets, and the loose livestock became such a public health problem and hazard that the city council passed an ordinance to establish an animal pound for "creatures running at large in the city." The order provided for the appointment of an inspector to apprehend loose livestock, with his salary fixed by the mayor and paid out of fines and forfeitures of owners who let their animals roam at will. The offending animals included hogs, horses, goats, and other members of the "rooting gentry." The new regulation exempted cows, specifically permitting them the run of the streets. "But it does look as though," complained the Mobile *Register*, "that they should be stopped from poaching on the wharves; but, however, the government is rich and can afford to feed all the cattle in the city."

Mobile remained well supplied with meat during the most difficult period of the Federal siege and throughout the last months of the war. In addition to local livestock, meat supplies regularly came to the Alabama port from the state's interior and sold for relatively reasonable prices. The *Register* in January 1865 could favorably report that "the meat crop is large this year" and had doubled from the year before. In some counties of Alabama, livestock producers had been furnishing Mobile with pork at a dollar a pound.[13] But Mobile's abundance of meat was an exception. Most urban dwellers and many residents in the countryside endured a lack of that commodity.

Among the more palatable substitutes for beef and pork and the protein they provided were fish, fowl, eggs, and peanuts. But supplies of these frequently diminished and at times disappeared. By late 1864 Southerners in some areas had resorted to eating cats, dogs, frogs, snails, snakes, and birds. Rats became part of some folks' diet, and President Davis himself compared them to squirrel meat. In besieged Vicksburg rats hung in the marketplace and sold for $2.50 each. The rodents were also on the menu in Richmond. In Vicksburg mule meat was sold daily, but it was expensive. Five dollars bought only a small portion.

An adequate substitute for salt was never found. Attempts at using wood ashes were unsuccessful. Boiling brine and scraping smokehouse floors did not produce any significant quantities either. For fats such as butter, oils, and lard there were no really good substitutes. Perhaps the best was oil from sunflower seeds, which was sometimes used in place of olive oil. More viable alternatives existed for sugar. The most popular was sorghum. Honey served too, and a syrup made from figs and watermelon could be used as a sweetener. Quality white flour became almost impossible to come by. Wheat imports had disappeared, and attempts to grow and mill the grain locally had mostly failed. The more common cornmeal replaced white flour in baking. A popular piecrust utilized white potatoes instead of flour. Rice, where it could be grown, and hominy were converted into flour, as were less-satisfactory substitutes such as pea meal.

A variety of beverages replaced coffee and tea. Coffee was a standard drink throughout the South, and families lucky enough to procure some through the blockade hoarded the beans and diluted the liquid to make it last. Blends and substitutes included brewed corn, rye, okra seeds, chicory, acorns, dandelion roots, rice, cottonseed, sorghum, sugarcane, peanuts, peas, and beans. Southerners did not drink as much tea as coffee, but those who did often had to console themselves with sassafras tea and various concoctions derived from the leaves of blackberries, raspberries, huckleberries, currants, willow sage, holly trees, several vegetables, and the coastal plant yaupon.

Milk too could be scarce, and households often thinned it with water to make it last. One beverage that never seemed to be lacking was distilled alcohol in various forms. The blockade inhibited the availability of imported wine, whiskey, and brandy, which commanded high prices. But whiskey could be made from virtually anything—from corn to sweet potatoes to sorghum seed—and it could be found in any setting, urban or rural. Disregarding state laws against wasting corn and other grains in the manufacture of whiskey, moonshiners did a thriving business and found a ready market for their product, despite its dubious quality. One consumer of the potent drink remarked that it "cauterizes the mucus membrane of the windpipe, sets the brain on fire, and sends a cold tremor through the system." Home-brewed beer—sometimes known as "Confederate beer"—emerged from a mixture of molasses, yeast, and ginger. Beer lovers called beer made from persimmons "possum beer." In Savannah, Georgia, a blend of juniper berries and whiskey sold as "imported Holland gin." Southerners consumed large quantities of alcohol during the war, and, as noted earlier, alcoholism became a severe problem.[14]

Industrially manufactured cloth became so rare for civilian clothing that virtually everyone wore ersatz garments at some point. For the first year and a half of the war, most of the population experienced no significant shortage of clothing. But eventually clothing wore out, and with industrial production limited, a scarcity of cloth for civilians prevailed. Spinning wheels and homemade looms appeared in most households, and the wearing of homespun cloth became virtually universal. Homespun for men's suits practically replaced the finer broadcloth by the end of the war. Women's dresses made from the material could be most attractive, incorporating a variety of checks, plaids, and stripes. Some homespun "was nearly as fine as muslin, while some was so coarse that straws might be shot through it without injuring it in any way." For some Southerners the wearing of homespun even became a symbol of patriotism. The chorus of the 1862 patriotic song "Homespun Dress" rang:

> Hurrah! Hurrah!
> For the sunny South so dear
> Three cheers for the homespun dress
> That Southern ladies wear

But for the poor classes, who suffered most from the lack of clothing and other necessities, such patriotic melodies had a hollow ring.[15]

When clothes were completely beyond mending and there was no homespun available, resourceful women converted other items into garments. These included curtains and draperies. Sometimes carpets, usually used for making ersatz shoes, were converted into coats and suits. A scarcity of wool led to a number of improvised alternatives, including a mixture of cotton and rabbit or raccoon fur, and cotton blended with dog or cow hair. If some wool was available, it could be combined with other animal fur or hair. To obtain dyes for clothing, people often resorted to searching among the woods and fields for berries, roots, nuts, leaves, and barks that produced colors that could substitute for commercial products. An insufficient quantity of tanned leather made it difficult for regular or amateur cobblers to make enough shoes. Nor were there ever enough of the tacks and strong needles necessary to craft the footwear. Shoemakers of various skills used an assortment of hides, including the skins of dogs, deer, sheep, goats, squirrels, and pigs. Shoes made of dog skins actually became fashionable, and some cobblers even advertised for the hides. Pigskin proved the least desirable because it stretched too much. Shoes frequently had wooden soles.[16]

Southerners derived replacements for many articles associated with day-to-day living. Ladies' hats were created from old bonnets or from straw, pine needles, and palmetto and adorned with feathers, flowers, berries, and even shavings from cow horns. For men's headgear, an ersatz felt could be made from wool, cotton, and animal hair. But most hats for males were fashioned of straw or pine needles. Knitted caps became common, even for President Davis, in the winter. The tall silk hats of the antebellum period practically vanished; some became dilapidated remnants of their former selves. Raincoats were cut from oilcloth or occasionally from "rubberized piano covers." Homespun was the last resort for making undergarments, old pillowcases and sheets being the first choice. Cut-up carpets served as blankets when none were to be had. Candles had various designs. They were usually made from strips of rags sewn together, twisted, and dipped several times in a mixture of beeswax, rosin, and turpentine. With little kerosene available for oil lamps, the home-front population turned to less-satisfactory "terebine oil," derived from "redistilled turpentine." Other substitutes included oil from peas, sunflowers, cottonseed, and corn. For illumination, some people attempted to use pine torches or lighted wicks in containers of various greases, oils, or fats, but these never performed adequately. Grease and fats were also collected to make soap at home. Wooden knives, forks, and spoons replaced lost or stolen silverware. Tin plates and cups substituted for broken china and glassware. As discussed earlier, a number of herbs and ersatz remedies were tried as replacements for unavailable medicines.

When paper and paper products became scarce, Southerners improvised. Scraps of wrapping paper, the backs of old letters, blank pages from books, and sheets from prescription pads were substituted for writing paper. Correspondents made envelopes from wrapping paper or folded their letters to serve as their own envelopes. To conserve paper people practiced "cross-writing," in which they wrote left to right as normal but then turned the paper upside down and wrote from bottom to top between the lines. Diaries were recorded on wrapping paper or other scraps or sheets of poor quality. Slates and shingles sometimes served for note taking. Rags, cornhusks, cotton, and sunflower stalks were used to make paper, but in insufficient quantities and of not-very-satisfactory quality. It was easier to find acceptable substitutes for ink, and most households had a recipe that worked reasonably well. They derived ink from a variety of barks, leaves, and fruits.

Other ersatz products appeared in lieu of common items. Goose quills replaced pens, and coal substituted for graphite in pencils. Gum from trees and a flour-and-water paste functioned as glue. In lieu of postal stamps, writers frequently paid the local postmaster the price of postage, and he then marked the letter "paid." Blacksmiths had only partial success in making ersatz needles and pins but did fairly well in hammering out knitting needles, which could also be made from wood. Bone and wood went into the manufacture of buttons, and wooden pegs often took the place of nails and screws.[17]

Inflation made it difficult to purchase whatever staples were available for sale. Without sufficient gold to back up its paper money, the Confederate government saw its currency fall in value as the war continued. When the conflict began, the Confederate Treasury Department issued millions of dollars worth of unsupported notes that were to be paid after the conflict ended. By the spring of 1862, Confederate currency had fallen to 65 cents on the dollar as measured by gold. Within a year it dropped to 30 cents, and there was very little silver and gold in circulation. As the war went on and the scarcity of hard currency increased, the Confederate government issued large numbers of treasury notes that could not be sold or redeemed. This further aggravated the decline in value of Confederate scrip. The problem became still worse as states, cities, banks, and some businesses also issued paper money. The supply of gold declined in the marketplace when wealthy investors began buying and hoarding it, especially in the final months of the war. "All of this . . . looks very much like gambling at a cock pit—40 to 1 that the Confederates lose the day," opined the Mobile *Register*. "Of course nobody would make such a wager in so many words, but the result is about the same."[18]

Predictably, when purchasing power declined because of inflation, prices rose. A woman shopping in Richmond complained that she "took my money in the market-basket and brought home the purchases in my pocketbook."[19] In the Virginia capital in February 1864, flour was selling for $225.00 to $250.00 per barrel, corn for $28.00 to $30.00 a bushel, meal for $30.00 to $35.00 per barrel, bacon for $6.00 to $6.50 a pound, apples for $90.00 to $110.00 per barrel, brown sugar for $11.00 to $12.00 per pound, sorghum molasses for $40.00 per gallon, and onions for $35.00 per bushel. Potatoes were relatively inexpensive at $10.00 to $14.00 per bushel. Prices varied from place to place and depended upon the success or failure of annual agricultural harvests, the size of industrial production, and a community's proximity to rail depots, mills, ports, and other supply facilities. Richmond had probably some of the highest prices anywhere. In June 1864 the Richmond *Examiner* noted that the prices in Columbia, South Carolina, were less than one-fifth of those in the Virginia city. But no matter where one lived, prices in general continued to soar as the war went on. In Charleston in 1861, beef sold for 15 cents per pound. Three years later the price was $3.00 per pound.[20] Cities had the largest crowds to stand in provision lines and make demands on retail merchants. But small communities were farther away from rail connections and main depots where supplies were delivered. In the small agricultural town of Louisburg, North Carolina, Anna Long Thomas Fuller noted in January 1864 that "the high price of provisions is alarming. Pork is selling at $2 per [pound], corn at $50 and flour $75 and $80, and everything else in proportion. Clothing, too, is enormously high. Calico is from $7 to $10 per yard and homespun $10 and $25." In April she reported that "the scarcity of all kinds is alarming."[21]

Although everyone on the home front, in town or country, felt the pain of hard times at some point, the inhabitants of cities and towns besieged by the enemy endured perhaps the most immediate hardships. Of those urban bastions, besieged Vicksburg probably suffered the most. As Union artillery and gunboats bombarded the town in the spring and summer of 1863, the inhabitants sought safety in the many caves dug in the streets and surrounding hills. Refugee Lida Lord Reed described the plight of civilians who scrambled underground to escape death and maiming.

> The people in our cave that night were not counted, but I have heard it stated since, that including three wounded soldiers, there must then have been at least sixty-five human beings under that clay roof; and I can say positively that they were packed in, white and black, like sardines in a box. A big store-box lined with blankets held several babies, and upon a mattress on the damp floor lay a lady accustomed to the extremest luxury, with an infant beside her only eight days old.
>
> All that Thursday night the shelling never ceased. Candles were forbidden, and we could only see one another's faces by the lurid, lightning-like flashes of the bursting bombs. Sometimes a roar, a more startling gleam, would cause us all to huddle closer together and shut our eyes, feeling that our last hour had come. Frightened women sobbed, babies cried, tired and hungry children fretted, and poor soldiers groaned; and a little girl, crushed by a fall of earth from the side of one of the caves, moaned incessantly and piteously. No wonder that the blessed daylight came like heaven.[22]

During bombardments some civilians never made it to the sanctuary of the caves unscathed. "A mother, rushing to save her child from a bursting shell, had her arm taken off by a fragment. . . . My own little brother," recalled Reed, "barely escaped being cut in two before our eyes, a Parrott shell passing over his back so close that it scorched his jacket. There were many other narrow escapes and frightful casualties." The victims of Vicksburg also faced starvation, and virtually anything edible was consumed. Reed noted that even a pet pony named Cupid, who was the "idol of every child in camp," was slaughtered and eaten. "Cupid had something of the look and all the peculiarities of a mule," she reported. "He would kick outrageously, and his capers provided fun for the whole camp. In the last days of the siege he disappeared. His fate was a mystery, over which, perhaps we had better draw a veil, for men were hungry, and Cupid was meat." When Vicksburg surrendered on July 4, the Union army immediately began dispensing emergency rations to the destitute. "[W]ithin twenty-four hours we were, with many others, receiving rations as 'a family in destitute circumstances,'" remembered Reed.[23]

In the final days of the war, Richmond and Petersburg, strangled by the entrenched Army of the Potomac, teetered on the brink of starvation. One resident of the capital reported in March 1865 that "the wolf is at the door here. We dread starvation far more than we do Grant and Sherman. Famine—that is the word now."[24]

By the second year of the war, food shortages were resulting in "bread riots" in Southern cities and towns. These demonstrations were frequently—but not exclusively—staged by women, upon whom the care and sustenance of children and the elderly fell, especially with draft-age husbands and sons in the army. The most notorious of these riots occurred in Richmond on April 2, 1863. Faced with a want of food—which recently had been made worse by a snowstorm that kept farmers and their produce out of the city—a group of women gathered in the morning at a local church to commiserate about their plight. They then marched to the Governor's Mansion and complained to Gov. John Letcher, who expressed his sympathy but failed to assuage the protestors.

A group of men and boys soon joined the women at Capitol Square, and the throng began to march down Main Street, shouting "Bread!" The rioters, who numbered about 1,000, broke into stores and shops, taking food, clothing, and shoes. Mayor Joseph Mayo, Governor Letcher, and President Davis all confronted the crowd and called for it to disperse. Although accounts vary as to which of the three officials threatened to have troops fire on the mob, it most likely was Letcher. The protestors did disperse, although a few were arrested by the police. Confederate and local authorities attempted to play down the seriousness of the uprising, claiming that the participants were thieves after only dry goods and luxuries, that destitution was much worse in the North, and even that the riot had been incited by Yankee spies. The mayor, however, feared further incidents and called on the Confederate army for support. Two battalions were placed on standby in case of future outbreaks.[25]

The Richmond incident was indicative of events taking place all over the South. A decline in food supplies had afflicted Mobile, Alabama, since the Union blockade was established. In April 1863 shortages led to a "bread riot" in that port city. The incident occurred not long after a surge of rumors regarding peace. "Rendered desperate by their sufferings," the rioters "met in large numbers on the Spring Hill road, with banners on which were printed such devices as 'bread or blood' on one side and 'bread and peace' on the other, and armed with knives and hatchets, marched down Dauphine Street breaking open the stores in their progress, and taking for their use such articles of food and clothing as they were in urgent need of."[26] Confederate officers called out troops to confront the rioters but quickly withdrew the soldiers when they began to mingle with the crowd. The protestors dispersed of their own accord, carrying their booty with them. Town officials and newspapers avoided drawing attention to the incident because they feared that such information might damage morale and incite further discontent. In Talladega, Alabama, women broke into a store to get at its stock of shoes. In Lafayette, Alabama, an armed group stormed a gristmill and made off with a supply of flour.[27]

In North Carolina in March 1863, a group of women in Salisbury walked en masse downtown and demanded to purchase supplies from local merchants at suggested government prices.[28] When the merchants declined to sell at those prices, the women "then forced our way in and compelled them to give us something." From stores and the local depot they "succeeded in obtaining twenty three blls of flour two sacks of salt and half a bll of molasses and twenty dollars in money, which was equally divided among us."[29] On April 8 women staged a similar raid in Greensboro. According to Nancy Mangum of nearby McLeansville, "a crowd of we poor women went to Greenseborough yesterday for something to eat as we had not a mouthful meet nor bread in my house. . . . I have 6 little children and my husband in the armey and what am I to do." Unlike their sisters in Salisbury, the women in Greensboro did not escape arrest. "[W]hat did they do but put us in jail," reported Mangum. "[T]hree and four men gatherd hold of one woman and took their armes away from them and led them all up to gail." Authorities "threatened to shoot us and drawed their pistols over us."[30]

Also in the spring of 1863, women determined to feed and clothe their children conducted raids on mercantile establishments and warehouses throughout Georgia. When a group asked a store owner on Atlanta's White Hall Street for the price of bacon, he replied that the nonnegotiable charge was $1.00 per pound. Their leader, "a tall lady on whose countenance rested care and determination," declared that such a price was extortion, and then she "proceeded to draw from her bosom a long navy repeater, and at the same time ordered the others in the crowd to help themselves to what they liked." The women departed with $200 worth of bacon. Women— called "Amazonian Warriors" by one editor—also seized dry goods from merchants in Augusta, Columbus, and Milledgeville.[31]

As the war continued, shortages spread, prices soared, and civilian raids to secure food and other provisions increased. In an attempt to alleviate their citizens' hunger, other needs, and growing dissatisfaction with the war, all the states of the South created relief programs for the destitute families of soldiers in Confederate or state service. Originally some county and city governments tried to provide such assistance. In June 1861 the *Memphis Daily Appeal* urged the Memphis City Council to "employ and pay a public almoner [charity worker] and contribute to a public relief fund." The newspaper warned that "owing to the absence of a considerable portion of the male community, many mothers and sisters will be left in very serious straits; and . . . there will be much difficulty in families hitherto exempt from privation."[32] But the demand soon exceeded the capacity of local governments, and state governments had to become involved.

The relief rendered by the state authorities included the distribution of money, salt, corn, bacon, flour, sugar, and other scarce provisions. Some state governments also authorized impressment of provisions and taxes-in-kind in order to secure sustenance for their poor. In addition to the millions of dollars collected by county governments for poor relief in North Carolina, the state added several million more. In December 1862 the legislature appropriated $400,000 to purchase provisions for the poor. It followed that appropriation with four additional acts "for the relief of the Wives and Families of Soldiers in the Army." These laws provided $1 million in February 1863, $1 million in December 1863, $1 million in May 1864, and $3 million in the last months of 1865. According to these acts, the county justices of the peace were responsible for distributing the relief, and they could claim state support in either cash or supplies.

Similar systems operated in other states. Georgia initially mandated that $2,500,000 be provided for direct relief in cash, $500,000 for the purchase of salt, and $100,000 to build factories for cotton and wool cards. In December 1863 the state set aside another $6 million for aid to the indigent families of soldiers. Louisiana's lawmakers authorized $5 million for a pension system that would give $10.00 monthly to soldiers' wives or widows. In Alabama in August 1863, the legislature appropriated $1 million for distribution, and in December it added another $3 million and included as recipients the families of substitutes and deceased and incapacitated soldiers. In November it also called for the shipping of 97,500 bushels of corn to mountain counties, where the crop had been destroyed by an early frost. In Mississippi, where large areas of the most fertile regions had been overrun by Federal troops, the legislature in December 1863 called for a cash sum of $500,000 to be dispersed and imposed a special tax to fund that amount. In August 1864 the legislature ordered that another $1 million be distributed. Private individuals and institutions also provided some assistance to the needy.

Governors such as Zebulon B. Vance of North Carolina and Joseph E. Brown of Georgia pressured their legislatures to pass relief laws. They called for state laws that outlawed the distilling of vital grain into whiskey. They issued proclamations that prohibited speculating merchants and manufacturers from exporting beyond state boundaries and selling for inflated prices items needed for the folk at home. But relief efforts, whether state supported or private, were never enough to assuage all the suffering of the Confederacy's poor.[33]

The situation could perhaps have been improved if the Confederate government had established some agency or bureau for providing assistance to the destitute. There certainly would have been support for such a national public welfare program among the common people.[34] Prior to the war, Southerners at large might have objected to an expansion of political power to create such a system. But the hardships of war and their growing desperation led many of them to turn more and more to their state and county governments for relief. They would have embraced help from the Confederate government with the same fervor. As historian Charles W. Ramsdell has written, at the state and local levels, the wartime "measures taken, generally with the approval and, in truth, at the demand of the people, involved an unprecedented extension of political authority and control which . . . would never have been tolerated before the war."[35] Many desperate people wrote to President Davis and the Congress, as well as to state and local officials, for help. In its regulation of the cargoes of blockade-runners owned by the states and private companies, the Confederate government had already ventured into the realm of what one historian has termed "state socialism."[36] If the Confederate government had applied the same effort to a national relief program, perhaps the suffering on the home front would have been alleviated to a larger extent and support for the Southern war effort would have been greater among the common folk. But, according to historian Mary Elizabeth Massey, the central government did not "ever become very sympathetic or helpful in solving the problems of shortages on the homefront. Most of what was accomplished was done through the channels of state legislation, gubernatorial proclamations, and city ordinances."[37]

In addition to a national public relief organization, a Confederate department of agriculture might have done much to relieve shortages and destitution on the home front. Such an office could have enforced state and Confederate laws requiring planters to grow crops to feed the population rather than cultivating cotton in anticipation of future profits. Department officials could have regulated the distribution of agricultural resources to ensure that they reached the people most in need. Some Southerners proposed the creation of a Confederate bureau of agriculture, with cabinet rank, and urged that it be "supplied with the requisite means to encourage agriculture in every legitimate and usual form." But the idea never received serious consideration in Richmond.[38]

Despite the deprivation that afflicted all areas of the Confederacy, there were probably enough food and other provisions available in the South to forestall destitution. The blockade, the inability to import goods from the North, an inadequate industrial complex, inflation, a poor transportation system, and an ineffective public relief system all contributed to deprivation on the home front. But they were not the only factors. Another major cause of the undue hardships experienced by many citizens, mostly the poor, was speculation, which occurred in just about any food, apparel, or other commodity needed or desired on the home front. Many wholesale and retail merchants, brokers, investors, entrepreneurs, opportunists, and outright extortionists seized on wartime conditions to turn sizable profits. Merchants usually ignored the government price guidelines, sold their stock at inflated prices and for large profits, and frequently would accept only gold and hard currency from their customers.[39] Various "money dealers," with sound money to lend, could charge exorbitant interest rates or claim cotton and other goods as collateral. In the final years of the war, many speculators, with a keen eye on the future, anticipated that Federal victory was likely. These "sharp fellows" bought up provisions and "held on to them hoping for starvation prices, or perhaps until such a time, as they may hope flour will bring its price in 'greenbacks.'" They realized that what could be bought at the time for a song and with virtually worthless Confederate money would turn a nice profit in better days, when sound Yankee dollars would once again appear in the South.[40]

One Georgia newspaper editor called upon merchants and speculators to cease their unscrupulous activities. "In the name of our beloved country—in the name of outraged humanity—in the name of the God they pretend to fear—we call upon these men to change their policy before it shall be too late," he pleaded.[41] Not all Southerners were so humble in their response to speculators. A band of "Regulators" in Bladen County, North Carolina, threatened that if wealthy local planters did not stop hoarding and charging unreasonable prices for corn, they intended to raid the plantations. The "Regulators" warned that they were "determined to have bread out of there [*sic*] barns & that at a pric[e] that we can pay or we will slaughter as we go."[42]

Everyone, from newspaper editors to poor refugees, denounced speculation and probably complained more about the practice than about any other problem afflicting the home front. In a speech in January 1863, Gov. John Letcher of Virginia condemned speculators as "drunkards, adulterers, and fornicators."[43] Nevertheless, speculation continued unabated. Efforts by state and local governments to stem it proved ineffective. Some Southerners blamed Jews for the unscrupulous trading and price fixing. Hoarding of various goods was also common in the Confederacy. Many inhabitants feared being without certain essentials and stockpiled them, hoping to avoid destitution. But hoarding never reached the same level as speculation.[44]

Confederate impressment policies contributed considerably to shortages and civilian suffering. Probably no law led to more resentment and anti-government feeling among the common folk than the Confederate Impressment Law of March 1863. To help supply and support the army, that act authorized the Confederate Commissary Department to impress (appropriate), with payment to the owners, food, forage, livestock, wagons, and other private property, as well as free blacks and slaves as a labor force. The Quartermaster Department collected the supplies and transported them to their destinations. Each state governor was allowed to appoint the impressment commissioner or agent for his state. A price schedule and arbitration by two "disinterested" parties—one appointed by the commissioner and the other selected by the property owner—decided the amount of compensation. But the system did not always work fairly. Payment for the supplies was not always rendered, and some impressment agents, or "pressmen," speculated with the goods taken. The governor of Florida protested that impressment agents were claiming too much of the state's produce and therefore were in violation of the law. Some unscrupulous impressment officers confiscated property without official authorization. Governor Brown of Georgia instructed his people to defy agents who could not show proper certification, and he called for a law to make such illegal activity a felony punishable by ten years in prison and thirty-nine lashes on the bare back of the perpetrator.[45]

A type of unofficial impressment was carried out by Confederate troops campaigning throughout the Southern states. As they passed through or made their temporary headquarters in certain areas, they simply took from the local population whatever food, forage, and other items they needed. This practice outraged many people, including the state governors. In December 1863 Governor Vance protested to Secretary of War James A. Seddon that Confederate troops—especially cavalry—were devastating North Carolinians with their summary appropriation of supplies and turning many Tar Heels against the Confederate war effort. The governor complained that "if God almighty had yet in store another plague—worse than all others, which he intended to have loose on the Egyptians in case Pharaoh still hardened his heart, I am sure it must have been a regiment or so of half-armed, half disciplined Confederate Cavalry! Had they been turned loose among Pharaoh's subjects, with or without an impressment law, he would have become so sensible of the anger of God that he never would have followed the Children of Israel to the Red Sea, No Sir not an inch!" Vance demanded that the Confederate army stop arbitrarily seizing food and other necessities from the people of his state.[46]

The Federal regiments that invaded the South also plundered and otherwise confiscated provisions from the fields, barns, chicken yards, livestock pens, larders, and houses of the home-front folk. After the Federals captured Vicksburg, isolated Mississippi and Alabama were vulnerable to Union supply raids. Huntsville suffered twenty-one raids by the end of 1863. Perhaps the most notorious U.S. military marauders were the troops of Gen. William T. Sherman, who cut a swath of devastation through Georgia and the Carolinas in the final months of the war.[47] As the prewar hotbed of secession, South Carolina suffered most at the hands of Sherman's men. Union general Alpheus Williams reported from that state that "all materials, all vacant houses, factories, cotton gins and presses, everything that makes the wealth of the people, everything edible and wearable was swept away."[48] Wherever the Union or Confederate armies marched and fought, deprivation usually prevailed in their wake. A Confederate surgeon passing through Culpeper, Virginia, in the autumn of 1863 reported: "The part of Virginia through which we have marched has been totally devastated, without a fence or a planted field of any kind. I do not understand how the people exist."[49]

A tax-in-kind imposed by the Confederate government added to the hardships endured by the home-front population. Congress passed a comprehensive tax act on April 24, 1863. The law called for assorted taxes, including a tax on some profits and an income tax on salaries and other earnings above certain amounts. But the most painful tax for the majority of the poor people was the tax-in-kind. It was a tax of one-tenth of agricultural produce, to be paid to the Confederate government in actual farm products such as wheat, corn, oats, rye, rice, sweet and Irish potatoes, hay and fodder, sugar, molasses, cotton, wool, tobacco, peas, beans, and peanuts. In addition a farmer had to give a small percentage of pork in the form of cured bacon and pay a tax of 1 percent on mules and on horses and cattle not utilized to cultivate his land. The War Department, through its quartermasters, and the Treasury Department administered the collection of the tax-in-kind. If farmers and government assessors disagreed over the amount of produce owed, arbitrators could be appointed to decide. Farmers delivered the produce in government sacks and containers to quartermasters at designated depots. The Confederate government considered the tax-in-kind to be the best means of supplying the army without printing more money and adding to the problem of inflation. But for many Southerners it imposed considerable hardship. Along with the impressment law and other wartime policies, it led many people, especially the rural poor, to resent the government in Richmond and become increasingly dissatisfied with the war effort.[50] Their disaffection grew as Confederate authorities made further demands on their lives and liberties.

FOUR

❧❧

CONSCRIPTION, DESERTION,
AND INTERNAL CONFLICT

Shortages and the impressment and tax laws did much to diminish popular support for the struggle for Southern independence. Confederate military conscription (the draft) further alienated the home-front populace. When the war began, the ranks of the Confederate army quickly filled with volunteers who signed up for one year's service. The states formed the volunteers into regiments, which were then turned over to the Confederate War Department.

But the short conflict that everyone had hoped for and anticipated did not occur. As the first year drew to a close, people had seen months of death, wounds, and destruction. Many soldiers who had marched off with enthusiasm holding visions of glory and a quick victory had been awakened to the horrors of killing and maiming and the rigors of hard marches and camp life. With their one-year enlistments about to expire, they were eager to return to their homes. The Confederacy, however, was nowhere close to winning its independence, and much hard fighting lay ahead. A large standing army was essential if the South was to prevail and establish a separate nation, and every month fewer volunteers signed up. The first year of the war was not yet over when upper-class South Carolina diarist Grace Brown Elmore lamented, "Where are the horsemen, the hunters, the gurillas so long talked of where is the daring courage of Carolina. My God was it but a dream has our's been the vain boasting of the fool."[1] Lt. Felix Buchanan, a young Confederate officer from Tennessee, complained that "there are those at home now that ought to be in service. I know several young, able boddied men and unmarried, now in their homes, laying up treasures which moth doth consume and rust destroy, relying upon the strong arms of others to establish a nation whose laws are to protect their person and property, such persons ought not to flourish."[2]

Because it could not secure enough volunteers to fill the ranks of the army, the Confederate Congress passed the First Conscription Act on April 16, 1862. The law provided for the drafting of all white males between the ages of eighteen and thirty-five for a term of three years or until such time as the war ended. Those soldiers who had enlisted for one year had their service extended to three years from the date of their original enlistment. The act gave the War Department the authority and responsibility for the direct induction of troops into the army. The department established one or two "camps of instruction" in each state. A "commandant of conscripts" commanded and supervised the collection and training of draftees at each camp.[3]

An amendment to the law exempted from conscription men whose occupations were considered vital to the war effort and operations behind the lines. Those exempted included "Confederate and state officers, and the clerks allowed them by law; mail carriers and ferrymen on post roads; pilots and persons engaged in marine services; employees on railroads and river routes of transportation; telegraph operators; ministers in the regular discharge of their duties; employees in mines, furnaces, and foundries; printers; presidents and professors in colleges and academies; teachers of the deaf, dumb, and blind; teachers having 20 pupils or more; superintendents, nurses, and attendants in public hospitals and lunatic asylums; and one druggist in each drug-store. Superintendents and operatives in wool and cotton factories would be exempted at the discretion of the Secretary of War." This exemption policy led many men of draft age to scramble to secure an exempt job or position. According to one expert on the Confederate draft, "Thousands of those who loved the good things of life, and who, because of a lack of interest in the war or through sheer cowardice were reluctant to go to the front, began to cast around for some way of sheltering themselves under the beneficent wings of the exemption act. In this process of 'agreeable adaptation' they exhibited a remarkable degree of resourcefulness. Those vocations which afforded exemption suddenly became popular, and were filled to the point of overflowing."[4]

A large number of draft-age males hoped that the War Department would not have the capacity to enforce conscription, especially in outlying regions and areas threatened by Union attack. "The conscription has caused a great commotion among the shirking stay-at-homes," Kate Stone, in Madison Parish, Louisiana, observed less than a month after the First Conscription Act was passed. "Around here, many are deluding themselves with the belief that the call will not be enforced in Louisiana now that New Orleans has fallen and Vicksburg is threatened." She also deplored the failure of volunteers to enlist. "We earnestly hope," she continued, "the coward souls will be made to go. They are not joining volunteer companies. . . . They will not even raise a guerrilla troop for home defense. Not a single man has joined for the last two months."[5] In South Carolina Mary Boykin Chesnut also remarked on the lack of enthusiasm with which draft-age men were embracing conscription. "The best and bravest went first," she noted. "Now the lag last do not want to be conscripted."[6]

Southerners objected to the conscription law also as a matter of principle. States had subjected their citizens to mandatory militia service, but there had never been a national draft prior to the war. Many people viewed military service forced upon them by the Confederate government as a usurpation of their individual liberties and a violation of states' rights. They feared that allowing a central government so much power was a threat to democratic ideals. Joseph Reid of South Carolina said of the conscription act that "a more oppressive law was never enacted in the most uncivilized country or by the worst of despots."[7] Gov. Joseph E. Brown of Georgia immediately objected to the conscription act, arguing that it gave the government in Richmond the power to "destroy the civil government of each state." Other states also protested that Confederate conscription impinged on state laws and rights, especially regarding the decision about who could be drafted. In response President Davis relied on the state supreme courts and Confederate district courts to decide the legality of the draft. All those courts that heard such cases ruled that Confederate conscription was constitutional.[8]

But neither the president nor the courts ever silenced the complaints of the disenchanted common folk, upon whom the injustice and burden of army service primarily fell. Those Southerners without wealth or influence resented that the vacant exempt jobs and positions usually went to the wealthy and influential who clamored for the safety of such havens to avoid combat. The poor found one provision of the First Conscription Act especially discriminatory: the provision of "substitution," which allowed a man of sufficient wealth to pay someone to serve in his place. A draftee who could not afford a replacement had no such option. The poor protested that this measure unfairly favored the rich, and the public outcry led Congress in December 1863 to approve a law abolishing substitution. A subsequent act in January 1864 declared that those men who had previously provided substitutes were now liable for service. But these adjustments came too late to prevent much of the resentment and disaffection growing on the home front.[9]

The Second Conscription Act, passed in September 1862, extended the draft to include men up to forty-five years of age. Poor families, who owned no slaves, felt this provision especially acutely. Many of them were already living at a subsistence level and needed the labor of every man. Alarmed by the news of the age extension, one distraught woman wrote to the governor of North Carolina:

> This is a great undertaking for me as i never wrote to a man of authority before necessity requires it of me as we are nonslave holders in this section of the State i hope you and our legislature will look to it and have justice done our people as well as the slaveholders i can tel you the condition of my family and you can judge for your self what its condition

woul be if my husban is called from home we hav eight children and the oldest is not
forteen years old and old aged mother to support, which makes eleven in our family
and without my husband we are a desolate and ruined family for extortion runs so hie
here we cannot support and clothe our family without the help of my husband i hope
you will look to the justice of peepils of this section of the state and i trust you will
hold the rane in your own hands and not let the confederate congress have the full sway
over your State i appeal to you look to the white cultivaters as strictly as cngress has
to the slaveholders and i think they men from 35 to 45 be hel as reserves at hom to
support ther families if they are calld from home its bound to leave a thoasn families in
a starving condition in our county we trust in god and look to you for some help for
our poor children.[10]

An October amendment to the second act increased the number of exempt classi-
fications to include an assortment of mechanics, artisans, professionals, and railroad
and navigation company workers, as well as physicians who had practiced for five
years, salt laborers who produced twenty bushels of salt per day, religious pacifists
who hired a substitute or paid a tax, and "other persons whom the President might
designate because of justice or equity." Another provision, the so-called Twenty-Negro
Law, raised great ire and discontent among the common people. It mandated that
every plantation holding twenty or more slaves have at least one white man remain on
the property to keep watch on the enslaved workers. Therefore, either the planter or
his overseer could be exempt from conscription. This measure, like substitution, led
to much class resentment and cries that the conflict was "a rich man's war and a poor
man's fight."[11] A disgruntled poor farmer in North Carolina complained to the governor in January 1863 that "the poor soldiers is fiting for the rich man's Negroes."[12]
In response to the clamor over the injustice of the twenty-slave act, Congress in
May 1863 modified it to apply to plantations of women alone, minors, the insane,
or men in the army. No overseer could be exempt unless he had been an overseer
before April 16, 1862. Planters also had to pay $500 to the Confederate treasury.
These modifications did little to convince the poor that the planter class was not
receiving special privileges and protection.[13] In parts of Arkansas, men "openly and
sometimes violently" resisted conscription authorities. Many turned out in protest
at the communities of Magnolia and Camden. Judge John Brown reported that the
conscripts displayed a "spirit of disloyalty beyond what was expected."[14]

The Confederate Congress approved its third and final conscription act on February 17, 1864. That law extended the age limits for conscripts from seventeen to fifty.
Those draftees who were over forty-five and under eighteen were to be utilized as
reserves to defend their respective states and to carry out special assignments. The
War Department hoped this maneuver would release more troops who were already
in the army for duty on the major battlefields. But because it created a further drain
on the male labor supply at home, it widened the gap of cooperation and support
between the yeoman class and the central government.[15]

Even though the Confederate government managed to draft a large segment of the South's white male population into the army, those men were not necessarily willing to remain there. As time went on, more and more discontented soldiers deserted, and desertion became a major problem for Confederate and state authorities. The majority of deserters came from the poorer classes, and many—if not most—of them were conscripts. Some draftees were "motivated, conscientious, and demonstrably good fighting men; but they appeared to be a distinct minority. Conscripts and substitutes as a rule had to be guarded in camp to prevent them from plundering their compatriots or deserting the army. In battle, they were an almost total liability. They would not fight under any inducement; and if somehow forced to the front lines, they would go over to the enemy at the first chance." The War Department first became concerned about desertion in the summer of 1862. At that time the department called on the state governors to use their militias to arrest deserters and return them to duty, and it assigned provost marshals to help prevent soldiers from stealing away home. The situation stabilized for a while, but beginning in the spring of 1863, the number of desertions began to rise.[16]

Men deserted for various reasons. Not the least of these was the horror of the battlefield. Major defeats, involving tremendous death and suffering, weakened the soldiers' will to continue in a seemingly hopeless struggle. Morale plummeted and desertion soared after the Confederate defeats at the bloody battles of Gettysburg and Vicksburg in July 1863. At that time the War Department estimated the number of deserters at 40,000 to 50,000. Other estimates were much higher.[17] Gen. Robert E. Lee wrote to President Davis, "The number of desertions from the army is so great and still continues to such extent that unless cessation of them can be caused I fear success in the field will be seriously endangered."[18] Illustrative of the common soldier's despair that ultimately led to desertion was the experience of Private John Futch of New Hanover County, North Carolina. During the severe fighting at Gettysburg, his regiment was virtually destroyed. Worse yet, Futch's brother Charley, who served in the same unit, was wounded and died in John's arms. On August 3, 1863, John Futch wrote to his wife, Martha, from Orange Court House, Virginia:

> Dear wife I take the plesher of riting you a few lines to informe you that I am well at present hopen thes few lines May reach and find you well. . . . I havent got Mutch to rite at present only it is harde times hear with us and mity hot. . . . I haven sean no plesher since charley got kild. he got wonded the 2 [July] and died the 3. he was shot in the head and suffered Mity Bad before he died. I toted him of[f] of the feald and stade with him tel he died. I am at a grate lost sence I lost charley tel I am all Most crasey but I hope that I will get a long with it the [best] I can. . . . I want to sea you the worse I ever did in My life. . . . I am a comin home the first chance I can get I think that this war will end before long for I think that the yankes will whip us before long. Charley never spoke after he got wonded and he wanted to go home Mity bad before he died—he was kild at gettiesburg PV pore feler he got kild a long wase from home. I was sary that I

codent get a cofen to beary him but I beared him the best I cod. It was something that I never expected to haft to do. . . .

Nothing More at present only I remain your lonely husband tel deathe.[19]

Devastated by Charley's death and weakened in body and spirit, John Futch wrote to his wife with increasing despair and loneliness. Eventually he deserted from camp in Virginia and headed home. Soon captured, Futch was shot for desertion by a Confederate firing squad on September 5, 1863.[20]

Unlike Futch, most deserters were not killed for unauthorized absence from duty. Courts-martial usually imposed lesser, even light, sentences, which could include a variety of punishments. At times the president, generals, and governors issued proclamations of amnesty to deserters who returned to ranks within a specified time. In the final desperate year of the war, however, punishment grew more severe in an attempt to force men to stand and fight.

Worry about wives and families who were destitute at home compelled many soldiers to leave their regiments. Hundreds of wives wrote to their husbands in the army reporting that they and their children did not have enough to eat and could receive no public assistance. They pleaded with their menfolk to come home. In Nansemond County, Virginia, a soldier's wife and mother of four small children wrote to her husband in December 1864:

> Christmas is most hear again, and things is worse and worse. I have got my last kalica frock on, and that's patched. Everything me and the children got is patched. Both of them is in bed now covered with comforters and old pieces of karpet to keep them warm, while I went 'long out to try and get some wood, for their feet's on the ground and they have got no clothes, neither: and I am not able to cut the wood, and me and the children have broke up all the rails 'roun' the yard and picked up all the chips there is. We haven't got nothing in the house to eat but a little bit of meal. The last pound of meet . . . is all eat up, and so is the chickens we raised. I don't want you to stop fighten them yankees till you kill the last one of them, but try and get off and come home and fix us all up some and then can go back. . . . We can't none of us hold out much longer down here.

Heeding his wife's call, the soldier went home without a furlough. Upon returning to duty, he was arrested as a deserter and sentenced to be executed, but he received a reprieve.[21]

Confederate troops were paid poorly and inconsistently, and the army had no program to send a portion of their pay automatically home to their families. In January 1862 Gen. John B. Floyd remarked that "one half of the fifty-first [Virginia Regiment] have never received one dollar since they entered the service [six months earlier]. They are generally poor men entirely without support for their wives and little children, except their wages. . . . They have not a single dollar to purchase the least little comfort, even for the sick." Furthermore, because of the manpower shortage, few furloughs were ever granted.[22] One young officer lamented the impact that the denial of furloughs was having on the number of men deserting. "There are a good many desertions all over the army," he wrote home in August 1863, and "all furloughs are discontinued. No reasons stated, and I don't think could be stated, unless some silly and foolish ones. The men can't be prevented from deserting when they think there is no prospect ahead for getting home. I don't think there are any in our Company that will ever run off, but it cannot be denied that, among the deserters are some of the bravest men of our army—men that have been tried under fire. Our leaders do not seem to think that the *morale* is as great a portion of an army, as Napoleon thought."[23]

A variety of other reasons compelled men to leave the army: a dislike of military discipline, the hardships and boredom of camp life, bad and insufficient food, poor health, and, of course, the fear of being killed or wounded. Conscripts from North Carolina thought they had legal justification for deserting. In 1863 a ruling by the chief justice of that state's supreme court convinced many of them that they had been drafted illegally. Chief Justice Richmond M. Pearson had ruled that the state militia could not be used to arrest deserters from the Confederate army. Such action, he argued, was the responsibility of the Confederate government. He issued writs of habeas corpus and ordered the release of those deserters who had been arrested by the militia. Although Pearson never ruled that Confederate conscription was unconstitutional, some Tar Heel conscripts interpreted his decision that way.[24] As Governor Vance wrote to President Davis in May 1863, "news of Judge Pearson's decision went abroad in the Army in a very exaggerated and ridiculous form, soldiers were induced to believe that it declared the conscript law unconstitutional and that they were entitled if they came home to the protection of their civil authorities—Desertion . . . broke out again worse than before."[25] Whatever the soldiers' motivations, however, the rate of desertion continued to grow throughout the South.

The army managed to slow the rate in the winter of 1863–1864. But by the autumn of 1864, desertion was reaching epidemic proportions. The fall of Atlanta to the army of Gen. William T. Sherman, the devastation and victories by Gen. Philip Sheridan's regiments in the Shenandoah Valley, and President Abraham Lincoln's reelection in November convinced many Confederate soldiers that the South could not triumph. The enemy's victories and unrelenting march into the heartland of their region persuaded them that the United States had the Confederacy by the throat. Lincoln's election victory indicated that Northern voters were willing to stay the course and see the war through to the end. In light of all that, the troops reasoned, why continue to suffer in a deadly struggle that could not be won? Why not quit fighting and go home? After all, such action had a good chance of succeeding. For an unhappy and disillusioned Civil War soldier, the odds for a successful flight from the army were about three to one.[26]

The exact number of Confederate deserters is not known. One official report puts it at 103,400, but the total was probably higher. At the end of the war, 359,000 troops were enrolled in the Confederate army. Of that number only 160,000 were present. Another estimate concludes that there was one desertion to every nine enlistments. With approximately 24,000, North Carolina apparently had the most verifiable deserters, followed by Virginia with about half that number. Alabama had 1,578, the fewest of the Southern states. Among the troops absent without authorized leave were 1,028 officers. North Carolina again had the highest number, at 428. Tennessee ranked second with 153, and Virginia was third with 84.[27] According to historian Paul D. Escott, "The large desertions from the southern armies represented an overall judgment by the common people on Jefferson Davis' policies. The action of thousands of soldiers proved that his government had failed to meet their needs and build the kind of morale necessary to endure a long and difficult struggle."[28]

The large number of deserters and men attempting to avoid conscription became a major component in the internal conflict that swept through the Confederate home front. Most deserters intended to return home and care for their wives and children, who were enduring the hardships of destitution, speculation, inflation, and ineffective public poor relief. Some fled to Union lines or the border states of Kentucky, Missouri, and Maryland, where they took the oath of allegiance to the United States. A few escaped to Mexico. But many of them banded together with draft dodgers, guerrillas, and an assortment of robbers, violent Union sympathizers, and other lawless types. Such bands roamed behind the lines, raiding towns and farms, stealing and burning property, and terrorizing and even murdering citizens and government officials. These outlaws, or "outliers" as they were often called, created havoc, fear, and social unrest in all the Confederate states. In Alabama they formed armed gangs in eleven northern counties, southward along the Gulf coast, and on the southeastern border with Georgia and Florida. They found excellent hiding places in the mountains of Georgia, North and South Carolina, Tennessee, and Virginia. The Tar Heel State had pockets of the renegades along the coast and in the Quaker Belt of the Piedmont. They also infiltrated Middle Tennessee, southwestern Georgia, western Florida, southern Mississippi, lower Louisiana, and northern Texas. These deserters, recusant conscripts, and other outliers proved adept at eluding capture and establishing camps, sometimes in caves, for shelter and subsistence obtained by raiding local farms and merchants. They created effective spy and communication networks, often with the help of their relatives and other sympathizers.

Efforts by Confederate troop details, state militias and Home Guards, and local authorities to subdue and apprehend the outlaws largely failed. Conscription officers attempting to seize recusant conscripts also had little success. Vicious fighting broke out between the outlaw gangs and the militias, as well as other troops dispatched to capture them. Civilians often got caught in the cross fire. The outliers deliberately raided and plundered the farms and homes of pro-Confederates. The troops retaliated against the families of the deserters and recusant conscripts. This violence became part of a widespread internal conflict between Unionists and loyal Confederates that swept through the home front.[29]

In 1861 support for secession and the creation of the Confederate States of America had been far from unanimous among Southerners. A significant portion of the South's population remained loyal to the Union and opposed the Confederate war effort. Unionism was most prevalent in the Upper South, especially the Appalachian Mountains that traverse western Virginia and North Carolina and eastern Tennessee and Kentucky and extend as far south as northern Georgia and Alabama. The individualistic inhabitants of the isolated Mountain region generally did not hold large numbers of slaves and consequently usually did not identify with the interests of the plantation economy that dominated along the Eastern Seaboard. Cut off from state governments as a result of poor transportation, mountaineers tended to go their own way, and they saw little purpose in fighting for a cause that offered them no benefit. They resisted conscription, taxes, and impressment. If drafted, many of them deserted at the first chance. Some served in Federal regiments. Throughout the mountains, guerrilla warfare raged between Unionists and Confederates. Sometimes called "bushwhackers," "tories," or "Yankees," the militant Unionists frequently raided Confederate camps and supplies and brutalized pro-Confederate civilians. Confederate sympathizers—known as "destructives" or "secessionists"—likewise committed violence upon the residents who remained loyal to the Union.[30]

One of the worst incidents of the internal war between the two mountain factions occurred in Madison County, North Carolina, in January 1863. The trouble began when a group of Union men, including some deserters, plundered the town of Marshall, the county seat. They were in pursuit of salt in particular, and they ransacked a number of pro-Confederate businesses and homes. In retaliation Confederate troops set out to punish the raiders and attacked the homes of several suspected Unionists in the community of Shelton Laurel. They sacked the houses and whipped and tortured a number of people, including women and children. They also took fifteen men and boys prisoner. Two escaped, but the soldiers gathered the other thirteen in a nearby ravine and shot them dead, burying their bodies in a shallow grave. The so-called Shelton Laurel Massacre outraged some North Carolinians and their governor, who called for an investigation by the War Department. The officers in command of the troops, however, received no, or only light, punishment.[31]

The Mountain region was not the only area where Unionists and Confederate sympathizers clashed violently. Conflicts perpetrated by one side or the other occurred in most areas where allegiances were divided. In Florida, for instance, pro-Union sentiment grew in the eastern, southern, and western parts of the state, but the central portion remained pro-Confederate. In the east particularly, Unionism was so prevalent that militia general Richard F. Floyd asked the governor to allow him to place sections under martial law. In September 1862 Gov. John Milton wrote to President Davis:

"You are apprised that in Florida a very large minority were opposed to secession, and in many parts of the State combinations existed to adhere to and maintain the United States Government, and even now in some portions of the State there are men who would eagerly seize any opportunity that promised success to the United States."[32] Jones County, Mississippi, became one of the locales most notorious for resistance to Confederate authority by deserters and Unionists. Confederate cavalry dispatched to the area failed to subdue the dissidents, who continued to defy authority and ravage the countryside.[33]

Counties throughout the South formed "vigilance committees" to keep watch on people who might be disloyal to the cause of Southern independence. These groups apprehended suspicious strangers or others who were suspected of treason and whipped, banished, or even hanged them. Some native critics considered these vigilante activities a dangerous violation of civil liberties and a prelude to despotism. An editor in Georgia cried that a vigilance committee was "an illegal irresponsible organization, usurping all the power it pretends to exercise." An infuriated Virginian declared: "A Vigilent Committee! Great God! and has it come to this that the friend[s] of the union are to be harassed by a Vigilent Commity? then let us have a Robespier to fill up our cup of iniquities that the vengeance of heaven may fall upon us at once; and give us a Merciful Bonaparte."[34] Just as they feared that unwatched slaves might betray or even murder them, many paranoid Confederates felt it necessary to train a close eye on neighbors who might harbor Union sentiments. In Augusta, Georgia, several people were reported to be disloyal. In that town in 1863, a policeman was jailed for treason, and subsequently several women and a newspaper editor were accused of communicating with the enemy and spying.[35]

The same sort of Southern mind that interpreted vigilance committees as a threat to civil liberties worried about the Confederate government's suspension of the basic democratic right of habeas corpus. The Confederate constitution protected the writ of habeas corpus, which was a decree by a judge instructing law enforcement officials to bring an arrested party before the court and specify why that person was being held. It guaranteed that citizens could not be arbitrarily arrested and imprisoned without charge. But the threat of Federal invasion and concerns about public safety, order, and loyalty compelled the Confederate Congress in February 1862 to authorize the president to suspend the writ in areas where Union attack seemed imminent and the imposition of martial law was necessary to maintain law and order and ensure an adequate defense. Habeas corpus thereby became entwined with the enactment of martial law, or law that suspends civil jurisdiction and imposes military authority over civilians.

President Davis immediately declared martial law in Richmond, which was under threat of attack by the U.S. forces of Gen. George B. McClellan. The heavy-handed restrictions, arrests, and military courts for civilians ordered by Gen. John H. Winder, Confederate commander of the district, outraged many Virginians, who cried that military rule was a violation of their individual liberties and constitutional rights. As a result Congress passed a bill on April 19, 1862, that stipulated that the February 1862 suspension law would expire thirty days after the beginning of the next congressional session, in September. On October 13, however, the lawmakers renewed the president's authority until February 1863. During the interim, army commanders in various locales imposed martial law and made arbitrary arrests. On January 29, just two days before the October act expired, Davis responded to a request by Gen. Theophilus Holmes, commander of the new Trans-Mississippi Department. As the general requested, the president suspended the writ of habeas corpus for the second time in Arkansas and the Indian Territory. Holmes reported that the region was "overrun with deserters, disloyal persons, and invaders," and that he could not enforce conscription. Davis issued the order on the same day the "Arkansas congressional delegation visited his office to complain about the previous impositions of martial law in their state."[36] The "previous impositions" had taken place under the tyrannical military rule of Gen. Thomas C. Hindman, who commanded the Arkansas District and infuriated many residents with suppressions of civil liberties and confiscation of private property.[37]

The home-front population's concerns about the suspension of the writ of habeas corpus became a volatile element in the controversy over Confederate conscription. In 1862 in Enterprise, Mississippi, for example, Louis Frenkel, who had earlier hired a substitute, claimed exemption from conscription. Nevertheless, conscript officers arrested him. Frenkel hired an attorney, who asked for a writ of habeas corpus from a state circuit judge. The judge ruled that Frenkel was being held illegally and ordered his release. The commandant of the conscript district, however, ignored the ruling, rearrested Frenkel, and placed him in a camp of instruction. The judge, William M. Hancock, then wrote to Mississippi congressman Ethelbert Barksdale pointing out the danger of having the War Department ignore rulings by state courts. "You are aware," Hancock told him, "that there has been for some time and is now a great deal of soreness & irritation existing in the public mind in this region in connection with the writ of habeas corpus & the assumption of military authorities over the liberty of the citizen." He informed Barksdale that his decision in the matter of Frenkel must stand, and that it was not legal for Confederate officials to circumvent it. Furthermore, "No appeal or writ of Error was prayed for, or sued out to the High Court, which is the only tribunal vested with the power to reverse the judgment of the current court." Indeed, because the Confederacy did not have a national supreme court, the final ruling on Hancock's decision, if appealed, would have been left to the state supreme court.

Frenkel's lawyer, David Chalmers Glenn, first appealed to the War Department to release his client from service, and he asked for an opinion on the case from the Confederate attorney general. Glenn did threaten, however, that if the Confederate government did not release Frenkel, "duty to my client will compel [me] to exhaust every remedy known to the laws of Miss to obtain the liberation of my client & for the consequences which may thus ensue I will not be responsible." Representative Barksdale, who customarily supported Confederate policies, protested to President Davis about the Frenkel case. "The privilege of the writ of habeas corpus," he avowed, "not having been authorized to be suspended in any case whatever, I can scarcely think that the course of the commandant of the camp of Instruction [for conscripts] is warranted by orders of the War Department." Davis instructed the department to give "prompt attention" to the matter. Unfortunately, extant records do not indicate the outcome of the Frenkel case. Nevertheless, the circumstances reveal the importance that people at home placed upon the writ of habeas corpus and the sanctity of their state courts.[38]

The issues of habeas corpus and the Confederate government's right to draft men into the army became further entangled in January 1864. On the fifth of that month, the Confederate Congress passed an act stating that all men who had earlier furnished substitutes were thenceforth liable for service.[39] In North Carolina a number of such men brought their cases before Chief Justice Pearson, who, as noted earlier, had defied the government in Richmond over the writ of habeas corpus involving the arrest of deserters. Pearson ruled that substitutes were not liable to conscription according to the conscription act of September 1862, and therefore the men for whom they had substituted could not be legally drafted either. He approved writs of habeas corpus and ordered the discharge of several conscripts who had previously hired substitutes. As a result of his decision, other draftees concluded that conscription was unconstitutional and that they could appeal to the state courts to avoid army service.[40]

At the request of President Davis, the Confederate Congress in February 1864 passed a third and final act suspending the writ of habeas corpus. The new act allowed the president to suspend the writ in thirteen situations, including desertion and defiance of conscription. The eleventh clause pertained to peace advocates. It provided for the suspension of habeas corpus for anyone arrested for "advising or inciting others to abandon the Confederate cause, or to resist the Confederate States, or to adhere to the enemy."[41] By early 1864 Davis had become seriously worried about the growing agitation for peace among the people in the Confederate states, and he wanted to quash pacifist sentiments or actions that might undermine the war effort.[42] The new law "may occasion some clamor," declared Davis, "but this will proceed chiefly from the men who have already too long been the active spirits of evil. Loyal citizens will not feel danger, and the disloyal must be made to feel it."[43]

Indeed, by early 1864 sentiments of disaffection and disloyalty had reached a high level in the Confederacy. The home-front population had grown weary and despondent over battlefield deaths, Federal invasion and devastation, shortages, inflation, speculation, and the oppressive Confederate policies of taxation, impressment, and conscription. Southerners everywhere had tired of the internal conflict between pro-Union and pro-Confederate elements and the violence involving deserters, guerrillas, and marauders. They also had come face to face with the reality that in all likelihood the Confederacy could never win its independence through victory on the battlefield. The failure of Lee's army at the Battle of Antietam in September 1862 and the subsequent issuance of the Emancipation Proclamation had closed the door on the possibility of foreign intervention on behalf of Southern independence. Then, overwhelming Union victories at Gettysburg and Vicksburg in July 1863 had proved the power and resolve of the Federal army, which, with the assistance of the U.S. Navy on the seacoasts and interior rivers, tightened its coils upon the Confederacy.[44] U.S. forces controlled the Mississippi River, cutting the South in half. The Confederacy's Trans-Mississippi Department, under the command of Gen. Edmund Kirby Smith, was cut off from Richmond, and the region was virtually being governed by the general and by martial law. The Federals held Tennessee, southern Louisiana, northern Arkansas, and various portions of the Southern states on the coasts. They raided into the interiors of Mississippi and Alabama, which became a "no man's land of dwindling support for the Southern cause."[45]

As 1864 came to a close, President Lincoln cleverly held out further incentive for a peaceful return of Confederates to the Union. His so-called Ten Percent Plan offered amnesty to any Southerner who would swear allegiance to the United States, and it would readmit to the Union any Confederate state in which 10 percent of the voting population of 1860 would take the oath of allegiance and form a loyal government. Such a proposal was more "grist for the mills of Southern pacifists."[46] In ever-growing numbers, people behind the lines began to agitate publicly for peace negotiations to end the terrible war that seemingly could not be won by armed conflict.

As public morale fell, peace movements and organizations arose all over the South. One of the three major peace organizations was the Peace and Constitutional Society, which began in Arkansas in the fall of 1861 and extended into Alabama, Georgia, Mississippi, and probably Florida. Another large peace organization was the Peace Society, which formed branches in Alabama, Georgia, Mississippi, eastern Tennessee, and probably Florida. A third major peace advocacy group was the Heroes of America, also called the Red Strings, which formed in North Carolina, southwestern Virginia, and eastern Tennessee. The Heroes organized in 1861 and were probably most active in North Carolina, where they had an estimated 10,000 members. They launched their activities in the state's Piedmont Quaker Belt region, where lived a number of Quakers, other pacifists, antislavery proponents, and Unionists.

These societies worked tirelessly to undermine the Confederacy. They encouraged and hid deserters and draft dodgers, supported Unionists, and assisted the Federal army in invasion areas. In politics they campaigned for and elected peace candidates to state and congressional offices. Their secretive rituals included a variety of messages, oaths, and signals. Smaller bands of peace proponents also appeared throughout the states of the Confederacy. In Texas the Germans particularly were noted for joining together in resistance to Confederate policies and authority. The scattered smaller groups did not have direct connections with the three major organizations, but in most sections of the South, opponents of the war could find a sympathetic band.

Members of peace organizations varied in the depth of their opposition to the Davis government, and some bands comprised largely lawless types set on plundering the countryside. A common motivation was to avoid army service.[47]

North Carolina had probably the most active peace movement in the Confederate states. A desire for peace had grown to such a level among the discontented Tar Heel population that peace negotiations became the major issue in the gubernatorial election of 1864. In that contest the leader of the peace movement, Raleigh newspaper editor William W. Holden, campaigned against pro-Confederate incumbent Zebulon B. Vance. Holden's call for peace talks with the Federal government led a worried President Davis to encamp a brigade of Confederate troops near Raleigh with the intention of arresting and retaining Holden under the authority of the Habeas Corpus Act of February 1864. Vance, however, persuaded the president not to invoke the law and take Holden into custody. Suspension of civil rights, Vance argued, would fuel rather than inhibit disloyalty and peace sentiment in North Carolina. He assured Davis that he was working against a peace convention, and that if he won the election, the president could count on his support. Through effective campaigning the governor defeated Holden overwhelmingly and managed to keep his state in step with the Davis government. Nevertheless, the people's discontent and desire for peace continued.[48]

Georgia closely rivaled North Carolina in the depth of peace sentiment among its populace. Its governor, Joseph E. Brown, protested Confederate policies—including conscription and the suspension of habeas corpus—as a violation of states' rights and an imposition on the welfare of his citizens. His defiance of the central authority in Richmond helped to bolster the peace movement in his state. Brown was joined in his attacks on President Davis by fellow Georgians Vice President Alexander H. Stephens and former Confederate general and short-term secretary of state Robert A. Toombs. When Congress authorized the suspension of the writ of habeas corpus in February 1864, Brown condemned the act as evidence of "military despotism" and a loss of "constitutional liberty." He proposed that the state legislature begin peace negotiations as soon as the Confederacy could secure a battlefield victory. Confederate independence, he and Stephens insisted, would be an essential part of any peace agreement. Both men hoped that news of their proposal would strengthen the position of peace Democrats in the North during the upcoming elections of November 1864. But a number of Georgia politicians, military officers, and newspaper editors condemned Brown's plan for ending the war as advocating "peace at any price." Furthermore, they argued, an offer for peace talks would divide the people of the South instead of helping the cause of peace in the North. In the end, rather than approving maneuvers for peace negotiations, the state legislature pledged "Georgia's continuing support for the war."[49]

Throughout the South state legislatures rejected suggestions for overtures for peace and persisted in passing resolutions in support of the Davis government. Still, the people behind the lines managed to elect a number of politicians who supported their hopes for a peaceful end to the war. According to historian Charles P. Roland, "The Congress that assembled on December 7, 1863, was a body of desperate, confused, and bitter men; desperate over the plight of the South, confused in their notions of a remedy, and many of them bitter in their hostility to Davis."[50]

Of the ten Confederate congressmen elected in 1863 from North Carolina, all but two favored some type of peace negotiations.[51] The most radical of these peace congressmen was James T. Leach. He won election overwhelmingly on a campaign platform calling for a "just, honorable and lasting peace." He opposed the president's call for suspension of the writ of habeas corpus and martial law as "mighty strides toward a military despotism." When Davis and like-minded lawmakers refused to consider peace talks, Leach called for separate state conventions to discuss an end to the hostilities.[52]

The most vocal and heated advocated for peace was Congressman Henry S. Foote of Tennessee. As a firebrand and an often inconsistent and despised opponent of Davis and other officials in the Confederate government, Foote opposed the suspension of the writ of habeas corpus and decided that the South could never win the war militarily. Therefore, he thought, Southerners should seek peace at any price; a peace agreement might at least make it possible to save slavery. Unable to sway the Congress, Foote actually fled across enemy lines to make overtures to Washington for peace negotiations. Lincoln and his cabinet, however, largely ignored him.

Despite the efforts of representatives such as Leach and Foote and clamors from the home front for peace, the Congress vowed to continue fighting until Confederate independence was achieved. In December 1864 it passed a law declaring secret meetings with the enemy punishable by a $5,000 fine and five years in prison.[53]

Any thoughts of a negotiated peace that the Confederate government might have entertained ended at the Hampton Roads Conference in coastal Virginia on February 3, 1865. At that meeting were Confederate commissioners Vice President Alexander Stephens, Assistant Secretary of War John A. Campbell, and Senator Robert M. T. Hunter from Virginia. President Lincoln and Secretary of State William H. Seward represented the United States. The conference quickly failed when the Southern commissioners refused to accept Lincoln's nonnegotiable terms that the Confederacy cease fighting, renounce its independence, and accept emancipation of its slaves.[54] Any hopes that the folk of the South had for an immediate end to the war were dashed. Fighting would continue until the Confederate surrender in April 1865. In the meantime, the bloodshed and suffering continued, in a cause that many Southerners felt had long since been lost.

FIVE

❧

SLAVES, FREE BLACKS, AND FOREIGNERS

In the South, where four million slaves lived when the war began, the relationship between master and bondman had always been a precarious one. Slave owners were convinced that slave labor was essential to the region's social and economic systems and must be protected and perpetuated. Slaves in general were equally certain that their bondage was an abomination, from which they would grasp any reasonable opportunity to free themselves.

Without the labor of the slaves to produce its food and fiber and build its military fortifications, it is doubtful that the Confederate States of America could have waged war for four long years. The contributions enslaved people made as agricultural hands, industrial workers, artisans, and laborers were substantial and helped the South to continue its struggle for independence. Slaves, however, usually did not perform their work willingly or out of loyalty to the Confederate cause or devotion to their oppressors. They labored in the fields, in the city streets, along the shipping wharves, and on the military ramparts because, as slaves, they had no choice. And when a promising chance to bolt for freedom presented itself, they inevitably seized it.[1]

Early in the war, a significant number of white soldiers took body servants to the army with them, but those slaves usually deserted at the first opportunity. One such servant was Robert Morrow, who escaped to Federal lines near New Bern, North Carolina, in 1864. Morrow joined a regiment of U.S. black troops, helped recruit other slaves into the Federal army, and, because he was educated, worked as a teacher among slaves who fled to Union lines in eastern North Carolina. He died during a yellow fever epidemic. Horace James, the Federal Superintendent of Negro Affairs, wrote of him:

> Robert Morrow at the time of his disease was a sergeant in the 1st North Carolina Heavy Artillery (Colored troops). He came into our lines at the time of an attack Upon New Berne, and had been for many years a body servant of the rebel General [James Johnston] Pettigrew, whom he deserted for Liberty and Union. He had a decent education, having been with Pettigrew at West Point, and [the university at] Chapel Hill, North Carolina, and was an enthusiastic and excellent teacher. He was of pure African blood, had an intellectual cerebral development, and a patriotic heart. He died suddenly, and in his bed, having retired at night as well as usual. He was then engaged in recruiting colored troops at Roanoke Island. It matters little to him that he left the world without warning, for he daily walked with God. He still belongs to the great army which marches under the banner of truth, but he wears a conqueror's wreath and sings the song of victory.[2]

Slaves who performed hard labor in the cotton, rice, cane, and tobacco fields or the turpentine and lumber forests of the South had the greatest motivation to escape from the exhausting work, poor diet and living conditions, and harsh punishments that they suffered at the hands of their masters and their overseers. But even those enslaved persons who lived an easier life were quick to avail themselves of any chance to escape from involuntary servitude. The Southern diarist Mary Boykin Chesnut noted on her family's plantation in 1863 that "Dick, the butler here, reminds me that when we were children I taught him to read as soon as I could read myself. . . . But he won't look at me now. He looks over my head—he scents freedom in the air. . . . He is the first negro that I have felt a change in."[3]

In the capital of the Confederacy, President Jefferson Davis himself had difficulty in preventing his servants from running away. When Davis and his wife, Varina, arrived to take occupancy of the Confederate White House in Richmond, they brought two slaves from their Mississippi plantation, Brier Field, with them. In urban areas both slaves and free blacks often were hired out, either by their masters or through their own negotiations. In Richmond the hiring season began shortly after New Year's Day with the letting of yearly contracts. Mrs. Davis originally hired about fifteen black servants—free and slave—to maintain the family and the executive mansion, including handling the social functions and obligations that went with being the Confederacy's first lady. Before the war ended, she would employ more than twenty black servants at various times, as some left when their contracts expired, were impressed by the military as laborers, or died. Davis and his wife probably treated their slaves as well as anyone did in the Confederacy. Some of them remained loyal to the family. But others fled their servitude or conspired against the president and his family.

William Jackson, a literate coachman, ran away from the Davis household in May 1862 and reported on morale and conditions in Richmond to Union general Irvin McDowell. He also noted disagreements between the president and Confederate general Joseph E. Johnston. The Confederate government offered a bounty for Jackson's capture. When several slaves stole twenty-dollar Confederate notes from the treasury, signed them, and attempted to pass them off as legal money, discovered among the culprits was the president's servant Dick, "who had access to the Custom-House." In early 1864 slaves Betsey (Mrs. Davis's maid) and Jim (probably James Pemberton Jr., whom Davis had brought with him from Brier Field) ran away. Shortly thereafter Henry, the butler, abruptly fled, and a suspicious fire in the basement of the executive residence coincided with his departure. In February Cornelius took his leave of his master and mistress. "These continued elopements," declared the *Daily South Carolinian*, "indue the belief that Mr. Davis's negroes are tampered with by abolitionists. This last runaway, Cornelius by name, had his pockets stuffed with money, preserves, ham, chicken, and biscuit, showing how kindly he was treated, or else how great a rogue he was."[4]

For many decades prior to the war, Southern slaveholders had feared the possibility of slave insurrections—bloody rebellions in which, they anticipated, their servants would rise up and rampage through the region, brutally murdering all whites they encountered. Those whites who owned slaves, and even those who did not, had good reason for their fears. Slave revolts, real and imagined, had been part of the history of the South since colonial days, as witnessed by the Stono Rebellion in South Carolina in 1739, the Gabriel Prosser uprising in Virginia in 1800, the Denmark Vesey plot in Charleston, South Carolina, in 1822, and other episodes of slave unrest and violence throughout the South and in the Caribbean. White anxiety intensified with the rise of the antebellum abolitionist movement in the North, the rebellion of the slave Nat Turner and his followers in Virginia in 1831, and the failed attack on Harper's Ferry by abolitionist John Brown and his little band of blacks and whites in Virginia in 1859.[5]

With the outbreak of the war, dread of slave violence swelled to almost paranoiac heights among the white home-front populace, slaveholders and non-slaveholders alike. The public clamored for greater control over slaves and their movements. States strengthened their laws regarding slave patrols. In Florida in 1861, biweekly patrols became weekly patrols. In the following year, Georgia canceled all exemptions from patrol duty, and Louisiana declared that all assigned patrollers who did not carry out their duties would have to pay a $10.00 fine or serve twenty-four hours in jail.[6]

Slaves tried to resist their owners and undermine the Confederate war effort in a variety of ways. They utilized theft, arson, espionage, feigned illness, and a stubborn refusal to work or submit to punishment. Their defiance rose with the onset of the war, which they quickly surmised involved them and might be turned to their advantage. At Brokenburn Plantation in Louisiana at the end of June 1861, Kate Stone recorded in her diary that "the house servants have been giving a lot of trouble lately—lazy and disobedient. Will have to send one or two to the field and replace them from the quarters if they do not settle down." Whites in the area worried that some type of slave escape or uprising might be planned for July 4. On the fifth Stone wrote: "The Fourth and today passed without any trouble with the Negroes. The general impression has been that the Negroes looked for a great upheaval of some kind on that day. In some way they have gotten a confused idea of Lincoln's Congress meeting and of the war; they think it is all to help them, and they expected for 'something to turn up.' I hope the house servants will settle to their work now."[7]

The most effective and widespread method of defiance and self-determination was running away. Historians John Hope Franklin and Alfred A. Moss Jr. prefer to call such flight "desertion." "It could hardly be called running away," they write, "in the sense that that term implied before the war."[8] Flight and other defiant activities increased as the war progressed and Union troops penetrated deeper and deeper into the heartland of the Confederacy. To prevent their slaves from fleeing to Union lines, many slaveholders resorted to "running the negroes"—that is, moving them away from areas occupied by U.S. troops. In the autumn of 1862, for example, slaveholders in Washington and Tyrrell Counties removed 2,000 slaves to the interior of North Carolina to get them away from Union lines in the coastal region of the state. According to historian Bell I. Wiley, "Travelers on the highways often met great droves of slaves, moving from the coast to the 'up country' in South Carolina, from Mobile to the environs of Montgomery, from Mississippi to Alabama, to Louisiana, or even to Texas."[9] As the war wore on and Federal armies seized and occupied large areas of the South, their occupation provided many slaves with a real chance for the liberty they had long awaited. For those bondmen, freedom was finally nearby, perhaps only down a road or across a river. They might hide in swamps or woods during the day and, under the cover of darkness, find their way to Federal lines.

An estimated half million slaves escaped or found refuge behind Union lines during the war. One such fugitive was Susie King Taylor of Savannah, Georgia. Born a slave in 1848, she secretly learned to read and write. In 1862 she and her uncle escaped to nearby Fort Pulaski. Under Federal protection she worked for the rest of the war on the South Carolina Sea Islands as a teacher for freedmen and a laundress for U.S. soldiers. Taylor recalled her first response to news of the invading Northern troops. She "had been reading so much about the 'Yankees' I was very anxious to see them. The whites would tell their colored people not to go to the Yankees, for they would harness them to carts and make them pull the carts around, in place of horses. I asked grandmother, one day, if this was true. She replied, 'Certainly not!' that the white people did not want slaves to go to the Yankees, and told them these things to frighten them. . . . I wanted to see these wonderful 'Yankees' so much, as I heard my parents say the Yankees was going to set all the people free."[10]

Federal troops captured and occupied much of the coastal region of North Carolina in early 1862. As word of their presence spread, slaves in large numbers fled the interior and sought safety and freedom at occupied coastal sites and towns. Hattie Rogers, enslaved in Onslow County, remembered how some local slaves made their escape. "When the Yankees took New Bern," she recalled, "all who could swim the [White Oak] river and get to the Yankees were free. Some of the men swum the river and got to Jones County then to New Bern and freedom."[11] By 1863 similar episodes were taking place in Union-occupied areas throughout the Confederacy. In Mississippi slave runaways flocked to Vicksburg and Natchez. In Louisiana they found refuge in large numbers in Baton Rouge and New Orleans. Since early 1862 Fernandina, Florida, had served as a center for black fugitives from Georgia and Florida.[12]

As escaped slaves came under Federal protection in occupied areas, the army began assigning them to camps or settlements supervised by the government, at first by army officers or appointed officials and then by agents of the Bureau of Refugees, Freedmen, and Abandoned Lands (the Freedmen's Bureau), after that agency was created in March 1865. An estimated one hundred camps or settlements existed throughout the South by the conclusion of the war. A few of them, such as the Trent River Settlement (also called James City) in eastern North Carolina, survived as black communities thereafter. Although an exact figure cannot be determined, one estimate holds that by the war's end approximately one-half million former slaves were living in areas controlled by the Union army, a large portion of them in camps supervised by the Federals.

The camps varied in size and characteristics. In general the army, and later the Freedmen's Bureau, gave slave families primitive housing, rations, clothing, and some degree of medical care, usually involving a makeshift hospital in the settlement. Northern missionary and benevolent societies dispatched teachers, mostly women, to the South to begin instructing the former slaves, called freedmen, in the basics of primary education. The newly liberated blacks enthusiastically embraced such schools and quickly established churches in their impromptu communities. Men found work as laborers for the U.S. Army building fortifications and other facilities, driving wagons, and occasionally serving as guides and spies. Many of them enlisted in the new black regiments formed by the Federal War Department. Sometimes a settlement included some type of crude industry such as a small sawmill, and some inhabitants learned skills including barrel making, shoemaking, blacksmithing, and shingle splitting. Many women found employment as laundresses, cooks, and seamstresses and in other domestic jobs for Union soldiers, their officers, and the missionaries. Others served as hospital nurses or attendants. Freedmen's camps, settlements, or "colonies" in the Upper South included the Fort Monroe camp in Virginia, the Roanoke Island and Trent River settlements in North Carolina, and those at various sites in Tennessee, Kentucky, Maryland, and the District of Columbia.[13]

Some freedmen's settlements in the Lower South became involved in large-scale agricultural enterprises, established under Northern supervision, on abandoned plantation land. When the U.S. Army occupied the South Carolina Sea Islands in the autumn of 1861, it established a number of camps for former slaves on Port Royal and Hilton Head islands. Large tracts of plantation land in the area had been abandoned by Southern owners. That land became part of a free-labor plan involving the camp residents, who had fled from the interior, and local slaves who had remained on the plantations after the whites left. Northern missionaries, teachers, and work supervisors from benevolent societies arrived to take part in a labor scheme intended to supplant slavery and provide profits for both African American workers and their Northern white overseers.[14]

A similar operation occurred at Davis Bend, Mississippi, in 1864. The abandoned land in that area on the Mississippi River included the plantations of President Jefferson Davis and his brother Joseph. Local slaves on the many abandoned plantations and those who fled to the camps nearby began laboring to produce a profitable cotton crop on 2,000 acres leased by the U.S. government to seventy of "the best negroes." In mid-August an infestation of worms destroyed a large part of their crop. Nevertheless, the enterprise earned a profit for the seventy lessees. They produced 150 bales of cotton, paid their debts for the year, and secured from $500 to $2,500 each. "Many had built comfortable homes and were well settled as small farmers," writes historian Janet Sharp Hermann. As a result the commanding general of the district issued an order to the military that the entire Davis Bend peninsula be "exclusively devoted to the colonization, residence, and support of the Freedmen."[15]

Not all residents of freedmen's colonies or settlements enjoyed such success, however. In some settlements in the Mississippi Valley, for example, conditions for former slaves were almost like those they endured under the old system. Government agents put men to work constructing fortifications or picking cotton for local planters who paid the government for their labor, although the black workers received little or nothing in the form of wages. In camps throughout the South, sanitary conditions were often bad and dwellings little more than shanties, crudely built of "shakes," or short boards split by hand. Yet most of the residents attempted to improve their living conditions as much as possible, maintaining their humble houses, churches, and schools and tending vegetable gardens for their personal use and for produce to sell to whites.[16]

In May 1861 at Fortress Monroe, Virginia, Federal general Benjamin S. Butler had established the precedent of protecting runaway slaves when he decided that they were "contraband of war" and refused to return them to their owners. He called them "contrabands" and began utilizing them as laborers to assist his army. In August 1861 Gen. John C. Fremont, commander of the Western Department, declared martial law in Missouri and announced that slaves in that state were free. President Lincoln, however, quickly revoked Fremont's order freeing the slaves. Lincoln feared alienating the border slaveholding states of Missouri, Kentucky, and Maryland from their pro-Union allegiance, and he considered any orders regarding liberation his sole prerogative as president. The U.S. Congress, however, moved a step closer to emancipating slaves with its Confiscation Act of August 6, 1861. That act declared that slaveholders lost all claims to their slaves if those bondmen were used for any hostile military action against the United States. In November 1861 Lincoln again revoked an army order liberating Southern slaves when he overruled Gen. David Hunter's proclamation freeing enslaved persons in Georgia, Florida, and South Carolina. Congress became more specific regarding the liberation of slaves with its Second Confiscation Act in July 1862. That legislation stated that the slaves of all persons who were actively participating in the rebellion were to be forever free. Nevertheless, it remained for Lincoln's Emancipation Proclamation to launch a major attack on slavery and signal the beginning of the end of the "peculiar institution." The preliminary Emancipation Proclamation, issued in September 1862, declared that all those rebellious states or parts of states that remained outside the Union when the final Emancipation Proclamation was issued on January 1, 1863, would have their slaves declared free by the Federal government.[17]

Besides proclaiming liberty for slaves in the rebellious states, the Emancipation Proclamation provided for the U.S. Army's enlistment and arming of black soldiers throughout the occupied South. Prior to the proclamation, some Federal generals, on their own initiative, had begun forming black regiments: Gens. James H. (Big Jim) Lane in Kansas, David Hunter in South Carolina, and John W. Phelps in Louisiana. In the Militia Act of July 17, 1862, the U.S. Congress had authorized the president to organize blacks and use them "for any military or naval purpose for which they may be found competent." But prior to issuing the Emancipation Proclamation, Lincoln remained cautious in authorizing the use of African American soldiers and would not approve Hunter's South Carolina troops (later formed and commanded by Col. Thomas Wentworth Higginson). After January 1, 1863, however, the Federal War Department began an active campaign to recruit blacks into the regiments of the U.S. Colored Troops, which included about 186,000 African American soldiers and white officers. According to the records of the U.S. adjutant general, about 134,111 of these black soldiers came from the slave states, and most of them were slaves or former slaves. These troops served and fought in engagements throughout the South and distinguished themselves in battles such as Port Hudson and Milliken's Bend on the Mississippi River; at Nashville, Tennessee; and in eastern actions in Virginia, the Carolinas, and Florida. Time and again they proved their worth and courage as fighting men, and their service was a decisive factor in the ultimate triumph of the Federal army.[18]

As news of the Emancipation Proclamation spread among slaves, the count of those who fled to Union lines continued to swell. In ever-increasing numbers they left plantations and farms and sought freedom and Federal protection. They fully understood what the proclamation meant, and as soon as possible, they availed themselves of the opportunity for a new life that it offered. In Union-occupied eastern North Carolina, Northern soldier George F. Winston observed this awareness among the fugitive slaves who sought refuge within his army's lines. "We visited one family in particular," he wrote home to Massachusetts,

> where several times we enjoyed breakfasts of which the principal portion was corn cake. They were very intelligent and although they could neither read nor write, yet had ideas upon matters pertaining to themselves & very correct ones too. They are quite well informed upon the President's proclamation at least that portion pertaining to their immediate change of condition, viz. freedom. There is no use in repeating that they are not capable of taking care of themselves, and that they do not desire their freedom, for it is wholly false. Necessity alone would soon teach them the former invention. The fact all of them who can run away from their masters is a sufficient answer to the latter assertion.[19]

Even those slaves who resided far from occupying Union regiments and had to wait for U.S. troops to penetrate their areas ran away at the first chance of success. When Sherman's army moved into the interior of North Carolina at the war's end, Anna Long Thomas Fuller of Louisburg noted in her diary that "the Negroes seem wild with excitement, they expect to be free.... None of ours have left us yet, but I expect they will." One week later she observed that "the Negroes are availing themselves of their freedom by leaving their former owners and setting up for themselves.... Lucy left us this morning."[20] Slaveholders often were surprised at the suddenness with which their servants fled. "All in all," historian Bell I. Wiley has written, "the reaction of slaves to the coming of the Federals was such as to reveal to the whites how little they knew of the real feelings so effectively concealed behind the veil of smiles and obsequious manners.... Before the war was over, most whites living in areas penetrated by Federal troops had abundant reason to feel as did an Alabaman who in 1863 complained that the 'faithful slave' is about played out."[21]

The Emancipation Proclamation and the enlistment of blacks into the Union army produced widespread alarm and anger among whites in the South. Many were convinced that the result would be a servile insurrection, that old nightmare that had haunted them for decades—except that now armed black soldiers would lead their enslaved brethren, filled with the proclamation's notion of freedom, in murderous uprisings. Some whites worried that the Emancipation Proclamation would turn non-slaveholders against slaveholders, because the war might, in the non-slaveholder's mind, suddenly become primarily a struggle to preserve slavery. In North Carolina the state legislature updated its law against insurrection by giving the governor broader powers to deal quickly with capital crimes committed by slaves. A committee of the Confederate Congress responded to Lincoln's proclamation by advocating that all captured commissioned and noncommissioned Union officers be imprisoned at hard labor until the end of the war. Some congressmen from the Deep South called for the Confederate army to abandon all civilized warfare and fight under the black flag. But neither measure gained congressional approval. President Davis vowed to transfer captured U.S. commissioned officers to the Confederate states to be tried and sentenced as "criminals engaged in servile insurrection." He never carried out his threat, however, apparently because he feared that the Federals would respond with similar action against captured Southern officers.[22]

When Confederate troops fought against the new black Union soldiers in engagements throughout the South, their racial hatred and fears of armed slaves led them to give blacks no quarter on the battlefield. African Americans were fugitives or insurrectionists, they claimed, not legitimate soldiers or prisoners of war. Consequently Confederate soldiers usually massacred black troops, even those who threw away their weapons and tried to surrender. In 1864 at the battles of Fort Pillow, Tennessee, and Plymouth, North Carolina, the Confederates summarily executed or murdered many black soldiers who surrendered or were captured.[23]

From the early days of the war, the Confederate army had, with the cooperation of the state governors and laws, been impressing slaves to assist the military as labor battalions for building fortifications. But it remained for the Impressment Act of March 1863 to authorize legal impressment of slaves. The law called for conformity with state laws regarding impressment and for compensation to slave owners for the use of their workers. Slaveholders and state governments frequently protested the drafting of their bondmen, especially during harvest time, but governors were more cooperative in providing a black labor force after the 1863 act was passed. Planters objected not only if their slaves were drafted during the harvest but also when the army failed to pay for the use of the bondmen, or kept them longer than the prescribed period, or returned them in poor physical condition and without the tools that the planters had provided. Then, too, working on fortifications near Federal lines gave slaves an opportunity to escape. In May 1864 forty-six planters in Randolph County, Alabama, complained to President Davis that it was unjust to impress their slaves to labor on Mobile's defenses. They claimed that one-third of their black servants between the ages of seventeen and fifty had been taken for that purpose, and those workers were sorely needed at home to produce the crop.[24] Before the Impressment Act, Gov. Zebulon B. Vance of North Carolina refused the War Department's request for slaves to work on the Greensboro-to-Danville railroad line. Planters were already volunteering their slaves to labor on the Wilmington-to-Petersburg line, Vance protested.[25] In May 1863 the slaveholders complained bitterly to their governor about impressment. As a result Vance asked Gen. William H. C. Whiting, commanding at the port of Wilmington, if he would release those slaves "at work under your command" to their owners, as "it would almost prove ruinous to keep them after the wheat harvest, which will be early June." Vance had heard rumors that some of the slaves were being assigned tasks other than the ones for which they had been impressed. He was not sure if the reports were true, but he cautioned Whiting "that negroes could not be taken from the fields for such purposes."[26]

By the autumn of 1864, a growing number of whites in the South were beginning to consider the feasibility of arming and emancipating their slaves to serve in the Confederate army. Blacks were desperately needed, the argument ran, to bolster the dwindling number of white soldiers and help halt Confederate battlefield defeats. The idea of enlisting slaves as Confederate combat soldiers had been mentioned by various newspapers and citizens since early in the conflict. But a serious, widespread discussion of such a proposal among the press, the public, and politicians did not occur until the last months of the war, when the tide turned decidedly against the Confederacy and defeat seem probable without drastic or heroic measures.

Several newspapers began clamoring for the use of slaves as Confederate fighting men. They argued that it was better for the Confederacy to use armed blacks for defense than for the Yankees to arm and deploy them against Southern forces. Some editors pointed out that it was worth losing some slaves to the war effort because if the Federals triumphed, slavery would be abolished anyway. In the Army of Tennessee in January 1864, Gen. Patrick Cleburne urged division and corps commanders to call for the use of black soldiers. A number of officers in Cleburne's division supported his idea, but most Southern generals opposed enlisting and arming slaves. Govs. Henry W. Allen of Louisiana and William Smith of Virginia expressed their support for turning some slaves into combatants, but the chief executives of the other Confederate states remained opposed. In November 1864 President Davis called for Congress to purchase 40,000 slaves and put them into war service as laborers and teamsters. He implied in his message that in the future it might be necessary actually to use slaves as fighting men. But Congress did not respond to Davis's request, and a number of newspaper editors expressed their alarm at such a suggestion.[27]

By February 1865, however, the argument for utilizing black soldiers had grown in acceptance and urgency. Gen. Robert E. Lee recommended the immediate emancipation and enlistment of slaves. He suggested that the black soldiers' families be freed after the war and allowed to continue living in the South. The options facing the Confederacy, he maintained, were "whether slavery shall be extinguished by our enemies and the slaves be used against us, or use them ourselves at the risk of the effects which may be produced upon our social institutions."[28] In his opinion "The negroes, under proper circumstances, will make efficient soldiers. I think we could at least do as well with them as the enemy. . . . Those who are employed should be freed. It would be neither just nor wise . . . to require them to serve as slaves."[29]

Despite the pleas of the respected and influential Lee, white Southerners, especially the large slaveholders, objected to the enlisting and arming of slaves. They considered Lee naive in his views on the reliability of slaves in the military. Blacks in Confederate ranks would simply desert to the enemy as soon as they had a chance, opponents asserted. "It proves to me that Gen Lee knows more of getting an army in the field than he does of Cuffee," declared plantation mistress Catherine Devereux Edmondston. "Should we take his advice, we but recruit for the Yankee Army." For slaveholders the idea that bondmen could be set free and made competent soldiers contradicted their contention that blacks were inferior beings fit only for slavery—the concept upon which the South's entire social and economic life was based. "We give up a principle when we offer emancipation as a boon or reward," insisted Edmondston, "for we have hitherto contended that Slavery was Cuffee's normal condition, the best position he could occupy, the one of all others in which he was the happiest, & to take him from that & give him what we think misery in the place of it, is to put ourselves in the wrong essentially. No! freedom for whites, slavery for negroes, God has so ordained it!"[30] Gen. Howell Cobb, one of Georgia's largest slaveholders, proclaimed that "If slaves will make good soldiers, our whole theory of slavery is wrong."[31] Slaveholders and non-slaveholders alike maintained that white soldiers would never serve alongside blacks in Confederate ranks. "The proposition to conscript negroes for soldiers may do to talk about but it will not answer to practice," concluded the *Milton Chronicle* in North Carolina. "We are satisfied of two things, 1st, that white troops would not companionship [*sic*] with them, and 2ndly, they could not be trusted if left to manage themselves. We regard the proposition as one to augment the Yankee army."[32] Some wealthy planters also probably hoped to retain their slaves after the war, regardless of which side achieved victory.[33]

Such opposition notwithstanding, on March 13, 1865, the Confederate Congress passed by a narrow margin a bill empowering the president to request the states to supply black troops for the Confederate army. Emancipation, however, could be carried out only by masters and the states that agreed to provide slaves for the military. Enlistment required the consent of both the slave and his master. But by March the war was nearly over. Even had there been more time, apparently few slaveholders would have agreed to relinquish their servants for military service, and few slaves would have been willing to volunteer. In the final days of the conflict, the Virginia legislature did authorize the formation of two companies of black soldiers in Richmond, but they never went into combat. No other state attempted to enlist slaves.[34] In the end, as much as anything, writes historian Bruce Levine, "The masters' stubborn opposition and resistance, which depicted the use of black troops as social and cultural suicide for the white South . . . prevented the proposal's enactment and implementation."[35]

Closely tied to the experience of slaves was that of the free blacks in the Confederacy. Among the population of the Southern states in 1860 were 250,000 free blacks. After the Confederacy formed, 132,760 free African Americans resided in the eleven seceded states. Virginia had the largest number, 58,042, followed by North Carolina with 30,463. With only 114, Arkansas had the fewest. As did most Southerners, white or black, the majority of free blacks lived in the countryside. But about 40 percent resided in the towns and cities of the Confederacy, with 15 percent of them located in the largest cities. New Orleans claimed 10,689, Charleston 5,478, Richmond 2,576, Norfolk 1,046, Mobile 817, Savannah 705, and New Bern, North Carolina, 689. In the Upper South on the eve of the war, some 32 percent of free blacks lived in urban centers (incorporated or unincorporated) with total populations greater than 2,500. In the Lower South, that figure was approximately 53 percent.

Free blacks worked in the fields on farms and plantations and as day laborers, factory hands, domestics, cooks, laundresses, peddlers, and waiters. They also filled skilled jobs as barbers, seamstresses, nurses, mechanics, tailors, carpenters, brick masons, wheelwrights, painters, blacksmiths, shoemakers, and plasterers. In urban areas they frequently found themselves competing with immigrants, particularly the Irish, for jobs. Their types of employment varied from city to city, depending on the local economy and demand. At the top of the hierarchy of free blacks stood free Creoles of color. The native-born, Roman Catholic Creoles were of French and Spanish and African descent, and they made up part of the free black population in the Lower South states of Louisiana, Alabama, and Florida. They lived primarily in the port cities of New Orleans, Mobile, Pensacola, St. Augustine, Key West, and Jacksonville. The Louisiana Purchase in 1803 and the acquisition of West Florida in 1810 and Florida in 1819 introduced Creoles into the United States.[36]

In most cases free blacks lived and worked only a step away from slavery. They enjoyed no voting rights and few civil rights. They were denied public education and access to most public accommodations. Laws forbade them from holding public meetings away from the watchful eyes of whites, and they could not testify in court against whites. Nor could they purchase liquor or possess firearms. They were required to wear badges or carry passes when in public and to observe curfews. In Richmond on June 3, 1861, the mayor's court ordered Susan Moxley, a free black, whipped for not obeying orders to go home and stay there.

Labor contracts and apprenticeship agreements sometimes bound free blacks in slavery-like arrangements, and state laws and city ordinances increasingly restricted their movements and privileges. For instance, the Alabama legislature of 1853–1854 passed a law requiring all free persons of color over fourteen years of age to choose a white guardian competent to teach them a trade. Each guardian had to make an annual report regarding his ward to the probate judge who bound over the free black to him. By 1855 more than 500 of Mobile's free blacks had guardians. Captains of ships bound for Mobile with free blacks on board as crewmen often saw them imprisoned by town authorities while their vessels were docked in the Alabama port.[37] In June 1861 the town commissioners of Charlotte, North Carolina, passed an ordinance stating: "All Free-Negroes now resident in the Town of Charlotte, or who may hereafter become residents of the same, being of the age of twelve years and upwards shall be required to appear before the mayor, enroll their names and upon satisfactory evidence of a peaceful character and industrious habits obtain from him a certificate of such enrollment together with a description of their persons characters and trade, or employment.... And if any free person of color liable to such enrollment shall be found without such certificate said free person of color shall be deemed guilty of a misdemeanor and on conviction before the Mayor shall be punished at his discretion by either fine, whipping, imprisonment, or hireing out for a time not exceeding six months for each offence." Free blacks had to pay a tax of $1.00 for each certificate.[38]

Free African Americans did have some advantages and privileges not allowed enslaved blacks, however. They could marry, own property, and engage in some trades forbidden to slaves. Perhaps most important, these free persons could enjoy the privacy and seclusion of their own homes and some type of family life. A number of free blacks themselves owned slaves. In Mobile in 1860, at least ten free blacks held slaves. One such owner, Burnadoz Rosieste, had sixteen slaves between the ages of twenty-four and thirty-six. Madam Bashong, a free woman, owned fourteen slaves who were thirty-six to fifty-five years old. The largest free black slaveholder in the antebellum South was John Carruthers Stanly of New Bern. The son of a wealthy white man and a slave woman, Stanly received his freedom and his wife's and launched a business career that included owning a barbershop, farms, property in town, and 160 slaves, mostly field hands and unskilled workers.[39]

Some free blacks rendered support for and service to the Confederate cause. A few sold their crops to the army and hired their slaves for work on building fortifications. Others volunteered to serve as noncombatants in various capacities for the Confederate military. Several states passed legislation authorizing enlistment and employment of free blacks and their transfer to duty under the authority of the Confederate government. In February 1864 the central government passed a law that impressed as laborers free black men between the ages of eighteen and fifty. Whether volunteering or impressed, these men were often organized as companies at camps of instruction and then detailed to work on fortifications and at various other sites, including factories and hospitals. They received the same pay as privates in the Confederate army. Some free blacks might have offered their services to the Confederate military out of local loyalties or the anticipation of better treatment, or as a result of pressure from whites, or to avoid impressment.

A number of free blacks even volunteered to serve as local and state troops. In Louisiana in 1861, Gov. Thomas O. Moore enrolled 1,500 of New Orleans's free blacks into the First Native Guards, Louisiana Militia. Ultimately 3,000 Louisiana black soldiers served in the state militia, but without arms and supplies and confined merely to drills. Both New Orleans and Mobile enlisted Creole companies into their city militia units. According to one interpretation, Creoles joined those companies as a way of protecting themselves from "violence, expulsion, and confiscation of [their] property." But after Union forces captured New Orleans, 3,122 Creoles and other blacks enlisted in the three Federal regiments of Louisiana Native Guards. Two of those regiments fought against the Confederates at the Battle of Fort Hudson in 1863.[40]

In the final desperate days of the war, when the Confederate army found itself suffering dwindling ranks in face of the Federal onslaught, some commanders began to call for the deployment of all eligible free blacks as combatants. On March 24, 1865, "All Creoles and other free persons of color between the ages of 16 and 50" received an order by Gen. D. H. Maury, the Confederate commander at Mobile, "to report at once at these headquarters to be organized into companies for local defense."[41] Other officers in the area endorsed the idea of using free blacks as soldiers. Gen. Randall L. Gibson, in charge of the defenses of Spanish Fort near Mobile, wrote to General Maury: "Have you any negro troops? I would be glad to get some."[42]

But if any free blacks actually bore arms and fought alongside white soldiers in the final throes of the Confederate war effort, their numbers were extremely small. Whites generally opposed giving weapons to free blacks and enlisting them in Confederate ranks. To make soldiers of African Americans would be to deny notions of their racial inferiority. "The proposition of the committee of safety to enlist companies of our free colored men, is not relished by our citizens generally," declared a Memphis newspaper editor in May 1861. He suggested that a few of the town's free blacks could be assigned to Confederate companies in the area "for cooking, washing, etc. This is their post, one of inferiority, not of citizen soldiers."[43]

Ever present was the fear that free blacks might unite with slaves and provide them with the leadership necessary to flee bondage or stage a successful revolt. After all, free blacks generally were more accomplished and worldly. Many of them could read and write. They might implant in slaves ideas about freedom and plans for rebellion. Indeed, some free blacks aided Federal troops, served as spies, and participated in minor uprisings. In Virginia during 1864–1865, their pro-Union organizations plotted to thwart the Confederate war effort. Consequently, many whites saw free African Americans as subversive, and as time went on, laws restricting the freedom and movement of free blacks and their association with slaves increased and tightened. Efforts were made to limit their economic opportunities. A free and successful black population ran counter to the concept of white supremacy and the foundation upon which the South's social and economic system rested—that is, that slavery was the proper and only sphere for African Americans. As historian Ira Berlin has written, "The free Negroes' fervent attempt to shake off the habits of slavery . . . and establish an identity as a free people heightened white fears. Ironically, the more the free Negro became like them, the more enraged whites became." As the war continued, white Southerners grew increasingly worried about the association between free blacks and slaves and made efforts to keep them apart. With their liberties curtailed and their racial equality denied, free blacks when the war concluded stood with their former slave brethren even farther on the outskirts of Southern society.[44]

Foreigners, too, frequently found themselves outside the mainstream of Southern life. According to historian Ella Lonn, "Probably no impression has been more deeply cherished by the population living south of Mason and Dixon's line . . . than . . . that in the veins of . . . southerners flowed the purest Anglo-Saxon blood in the New World and that their soil was the freest from the tread of foreign races." In actuality, as Lonn has demonstrated, the states of the South had a significant number of foreign-born persons, who played an integral part in daily life on the Confederate home front. Although 86.5 percent of the foreign-born population of the United States in 1860 resided in the free states and only 13.5 percent inhabited the slave states, the latter figure nevertheless represented "a very appreciable and important number."[45]

In the slaveholding states in 1860, the Irish dominated the foreign-born population at 84,763. Germans ranked next in number at 73,579. They were followed by 53,304 British other than Irish. The Irish accounted for the largest number of foreigners in each of the Southern states except Texas, which had more Germans. Texas also was home to 12,443 Mexicans. Scattered throughout the South were an undetermined number of immigrants of other nationalities, including Polish, Italian, Spanish, French, Swiss, Norwegian, and other, mostly European, people. Missouri had the largest percentage of foreigners at 13.59 percent, the majority being German. Louisiana followed with 11.44 percent. North Carolina had the smallest percentage of foreign-born inhabitants at .33 percent. The eleven states that formed the Confederacy included about 5.5 million white people. Of that number about 250,000—between 4 and 5 percent—were born abroad.[46]

Throughout the antebellum period, immigrants arrived in the coastal and river port cities of the South: New Orleans, Galveston, Mobile, Savannah, Charleston, Richmond, Memphis, and Louisville. As the most populous city in the Confederacy, New Orleans had almost 65,000 foreign-born inhabitants when the war began. Richmond had close to 38,000 inhabitants, of whom nearly 5,000 were foreigners, representing about 23 percent of the white population and 13 percent of the total population, white and black. In Alabama 63 percent of all foreigners lived in Mobile. That port city's aggregate population—29,258, of which 20,854 were white—included 7,023 foreign-born residents, 7,587 slaves, and 817 free blacks.[47] Irish and Germans constituted the largest numbers of foreigners in Mobile, but there were a good many immigrants from England and Wales as well. They were dispersed throughout the city, except that one ward held more than a third of the community's immigrants. The foreign residents of that ward were mostly "recent immigrants" who grouped together because of "common customs and religions, language difficulties, and economic necessities."

Foreigners made up a vital part of the urban labor force in the Confederacy. The Irish particularly gravitated toward manual jobs. They found work as laborers, cab drivers, draymen, brick masons, stonecutters, carpenters, hotel employees, and house servants. Some held municipal jobs as policemen, watchmen, and street inspectors. They established small businesses, including grocery stores, which also frequently served as grog shops. Their occupations were sometimes the same as those of urban slaves and free blacks.[48]

To a large extent, the South's mechanics and munitions workers were foreign born, and their skills were important to the Confederate war effort. Germans, who had learned their skills in their homeland, became the "most important and valuable workmen in the Confederate armories, arsenals, and ordnance foundries."[49] A few foreigners—mostly Irish and English—worked on Southern railroads in various capacities. But the Confederate rail lines suffered from a shortage of mechanics, most of whom before the war had come from the North. At the outbreak of the conflict, foreigners who worked as railroad mechanics left the Confederacy along with skilled Northerners.

The war virtually ended the flow of immigrants into the South, thus denying the Confederacy an important element of its skilled labor force. But as the fighting continued and turned decidedly against the South, and as conditions worsened at home, native white Southerners increasingly looked for scapegoats on which to blame their region's dire circumstances. Foreigners often became objects of local frustration, resentment, anger, and prejudice. In the port cities, immigrants tended to live in the poorest neighborhoods near docks and warehouses, where they found work. Poverty and disease afflicted them, and they found themselves easy victims of native whites, who were quick to blame them for social ills and downturns in fortune.

Although nativism did not exist in the South to the same extent as in the North, it was present among the white home-front populace. The Irish especially came in for condemnation, reportedly for drunkenness and rowdy behavior. Their association with blacks—against whom, ironically, they often competed for laboring jobs—also led to suspicion and denunciation by native whites. Nevertheless, large numbers of the foreign born served in the Confederate army and in civil government. Others achieved prominence in business and the professions of law, medicine, religion, education, and politics, and in the skilled vocations. German-born Christopher Gustavus Memminger became secretary of the treasury for the Confederacy. The two foreigners to attain the rank of major general in the Confederate army were Patrick R. Cleburne, an Irishman, and the Frenchman Camille A. J. M. Polignac. Several immigrants attained the rank of colonel, including the dashing Pomeranian cavalryman Heros von Borcke, chief of staff for Gen. J. E. B. Stuart.[50]

Mainstream Southern society frequently suspected and denounced Jewish bankers and merchants, who it claimed had invaded the South to cheat the people and profit from their misfortune. Before the war Jews in the South, although they remained outside the largely Protestant mainstream, found a place in society. Some owned slaves, others were slave traders, and many defended the institution of slavery and Southern values and culture. About two-thirds of the Jewish people in the Confederacy were recent immigrants, but they and native-born Jews did not differ in their identification with the South and its cause. Jews served in the Confederate army, and a significant number became officers and noncommissioned officers. Some earned high rank in the army and Confederate government. David Camden De Leon became the first surgeon general of the Confederate army. Levy Myers Harby commanded the port of Galveston. Lionel Levy held the position of judge advocate of the army. Abraham C. Myers became quartermaster general. Perhaps the best-known Confederate official was Judah P. Benjamin, a former U.S. senator who served the Confederate government consecutively as attorney general, secretary of war, and secretary of state.

Other Jews lent their support to the Southern cause as businessmen, manufacturers, and government agents. David (Levy) Yulee, another former U.S. senator and passionate secessionist, became president of the Florida Railroad during the war, although he had renounced his Judaism and converted to Christianity. Some Jewish factory owners converted their facilities to produce arms. The Harmon brothers of Columbus, Georgia, for example, were the largest manufacturers of swords and pistols in the Confederacy. Nathan Lazarus became a Confederate agent for purchases in England.

Despite such contributions to the Confederate war effort, Gentile Southerners frequently accused Jews of being "Shylocks" who were profiting from the war and undermining Confederate success. That stereotypical prejudice manifested itself in suspicion and accusations that Jewish merchants and traders were price gouging, speculating, profiteering, and even spreading counterfeit money. Christian whites claimed that Jewish storekeepers seemed to have little to sell when inflation-riddled Confederate scrip was offered but suddenly discovered desired goods when gold was produced for payment. Charges and taunts of Jewish disloyalty grew, especially as fear and anxiety over Federal invasion increased.[51]

While Vicksburg suffered under Union siege in 1863, some inhabitants accused the town's Jews of speculating in real estate that was being sold cheap to avoid losses from Federal bombardment or occupation. Benjamin L. C. Wailes wrote to President Davis that "the shopkeeper Jews in Vicksburg are buying up real estate—one bought the Washington Hotel and other property has fallen into their hands."[52] In the lower house of the Confederate Congress, Henry S. Foote of Tennessee maligned Judah Benjamin and decried the permissiveness of Southern society in allowing so many Jews to infiltrate the South and practice extortion. "In every city and village," he declared, "it might be safely estimated that at least nine-tenths of those engaged in trade were foreign Jews, spirited here by extraordinary and mysterious means. In this city [Richmond] one had only to explore the streets to convince him that four out of five of the tradesmen in our principal thoroughfares were Jews." Indeed, for years German Jews had been settling in Virginia county seats. Their numbers in Richmond had become large enough to establish a synagogue in that city in 1840 and a commercial college on the eve of the war.[53] A British merchant noted the large number of Jews in Charleston. At a hotel, he observed, "Fully one-half the large number of guests . . . seemed as if they had just stepped out of Houndsditch, and reminded me of what a friend in Mobile had said, that, 'I should meet more Jews in Charleston than I would see in Jerusalem.' They all seemed absorbed in the study of the auctioneer's pamphlets, and the long advertisements of sales which half-filled the papers. I found these sales were all of goods which had run the blockade, and the quantity seemed very large, and very varied."[54] A refugee from Charleston who fled to the town of Sumter was shocked at the high cost of living and abhorred "the prevalence of sand and Jews."[55] Edward A. Pollard, editor of the Richmond *Examiner* and author, declared that the largest volume of speculation and extortion in manufacturing and trade was carried out "by Jews and foreign adventurers who everywhere infested the Confederacy."[56]

Despite the bigotry and xenophobia that the white home-front population showed toward immigrants, most foreigners remained loyal to the cause of Southern independence. Texas was the only Confederate state in which a significant portion of the immigrant population opposed the Southern war effort. In Texas Germans predominated among the large foreign-born populace. Some areas of the state became German belts. Most Germans in the state opposed slavery and saw no reason to fight to defend and protect the institution. Many were small farmers with no desire for slave labor. Still others objected to slavery on moral grounds and considered disunion to be folly.[57] They were among the many Southern folk who did not embrace the Confederate cause. But willing or not, everyone in the South—black or white, slave or free, foreign or native born—was swept up in the war waged by the Confederacy.

Confederate soldier Sam Eller had his leg amputated after the Battle of Gettysburg in 1863. He is shown here in the early 1900s wearing a wooden replacement. (Courtesy of the North Carolina Office of Archives and History, Raleigh)

During the siege of Vicksburg in 1863, civilians sought refuge from Union bombardment by living in caves. This drawing of a woman praying in her earthen dwelling was made by Adalbert Johann Volck. (Courtesy of the Lincoln Museum, Fort Wayne, Indiana [#3686])

The Johnson-Jones family of Georgia was photographed while visiting relatives at an army camp near Richmond in the spring of 1862. (Johnson-Jones Family Portrait, Pictorial File BVIII, Manuscript, Archives, and Rare Book Library, Emory University)

With wooden flooring and a second story, the slave quarters at Horton Grove on Stagville Plantation in North Carolina were more elaborate than most. This structure had four rooms and housed four families. (Photograph by Paulette Mitchell)

At her own expense and with female volunteers, Sally Tompkins operated a military hospital in Richmond. (The Museum of the Confederacy, Richmond, Virginia)

Tredegar Iron Works in Richmond became a major manufacturer of cannon and other war material and employed as many as 2,500 workers. (Library of Congress. Copy print courtesy of the Museum of the Confederacy, Richmond, Virginia. Copy photography by Katherine Wetzel)

Cards for combing cotton and wool fibers in preparation for spinning remained in short supply throughout the Confederacy. (Courtesy of the North Carolina Museum of History, Raleigh)

This homemade leather shoe had a hand-carved wooden sole reinforced with iron. (Courtesy of the North Carolina Museum of History, Raleigh)

A Northern artist created this interpretative image of the Richmond bread riots of 1863. (The Museum of the Confederacy, Richmond, Virginia. Photography by Katherine Wetzel)

As the war continued, peace movements arose in the Confederate states. North Carolina's peace advocates found a spokesman in newspaper editor William W. Holden. (Courtesy of the North Carolina Office of Archives and History, Raleigh, North Carolina)

TRENT RIVER SETTLEMENT, OPPOSITE NEWBERN, NORTH CAROLINA.—[Sketched by Theodore R. Davis.]

SCHOOL-HOUSE AND CHAPEL AT TRENT RIVER SETTLEMENT.—[Sketched by Theo. R. Davis.]

NEGRO HUTS AT TRENT RIVER SETTLEMENT.

GENERALS STEEDMAN AND FULLERTON CONFERRING WITH THE FREEDMEN IN THEIR CHURCH AT TRENT RIVER SETTLEMENT.—Sketched by T. R. Davis.—[See Page 36.]

Many slaves escaping to Federal lines lived in camps such as the Trent River Settlement near New Bern, North Carolina. (From *Harper's Weekly*, June 9, 1866)

Mary Jane Conner, a freed black woman, operated a boardinghouse in Union-occupied New Bern. (Courtesy of Tryon Palace Historic Sites and Gardens, New Bern, North Carolina)

SIX

❦

REFUGEES, CITIES, AND TOWNS

The war displaced vast numbers of Southern civilians. Possibly as many as 200,000 became refugees.[1] The reality or threat of federal attack compelled most of these people to flee their homes and seek safety elsewhere. When they first took flight, refugees generally "fell into one of three categories": those who had planned a destination in advance, those who were not exactly sure where they would end up but hoped for lodging with relatives or friends, and those who had no definite destination but were just fleeing to escape danger. It was not unusual for refugees to experience all three situations as the war continued to disrupt their lives. According to historian Mary Elizabeth Massey, "Very few refugees were permitted to remain in one spot long enough to feel at home, and as they migrated from place to place within the contracting Confederacy they created problems for themselves and others. This floating population contributed appreciably to the breakdown of homefront morale as it aggravated the economic and social conditions in the wartime South." No particular characteristic defined all refugees. Rather, "a person's financial situation, personal contacts, place of refuge, ingenuity, adjustability to changing conditions, and his good fortune or lack of it combined to make each refugee's circumstances distinctive."[2]

The year 1861 produced few refugees, and most of those came from the border areas of western Virginia, Kentucky, and Missouri and from certain coastal regions. As Union armies penetrated into the border states, Confederate sympathizers fled farther south. When Federal army and navy expeditions began capturing coastal sites, some residents moved inland. By 1862, however, the flood of refugees began in earnest. "The real meaning of the war dawned on the people in the late winter and spring as thousands left their homes and fled before the advancing Federal armies."

The poorer classes of people of the Confederacy composed the largest proportion of refugees, and the majority were women, children, and men too old for military service. Mostly uneducated, they left few descriptions of their plight. The surviving military, newspaper, and upper-class accounts describe them "collectively as a 'swarm,' 'horde,' or stream of humanity seen trudging along the roads of the Confederacy or infiltrating a community." The poor classes might have contributed the greatest number of refugees, but a larger percentage of the upper class joined their ranks. Upper-class civilians had the most to lose to Federal raids and occupation and therefore were more inclined to seek safety elsewhere. Then, too, the wealthy had the means to move their families and possessions to new sites away from the ravages of war. Some of them owned additional houses or plantations in other locales, and many had friends or relatives with whom they could live temporarily in relative comfort.[3]

When Halifax County plantation mistress Catherine Devereux Edmondston went to her father's home for dinner on February 15, 1862, she found the house filled with refugees from coastal North Carolina. "As we stopped at the door," she recorded in her diary, "we were surprised to see the window crowded with little faces watching our descent from the carriage. On entering the Drawing Room two strange ladies sprang up & met us with the exclamation—'where did you come from!?' We soon found they were Refugees & thought we were in the same sad situation! Poor people they have been driven from their homes by the advance of the enemy and are now seeking an asylum, a shelter for their heads—Mr. and Mrs. Leary, his sister, Mrs. Carlton, his daughter, Mrs. Skinner, & children & grandchildren, to the number of nineteen whites and seventy negroes, all homeless & houseless." On the following day, she recorded that as U.S. troops commanded by Gen. Ambrose E. Burnside captured territory in the Carolina Coastal Plain, "the roads were crowded with Refugees in vehicles of every description, endeavoring to move what of their property they can to save it from the grasp of the invader." The invasion was causing a "disaffected state of feeling" throughout the coastal counties, she wrote, "so greatly does fear affect principle."[4]

The immediate dilemma facing people who chose to take flight was where to go. Most refugees were at first reluctant to leave their homes and did so only as a last resort. Once on the road, they wanted to remain in their own state. They preferred to stay as close to home as possible, edging "away by degrees, keeping a short distance ahead of the Federals."[5]

Having decided to leave their homes, refugees were forced to choose what to take with them. Most attempted to include as many of their household possessions as possible—furniture, bedding, clothing, cookware, provisions, and other necessities—and had to leave treasured items behind. It was not unusual for those who were heavily burdened to abandon some of their cargo on an arduous journey. Those who carried fewer possessions generally found travel easier. But refugees who traveled light had fewer comforts of life once they arrived at a safe destination. Wagons, carts, and all other wheeled conveyances were much in demand, and they were expensive to buy or rent. Transportation by water or rail grew increasingly expensive with the growing mass movement of displaced persons. There never seemed to be enough means of transportation. Once on the move, refugees had to endure bad roads, swollen rivers and streams, unpredictable weather, lack of food and water, overexertion, illness, fear, and a multitude of other hardships. They frequently had difficulty procuring lodging and assistance from locals whose homes they passed en route. Not surprisingly, travelers who could afford to pay for transportation, food, and lodging fared better than those who were not so well heeled.

Most refugees settled in villages, towns, and cities. They were attracted to urban areas for a number of reasons. Towns offered them the protection and psychological comfort of being among masses of people and sometimes made charity services available. Initially urban centers provided greater housing possibilities, although that situation changed as the war continued and cities and towns filled with more and more displaced people. Refugees also gravitated to urban environments for the pleasures and conveniences of social life, mail service, churches, schools, and theaters. In general, it was more economical to live in the countryside, and some refugees did leave towns and cities to resettle in rural areas for that reason. Most refugees who settled on plantations and farms moved in with relatives or friends. Nevertheless, the number of them arriving in urban centers always exceeded the number departing. With thousands of the homeless arriving, some towns and cities doubled or tripled in population by the end of the war.[6]

Even in cities under threat of Federal attack, the number of people arriving tended to exceed the number fleeing. At Vicksburg, Mississippi, in May 1863, "a paradoxical situation developed; some people were desperately trying to flee the city while others were eager to come in. Most of the ones who were arriving were from New Orleans and the vicinity already occupied by Union forces—they were glad to exchange life in an occupied territory for the meager comfort they could find in Vicksburg, which was only threatened with attack and capture."[7]

No city attracted more refugees than did Richmond, which in 1860 had a population of 40,000. That number doubled in the first year of the war, and refugees continued to come in droves. As the Confederate capital, Richmond attracted large numbers of government and military officials and their families. Many people also flooded the capital in hopes of filling one of the city's new government or industrial jobs. Richmond became so congested that towns and villages in the vicinity of the capital served as (in present-day parlance) "bedroom communities" for commuters who made daily treks into the city to work in government offices and at other jobs. With direct rail lines to Richmond, the towns of Ashland and Petersburg particularly housed a significant number of commuters as their populations swelled with hundreds of refugees. Throughout Virginia other towns and villages of various sizes became settlement sites for the homeless and dispossessed. Most desirable were those with railroad connections. Danville, for example, attracted so many refugees that by June 1862 its population had doubled. Large numbers of displaced persons were among the inhabitants of Fredericksburg when that town had to be evacuated in 1862. Amelia Courthouse, Farmville, Staunton, Lynchburg, Gordonsville, and Charlottesville also filled with newcomers uprooted by the war. In southwestern Virginia refugees from Tennessee, Kentucky, and North Carolina sought safety in Bristol and Abingdon. As Union forces overran Virginia in the final year of the war, the homeless found fewer and fewer places where they could escape the Federal onslaught. But even then the urban centers continued to attract them.

North Carolina experienced less dislocation than Virginia, primarily because only the eastern part of the Tar Heel State was invaded and occupied for most of the war. Even so, as Federal troops in 1862 captured coastal towns such as New Bern, Elizabeth City, Plymouth, and Beaufort, many residents of those municipalities sought refuge in the interior. Located in the southeastern region known as the Cape Fear and guarded by the formidable Fort Fisher, the port of Wilmington, North Carolina's largest city, remained in Confederate hands and open for blockade-running for most of the war. It attracted a sizable number of refugees. Some of them came to the city in search of employment, to profit in the bustling blockade-running business, or seeking passage abroad. In the final weeks of the war, some residents fled to the interior of the state when a joint Federal army and navy expedition captured Fort Fisher and then occupied Wilmington. Already in 1862 a number of Wilmingtonians, especially the affluent, had hurried away from the city when yellow fever struck. New Bern too experienced an exodus when yellow fever broke out there in 1864.

Refugees who abandoned their coastal homes for sites in the interior of North Carolina sought shelter and safety in such urban centers as Goldsboro, Raleigh, Chapel Hill, Hillsborough, Greensboro, Salisbury, Charlotte, and numerous other small towns and hamlets just out of Yankee reach. Those who took flight tended to push farther westward as Federal raids threatened from the east, and especially when Gen. William T. Sherman's army invaded the state from the south in the spring of 1865.[8]

One of North Carolina's most famous refugees was Varina Davis, wife of the Confederate president, who became a temporary resident of Raleigh in May 1863 when a Federal campaign threatened Richmond. The flight of Mrs. Davis and her children annoyed Catherine Edmondston, who accused Mrs. Davis of abandoning her husband in a time of peril. "I fear she does not strengthen her husband, or she would never have abandoned her post & set such an example for the women of the Confederacy," complained the plantation mistress.[9]

As Sherman's columns invaded Columbia, South Carolina, in February 1865, refugees from that city poured into Charlotte, North Carolina. But fearing that their town would be captured next by Sherman, many permanent residents of Charlotte began moving toward mountain towns such as Lenoir, Asheville, Flat Rock, Morganton, and Shelby. Mrs. Joseph E. Johnston, wife of the Confederate general, arrived in Charlotte from Columbia aboard a train with 300 women who could not find shelter in the North Carolina city. "The sight of the town is lamentable," she noted, "women hunting in every direction for shelter—and the people themselves beginning to move off." Probably the most desired place of refuge for the displaced from Columbia was the North Carolina town of Lincolnton. It became a haven for Mrs. Johnston, the diarist Mary Boykin Chesnut, and other prominent South Carolinians.[10] But even those refugees who reached the safety and isolation of western North Carolina's mountains discovered that there was no complete escape from the Federal advance when cavalry commanded by Gen. George H. Stoneman invaded the Tar Heel State from Tennessee in the final weeks of the war.[11]

As in North Carolina, refugees in South Carolina initially fled from the coastal region, largely because prior to 1865 that was the only area of the state held by the U.S. Army. Some refugees sought safety in the port city of Charleston, but it did not become as congested as other cities in the South. Thousands of low-country residents settled anew in the Piedmont or upcountry, in such towns as Sumter, Cheraw, Orangeburg, Barnwell, Greenville, and Spartanburg. Sumter was the first urban center to become inundated with new arrivals, but eventually Columbia hosted the largest number of displaced persons. The state capital's rail connections, hotels and boardinghouses, and potential employment in government offices and factories made it particularly attractive to folk on the run. In early 1865 many South Carolinians, and also a number of refugees from Georgia and other invaded areas, flocked to Columbia to avoid Sherman. Initially they believed that his troops were not marching toward the state capital. But when it became obvious that Columbia was Sherman's destination, the escape routes from the capital were crowded with refugees, permanent residents, and government workers, many of whom pressed northward into North Carolina.[12] In February Mary Chesnut "took French leave of Columbia, slipped away without a word to anybody" and settled in Lincolnton. "The day I left home," she recalled, "I had packed a box of flour, sugar, rice, coffee, &c &c, but my husband would not let me bring it. He said I was coming to a land of plenty. Unexplored North Carolina, where the foot of Yankee marauder was unknown—and in Columbia they would need food." But she soon was writing back to Columbia for someone "to send me that box and many other things . . . or I will starve." As Sherman neared the South Carolina capital, Mrs. Chesnut was joined by a number of friends. "The Middletons have come," she exclaimed. "How joyously I sprang to my feet to greet them. Mrs. Ben Rutledge describes the hubbub in Columbia—everybody flying in every direction, like a flock of swallows. She heard the enemy's guns booming in the distance."[13]

In addition to its own inhabitants, Georgia drew a large number of refugees from the Deep South and from Tennessee and Kentucky. Out-of-state refugees from Alabama, Louisiana, and Florida crowded into such Georgia towns as LaGrange, Columbus, and Lumpkin. Atlanta became the primary site for the dispossessed seeking refuge. Many persons were attracted to its urban and cosmopolitan advantages, and they doubted that the city was vulnerable to Union capture. After all, they reasoned, the Confederacy could not afford to lose such a valuable transportation and manufacturing center. At the outset of the war, Atlanta accommodated refugees without too much difficulty. But by the second year, it was becoming overwhelmed as more of the homeless competed for housing, food, and other necessities. As the conflict wore on, many refugees began living in tents and other impromptu shelters. The state capital of Milledgeville was a major destination for refugees for much of the war. Among its itinerant residents were homeless people from Tennessee and Kentucky. Athens experienced a similar influx. Some arrivals found shelter in the town's Franklin College buildings. Although the college was closed, two "institutes" remained open, and refugee children could attend. Augusta, with its factories, also attracted large numbers of people in search of dwellings, employment, and safety. Some inhabitants of Savannah evacuated that city after a Federal expedition captured nearby Fort Pulaski in April 1862 and closed the port to blockade-running. But the city itself remained in Confederate hands until Sherman's army arrived in 1864. Many residents then fled to Augusta. As Sherman approached Atlanta in the fall of 1864, the first residents to take flight secured shelter in Macon, but those who left after the Union general issued an evacuation order were hard pressed to obtain a place to live in Macon, Milledgeville, or Athens.[14]

Florida had a smaller population than other Southern states and consequently had fewer native refugees. Inhabitants of the coastal region moved inland or out of state when Federal invasion first occurred. In northeastern Florida the Federals banished a number of residents to the areas of Savannah and Charleston in Georgia and South Carolina. Madison, St. Augustine, and Jacksonville proved to be only temporary sites for refugees to find shelter. Displaced residents from eastern Florida who went to Tallahassee soon found that they had to move again when Union troops threatened that city. In the end most Florida refugees moved out of state, and few displaced people entered the state.[15]

The northern region of Alabama was settled by hundreds of displaced persons from Tennessee after the Federal capture of Fort Henry in February 1862. They relocated to mountain communities and resorts and to Huntsville. Many new arrivals fled from that town when the Union army seized it, but some of them returned after the Confederates reclaimed the area. Selma provided refuge for hundreds of homeless Mississippians who wanted to get away from the Federal advance or find employment in the town's government factories. Hundreds also flocked to the university town of Tuscaloosa. The university there remained open, but housing was difficult to procure. Because the U.S. Army did not penetrate into central Alabama, many refugees relocated to that region. Montgomery was the chief center for those displaced people, most of whom were residents of the state. Throughout the war Mobile was the major refugee center on the Gulf coast. In 1862 and 1863 a large number of inhabitants of New Orleans were banished from the Crescent City by the Union army, which had captured the Louisiana port in April 1862. Those exiles went to Mobile, and in 1863 the Louisiana Exile Relief Committee was formed in the Alabama town to aid them. The British military observer Lt. Col. Arthur James Lyon Fremantle of the Coldstream Guards commented on the horde of exiles from New Orleans and the problems confronting the city authorities in Mobile in finding "accommodations and provisions for the poor and homeless people." He wrote in 1863 that, as a result of the large number of displaced moving to the port city, Mobilians were seriously considering prohibiting the entry of any more refugees. Nevertheless, hundreds of refugees continued to flee to Mobile from the coastal area and the Alabama and Mississippi countryside, even after the port was closed to blockade-running by a joint U.S. Navy and Army expedition in August 1864.[16]

Because Mississippi was a major battle zone, its earliest refugee centers had been abandoned by the final two years of the war. Among the displaced people in the state were transients from Tennessee, Missouri, and Arkansas. Jackson was the largest refugee site in Mississippi, but just before the city fell to Union attack in May 1863, outgoing trains were crowded with people bound for Mobile, Meridian, and Vicksburg. Other refugees fled to Columbus or over the Alabama border. Those who chose Vicksburg soon found themselves in a besieged city, which surrendered to Federal forces in July. Prior to Vicksburg's capture, some homeless Mississippians had journeyed to the Trans-Mississippi west. But after the Vicksburg collapse, most refugees traveled toward the east.

Probably no state in the Confederacy was more sharply divided in its loyalties than Tennessee. East Tennessee harbored strong pro-Union sentiment, but people in central and western Tennessee tended to support secession and the Confederacy. In the first year of the war, refugees from Missouri and Kentucky arrived at Memphis, Nashville, and Knoxville, but that influx soon ceased. Federal victories at Fort Donelson and Shiloh in the winter and spring of 1862 forced the pro-Confederate state government and Gov. Isham G. Harris to evacuate the capital at Nashville. President Lincoln then established Andrew Johnson as a Federal military governor, with the mission of restoring Tennessee to the Union. A number of civilians were banished from the capital for refusing to take an oath of loyalty to the United States. Fighting continued in Tennessee, but by November 1863 Confederate forces—except raiding cavalry and guerrillas—had largely been driven from the state. After the surrender of Fort Donelson, a large number of Tennesseans fled to Nashville, only to flee that city when it, too, fell. The pattern was repeated when the Federal army captured Memphis in June 1862 and Chattanooga in the fall of 1863. Folk who evacuated these areas ahead of the Federal onslaught traveled to Alabama, Georgia, and Mississippi or found havens in western or southern Tennessee.

In Arkansas Little Rock drew the most refugees. Many of them came from the southern part of the state or southern Missouri. Planters whose property stood along the Mississippi River and who wanted to migrate into Tennessee found their plans thwarted when Memphis surrendered. They then sought out Little Rock as an alternative. When the Federals seized that city, refugees went to the village of Camden, which contained ordnance factories, and to Washington, which became the temporary state capital. Hundreds also crossed into Louisiana and Texas.[17]

As mentioned earlier, hundreds of Louisianans found themselves on the move after the Union army and navy captured New Orleans in the spring of 1862. That port city had been a major refugee center prior to its fall, and few of the inhabitants were able to escape before the Federals arrived. Those who did manage to leave joined the multitude of dispossessed folk throughout the state who struggled to find places to live. A large number of refugees from Union-occupied New Orleans fled to Mobile. Still others went to Tangipahoa Parish or the villages of Arcola and Amte. In the end, as Mary Elizabeth Massey has written, "New Orleans citizens managed to stray all over the Confederacy." After the surrender of the Crescent City, the state capital of Baton Rouge soon fell, and few residents could evacuate before Federal troops took the city. Those who later left crowded into the new state capital at Opelousas and then, when it was threatened, into another state capital at Shreveport. Moving from place to place as the Union army encroached, these Louisianans seldom had the luxury of staying long in one location in their native state. Ultimately many fled across the border into Texas.[18]

Perhaps Louisiana's best-remembered refugee was Kate Stone of Brokenburn, a large cotton plantation in northeast Louisiana. Kate began recording her life experiences in a journal in May 1861. As Union troops invaded her home and slaves threatened violence, she and her family and two servants began a flight that took them through Louisiana and ultimately to Tyler, Texas. Along the arduous journey, she described the chaos of masses of refugees crowding into the town of Delphi, Louisiana, seeking railroad transportation away from the Federal advance.

The scene there beggars description: such crowds of Negroes of all ages and sizes, wagons, mules, horses, dogs, baggage, and furniture of every description, very little of it packed. It was just thrown in promiscuous heaps—pianos, tables, chairs, rosewood sofas, wardrobes, parlor sets, with pots, kettles, stoves, beds and bedding, bowls and pitchers, and everything of the kind just thrown pell-mell here and there, with soldiers, drunk and sober, combing over it all, shouting and laughing. While thronging everywhere were refugees—men, women, and children—everybody and everything trying to get on the cars, all fleeing from the Yankees or worse still, the Negroes.[19]

More than any other state in the Confederacy, Texas offered refugees the allure of space in which to settle. Large numbers of Missourians, Louisianans, and Arkansans streamed into the state. Most new arrivals established themselves in the eastern part of Texas, near the coast or on the Brazos, Trinity, and Sabine Rivers. Some planters moved their slaves to Texas to work on newly purchased or rented land. Those migrants who chose urban areas for relocation settled in eastern and central Texas in such towns and villages as Tyler, Rusk, Marshall, Waco, and Corsicana. Houston became the chief destination in the coastal area, and the largest number of refugees who settled in that city came from the port of Galveston. Also in that region, San Antonio witnessed a sizable surge in its population.

Whether the destinations of hordes of refugees or the homes of permanent residents, the cities and towns of the Confederacy offered a life different from that in the countryside. In the United States in 1860, 102 cities had populations of 10,000 or more. Of those only ten were located in the Confederate states. Neither North Carolina, Florida, Mississippi, Arkansas, nor Texas had a city of that size. Of those cities that did have populations of 10,000 or more, New Orleans was the largest, with a population of 168,675. Charleston had 40,522 and Richmond 37,916 residents. Mobile boasted 29,258 people, and Savannah could claim 22,292 inhabitants. With a population of 12,493, Augusta was the smallest of these Southern cities. A prosperous agricultural economy, a growing urban commercial class, and the steamboat, railroad, and shipping industries had enabled these urban centers to grow in the antebellum era. Small towns and villages, with some of the commercial activity and amenities of urban living, were scattered throughout the Confederacy, but for most Southerners, daily life was largely rural.[20]

Cities and towns provided cultural and educational advantages and entertainment and diversions that were not directly available to folk in the hinterland. They usually contained a more diverse population than did the rural South. They were the sites of schools and colleges, theaters and concert halls, social and fraternal clubs, writers and artists, and large church congregations. Mercantile companies, banks, industries, and commercial interests of all kinds formed part of the urban milieu. At the outset of the sectional conflict, the cities' land transportation depots and seaports connected them to each other and the outside world.

Probably no Southern city embodied the panorama and allure of urban life more than the Confederate capital, Richmond. Established in the 1730s at the falls of the James River, Richmond had become a thriving and prosperous mercantile and industrial city by the outbreak of the Civil War. Among the products of its factories were tobacco (the city's most profitable commodity at $5 million in 1860), iron, flour, and meal. In manufacturing the Virginia capital ranked first among Southern cities and thirteenth in the entire United States. It did a significant business in the slave trade, its market being second only to New Orleans's. During the war Richmond's Tredegar Iron Works produced the bulk of the Confederacy's cannon and rails. The city was also a transportation hub. Five railroad lines had terminals there, and steamships made connections from Richmond to Washington and Baltimore. Coastal vessels tied up at its docks, and the James River and Kanahwa Canal ran westward beyond Lynchburg, transporting huge quantities of freight into the capital for sale and export. The city had six daily newspapers and a number of journals during the war. In May 1861 the Confederate government abandoned its offices in the first capital, Montgomery, Alabama, and moved to Richmond. With that transfer the Virginia capital became the center of bureaucratic, military, and social activity in the South.[21]

Richmond's downriver neighbor Norfolk was home to the Gosport Navy Yard, the United States's main naval base and the largest shipbuilding site in the South. The Virginia militia seized the facility in April 1861, after the Federals attempted, with only partial success, to burn the yard and scuttle its vessels. The Confederates raised the USS *Merrimack* and rebuilt it as the famed ironclad *Virginia*, which preyed upon Union ships in the Hampton Roads area. In March 1862 the *Virginia* fought its famous stalemate battle with the USS *Monitor* and withdrew. Shortly thereafter, the U.S. Army and Navy captured Hampton Roads and began invading along the peninsula between the York and James Rivers toward Richmond. In response the Confederates evacuated Norfolk in early May and pulled back to defend their capital. The crew of the *Virginia* floated the vessel a short distance upriver, where they burned and scuttled it. Thus Norfolk's career as a Confederate urban stronghold was short lived. Many of its residents fled to inland locales, and the town remained in Union hands for the rest of the war.[22]

Although they never surpassed Richmond, a number of the South's coastal ports and urban railroad hubs rivaled the Confederate capital in activity and strategic significance. With its blend of French, Spanish, African, and Anglo cultures, New Orleans, established as a French outpost in 1718, was the South's most worldly, diversified, and cosmopolitan city. Located at the mouth of the Mississippi River, antebellum New Orleans was a bustling commercial port, exporting cotton and other products of the Mississippi Valley. Cotton arrived in the Crescent City on steamboats and coastal ships and via rail lines that ran through Mississippi to Memphis and as far north as the Ohio River. In 1860 nearly two million bales of cotton from Texas, Louisiana, Arkansas, Tennessee, Mississippi, and western Florida cleared the port. New Orleans was surpassed only by New York in the volume of export trade. New Orleans also operated as the slave-trading capital of the South and as the region's third-largest manufacturing center. Because of its strategic value as the gateway to the Mississippi, however, its tenure as a Confederate city soon ended. A joint U.S. Army and Navy attack, featuring the famed admiral David G. Farragut, captured the port city in April 1862. It remained under Union control for the rest of the war and became a headquarters for Abraham Lincoln's attempts at emancipation and reconstruction in wartime Louisiana.[23]

As another Gulf Coast port, Mobile also thrived in the antebellum era. Strategically located where the river system of Alabama flows into the sea, the city served as a cotton-export and supply-import center for the Alabama-Tombigbee River Basin. It was second only to New Orleans as the largest cotton-shipping port in the United States. Its economic boom began with the arrival of the steamboat ca. 1818–1820, which made river travel, especially upstream, much faster and thereby increased trade with planters and merchants in the interior. In 1860 more than 800,000 bales of cotton arrived in Mobile, of which two-thirds came by river. Most of this cotton went to foreign markets, bringing a price of $38,333,576. England was the largest customer, followed by France and then the rest of Europe. But the domestic trade also flourished, and although the New England textile industry had to compete with British mills, it nevertheless bought more Southern cotton each year. Mobile's trade with the northeastern states amounted to 200,000 bales in 1860. This commerce was enhanced when the Mobile and Ohio Railroad was constructed on the eve of the war. That line tied the port city to the Ohio River. From 1857 to 1860, the railroad carried more than 100,000 bales of cotton to Mobile. Thus life in the Gulf port city revolved around cotton and the goods and services connected with it. Not only was cotton prepared there for shipment, but Mobile was also the center for factors who sold their clients' crops and furnished those clients with provisions. The port was filled with brokers and buyers. Hotels, retail merchants, theaters, banks, and the freight industry all flourished during the late antebellum period. The war, featuring a strangling U.S. blockade, brought the great prosperity and activity to an abrupt halt and inflicted considerable suffering on the inhabitants of Mobile and its environs.[24]

Port cities such as Savannah and Charleston too saw their economic life and urban advantages severely curtailed by the war and the Federal blockade. Savannah had languished during the early antebellum era, but during the 1850s its population expanded by 45 percent and it became the third-largest exporter of cotton in the United States, shipping 500,000 bales overseas in 1860. The cotton arrived on steamboats from Augusta, a major depot for the staple, and aboard the Coastal Georgia Railroad, which connected Savannah with Macon and Columbus in the interior. Much lowland rice was also shipped from the city's docks. The Georgia port teemed with wealthy merchants, brokers, factors, and others associated with the booming export-import business. In 1860 nine banks, with a capital of $10 million, operated in Savannah. The town included a number of public and private schools, and most of them managed to remain open for much of the war. The grandiose houses of the urban mercantile class exhibited a "New York Fifth Avenue character." The city's waterfront commercial district, cultural life, attractive shady streets, and town squares all reflected its antebellum prosperity and importance. After the Federals captured Fort Pulaski in 1862 and closed Savannah to blockade-running, the arsenal in the city was moved to Macon. The inhabitants of the seaport endured the shortages and other hardships of a population under siege.[25] Nevertheless, after the city fell to Sherman in 1864, Union occupiers remarked on its antebellum elegance. According to one Federal officer, Savannah was the "finest [city] in the south." He wrote to his wife that instead of his customary tent, he lodged in rooms in a fine mansion that included "gas light, coal fires, sofas, fine beds, bath room with hot and cold water and all such luxuries."[26]

Charleston served as an Atlantic port for shipping South Carolina lowland rice and cotton, as well as for importing supplies for planters and farmers in the interior. But the city's trade had been declining since the 1820s. As much as anything, it was the drop in the retail supply trade to the agricultural interior that made Charleston commercially static. Ironically, the coming of the steamboat contributed considerably to that situation. Before the steamboat planters in the southwest had procured their supplies by hauling them overland from Charleston by wagon. But with upriver travel made easier, interior towns located on the fall lines of major rivers in the hinterland became important commercial centers for the first time, depriving the Palmetto State's chief port of much trade. The arrival of the railroad further siphoned trade away from the city, which had poor railway connections. Although Charleston's antebellum population might not have been growing and prospering as a whole, the wealthy elite merchants of the city and the lowland rice and Sea Island cotton planters reaped profits that enabled them to enjoy an extravagant lifestyle in the port city. They built grand houses along the Battery and streets of the lower peninsula. They gave elaborate parties and attended balls, the theater, concerts, and races, establishing the social scene and hierarchy in Charleston.

Early in the war, Charleston served as a vital blockade-running port for the Confederacy. To close the harbor to blockade-runners and halt the building of ironclads and the manufacturing of ammunition at the South Carolina port, the Federals launched several army and navy assaults, but their attacks failed. Then in July 1863, a joint operation managed to capture most of Morris Island at the mouth of the harbor and began bombarding Fort Sumter and Charleston. The occupation of Morris Island and the U.S. Navy's increased activities severely stymied blockade-running. The city itself did not succumb to Union occupation until February 1865. During the siege, however, the residents suffered the devastation of bombardment and the hardships of shortages and destitution.[27]

Wilmington, North Carolina, was no New Orleans, Mobile, or Charleston in size or activity. But with the demise of all other blockade-running ports, the Tar Heel coastal town took on a high level of importance as the Confederacy's only viable open seaport in the final months of the war. As mentioned, New Orleans, Mobile, Savannah, and Charleston had all been closed, or nearly so. The Union navy secured possession of the harbor at Galveston, Texas, in the fall of 1862. But even after the Confederates recaptured that port in January 1863, the tightening of the blockade inhibited the success of blockade-running. Between January and March 1864, seventy ships attempted to depart from Galveston, but fewer than twelve managed to return. The procurement of supplies through the Mexican port of Matamoras was severely hampered by problems with the Mexican government and the difficulties of transporting cotton and supplies to and from Matamoras over long distances by wagon.[28] Consequently, after the Union forces effectively shut down most of Charleston's blockade-running, Wilmington remained as the major lifeline of the Confederacy.

On the eve of the sectional conflict, Wilmington had a population of 9,552, and African Americans made up 45 percent of that number. Located at the mouth of the Cape Fear River, the only North Carolina river to flow directly into the Atlantic Ocean, Wilmington was the state's largest city and dominated North Carolina's overseas trade. For much of the antebellum period, its commerce had centered on the export of naval stores and wood products. A number of sawmills and turpentine distilleries operated in or near the port. But by the 1850s, cotton exports had also become a vital part of Wilmington's foreign commerce. The advent of the steamboat and improved navigation on the Cape Fear River enhanced Wilmington's economy, and the arrival of three railroads brought more traffic and profits. The Wilmington and Weldon Railroad connected the port with the Petersburg and Richmond area in Virginia, and during the war it served as a main supply artery for Gen. Robert E. Lee's Army of Northern Virginia. The Wilmington and Manchester Railroad ran southward to Charleston, and by 1861 the eastern section of the Wilmington, Charlotte, and Rutherfordton Railroad had been completed into the interior nearly as far as Rockingham. Wilmington's antebellum growth, prosperity, and cultural sophistication were reflected in such residences as the Bellamy Mansion, the DeRosset House, and the grand Italianate City Hall–Thalian Hall, a combination municipal building and theater.[29]

Located 570 miles from Nassau and 674 miles from Bermuda, Wilmington occupied an excellent position for blockade-running. As long as the entrance to the Cape Fear River remained protected by the powerful guns of Fort Fisher, Federal forces could not close the port. Not until January 1865 did a U.S. Army and Navy expedition capture the fort and close Wilmington completely to blockade-running.[30]

The interior river towns of the Confederacy had thrived as antebellum depots for export and import commerce. Located on the Cumberland River, Nashville, Tennessee, had benefited from river trade since the late eighteenth century. With a population of nearly 30,000 in the 1850s, it had become one the busiest cities south of the Ohio River. Five railroads connected it with "most of the major markets in the South and East." The city prospered by selling imported supplies to the planters and farmers in the region. Its exports of cotton and other agricultural produce went to the markets in the South and Midwest. Nashville also had seventy-three manufactories, which employed 1,318 workers and contributed more than $1.5 million to its economy. Those industries produced lumber and wood products, tobacco and leather items, stoves, carriages, railroad cars, farm equipment, and iron castings. Education and religion thrived in the city, which could claim two medical colleges and a female academy, as well as a number of Protestant, Catholic, and Jewish churches and congregations. As the capital of Tennessee, the city was home to the offices and workers of state government. Its operations included asylums for the blind and mentally ill and a penitentiary. A new state capitol building was constructed just before the war began. During the conflict local factories turned out ammunition, weapons, uniform cloth, and other military equipment and accoutrements. After the fall of Forts Henry and Donelson in February 1862, Nashville's days as a Confederate bastion were numbered. On the twenty-fifth of that month, the mayor surrendered the city to Gen. Carlos Buell. It was the first Southern state capital to succumb to Union forces, which held the city for the rest of the war and utilized it as a supply center for U.S. troops in the western theater—"the longest uninterrupted occupation experienced by any Confederate city."[31]

Standing on the Tennessee River, Chattanooga, Tennessee, never achieved the antebellum size and significance of Nashville. It was a small commercial and man-ufacturing site that relied on the river trade until the railroad arrived in the decade before the war. Its population totaled 2,500, of which one-fourth were slaves and 10 percent were free blacks. But once the war began, Chattanooga's location made it strategically important to both sides. It was the hub for railroads connecting the eastern and western sections of the Confederacy. The Confederate army first oc-cupied the town and made it into a main supply depot. Chattanooga became a virtual military citadel, with warehouses, barracks, and other army buildings. The population surged to several times its prewar size. In the late summer of 1863, the Union army captured and occupied the town. But following a victory at the Battle of Chickamauga in September, Confederate forces besieged the city and cut its supply lines. Soldiers and civilians inside its defenses suffered from shortages of supplies. The Union army, however, broke the siege in November, giving the Confederates a decisive defeat at nearby Missionary Ridge. From that time until the war's end, Chattanooga remained in Federal hands. But many of its buildings had been de-stroyed in the fighting. The residents—strongly divided in their loyalties, some being Unionists, others Confederates—persecuted each other and experienced much social, as well as economic, disruption and unrest. Such problems were exacerbated when large numbers of escaped slaves crowded into the town and vicinity. To keep order, the army imposed strict martial law.[32]

Located strategically on the vital Mississippi River, prewar Memphis, Tennessee, was a bustling river port for the shipment of cotton to textile mills in the northeast-ern and midwestern United States. Associated with the cotton trade were the city's gins, warehouses, oil processors, and mills. Memphis did a thriving business in the distribution of wholesale supplies to the surrounding countryside of the Mississippi River Valley. Its 1860 population of 22,263 included retail merchants; factors; buyers; brokers; slave dealers; wagon, carriage, and railway car builders; and printers. The city boasted four iron rail manufactories, three flour mills, two brass and iron foundries, a sugar refinery, and a brewery. In the winter and spring of 1862, Union troops and naval gunboats conducted a campaign to gain control of the Mississippi River. They captured New Madrid, Island No. 10, and Corinth, which surrendered in May. The Federals then took Fort Pillow, fifty miles above Memphis. At Memphis the Confederates attempted to make a stand, and from the bluffs many of its inhabitants watched the ensuing battle on June 6. But the Yankees quickly carried the day. They occupied the city for the rest of the war, using it as a base for subsequent operations in the western theater.[33]

Atlanta owed its impressive rise as an antebellum city to the arrival of the railroad. As a hub for four rail lines, the town, with a population of 9,723 in 1860, was Georgia's fastest-growing urban center, surpassed in size by only Savannah and Augusta. The rail lines tied Atlanta to such vital points as Chattanooga, the Mississippi River Valley, and locations in the east. A number of industries supported the railroads by manufacturing steam engines, cars, iron rails, and other equipment necessary to maintain the thriving rail traffic. The prosperity produced by the railroads and the accompanying industries and businesses created a prosperous middle class, whose success and wealth were reflected in the houses of Atlanta's tree-lined neighborhoods. The city was overwhelmingly Protestant. That group had thirteen churches, but there was only one Catholic congregation. Two daily newspapers kept the population informed. The small Atlanta Medical College provided instruction for potential physicians, but primary and secondary education was largely private. An apprentice system existed to train young workers. During the war the city's factories labored to fill government contracts for cars and other railroad equipment. Bakers prepared hardtack for the troops. Small industries produced saddles and harnesses, as well as other war materials and weapons. Several Confederate bureaus, including the Quartermaster Department, established headquarters in the city. Because of its importance as a major transportation and manufacturing hub for the Confederacy, Atlanta became an important objective for the Union army early in the war, and Confederate authorities took considerable pains to fortify and protect it. Sherman's capture and partial destruction of Atlanta in the fall of 1864 struck a major blow to the South, and many of the inhabitants fled as much of the city burned.[34]

Augusta also benefited economically from the railroad, which ran from its depot to Savannah and points westward. In 1860 six banks with capital of $3.4 million did financial business in the town. A U.S. arsenal operated there, and state troops seized that facility at the outbreak of the war. Georgia turned the arsenal over to the Confederate government, which expanded its capacity to produce large quantities of ammunition and small arms. Under the direction of Col. George W. Rains of the Confederate Ordnance Bureau, a large gunpowder factory just west of Augusta manufactured as much as 5,000 pounds of powder per day. Two cotton mills in the town operated at full capacity, and Augusta quickly became a center for the manufacture of clothing, shoes, wagons, and other supplies for the Confederate army. Augusta had the advantage of institutions for secondary education. Its Academy of Richmond County and the Augusta Select Academy for Boys and Girls remained open for much of the war. Augusta also served as the headquarters for the Georgia Hospital and Relief Association, a statewide volunteer organization that provided money, clothing, and medicine for wounded and sick soldiers from Georgia who were in hospitals in Richmond.[35]

The cities and towns of the South were the commercial, governmental, and cultural centers of the Confederacy. But they also became hotbeds of crime, violence, and vice, conditions exacerbated by the disruption of war. Here again Richmond was probably the leader. According to one historian, the capital grew to a population of 140,000 and became "the most corrupt and licentious city south of the Potomac."[36] Throughout Richmond as the war continued, the ever-growing shortages of food and other essentials led to increasing numbers of violent confrontations over available supplies. The large numbers of troops and refugees who visited the city and its many saloons contributed tremendously to the rowdiness and frequent thefts, fights, knifings, shootings, and murders. Robberies and vandalism—sometimes committed in broad daylight—were common. President Davis himself had one of his horses stolen, and vandals even ransacked the Confederate House of Representatives. Drunken soldiers crowded into theaters and public buildings and became disruptive and often violent. On the streets they cut vendors' watermelons with bowie knives or tossed and speared them on their bayonets. Every day the mayor's court was filled with arrested soldiers. The number of gambling establishments swelled during the war, especially along the main street, where many stores had upstairs gambling dens, most of which specialized in the game of faro. Such establishments were called "hells," and both rich and poor gambled there, although they were usually segregated in separate rooms. Whiskey flowed, and fights broke out. Police raided the rooms but never had much success in closing them.[37]

Prostitution was rampant in all Confederate cities. In Nashville in 1860, for example, 207 women were listed in the census as prostitutes. The number was probably higher because such women did not always list their true vocation but instead claimed phony occupations such as seamstress.[38] But according to historian Bell I. Wiley, Richmond was "the true Mecca of prostitutes."[39] By 1862 their numbers in the Confederate capital had grown by leaps and bounds. One observer "estimated that wartime Richmond had more harlots than New Orleans and Paris combined." They appeared on streets, in theaters, on foot and in carriages. The better class of working women plied their trade above the gambling houses and along Locust Alley. A lower class operated west of Broad Street, in the suburb of Screamersville, "named after the shouting men tormented by the hallucinations of delirium tremens," where "sallow-faced, doped drugged, booze-sotted harlots of the most desperate sort served a clientele little better than themselves." To the east of downtown, "along Main and Cary Streets was another rowdy area of illegal liquor sales, alcoholic whores, pickpockets, and cutthroats. Drunkenness and fighting were normal; love and good manners were not even on the agenda." On the Capitol Square, "there was a perennial shortage of cabs, as most were on permanent hire to the courtesans for their assignations."[40] One madam's employees even advertised their services from the windows of a building across the street from the YMCA Soldiers Hospital. The police eventually gave up on trying to close down the many houses of ill repute and merely attempted to keep the prostitutes away from respectable areas.

For many years Richmond had gangs of warring youths known as "cats." Their turf battles increased as the war went on. In one rock battle, the "Hill Cats" from Shockoe Hill fought the "Butcher Cats" from Butcher Hill. President Davis himself attempted to mediate their dispute but failed, and the gang struggles continued. In an effort to combat the soaring rate of crime and vice, the city council increased the number of day policemen and by the end of 1861 had employed seventy-two night watchmen to patrol the streets. The mayor reinstated the city's chain gang to help correct overcrowding in the jail, the walls of which were raised to prevent escapes. Such measures, however, did little to check criminal activity. Between April 1863 and January 1864, 11,494 arrests were made in Richmond, 1,784 of them felonies. When Gen. John H. Winder attempted to enforce martial law in the city in 1862, he established a force of undercover detectives to investigate crimes, but he had to disband the group when the detectives themselves proved corrupt. Winder also assigned an armed soldier to accompany each night watchman, and he tried to control the importation and manufacture of alcoholic beverages. He received some credit for improving law and order but, like the police, never gained control over crime. Furthermore, some Richmond citizens objected to other aspects of his enforcement of military law.[41]

All the social ills that afflicted Richmond existed in the other cities and towns of the Confederacy. Charleston, for example, was infested with gambling rooms and bars. The port city, "already notorious for its brothels," saw prostitution soar during the war as "free colored street walkers" and white "loose women impudently accosted passers-by, and filled the hotels with their presence." Police could not control the drunken and disorderly soldiers who fired their guns, fought in the streets, and stole and destroyed property. The mayor's appeal to military authorities for help produced little corrective action.[42]

As a port city, Wilmington had always been bedeviled with similar crime and social problems. Its difficulties intensified when the war brought an influx of new arrivals, some engaged in legitimate businesses and others in illegal activity. Among the latter was a "'gang of foreign and domestic ruffians' who made a livelihood out of robbery and murder." It became dangerous to wander in the suburbs at night. During the day fights broke out on the streets among and between the many sailors and soldiers in the town. In these clashes "knives and pistols were used; and not unfrequently a dead body would rise to the surface of the water in one of the docks." In one incident just outside his window, shipping company clerk James Randal witnessed the murder of a blockade-runner's sailor by a "notorious" barroom keeper. Neither civil nor military authorities had much success in controlling the violence and other crime. A Wilmington newspaper editor encouraged the local residents to arm themselves for self-defense.[43]

Mobile endured similar difficulties. Almost every session of the mayor's court handled cases of drunken and disorderly Confederate soldiers, and often local inhabitants as well. The numbers of larcenies, burglaries, and incidents of receiving stolen goods continued to grow, especially after the closing of Mobile Bay, when the town remained under siege in the fall and winter of 1864–1865. Thefts occurred in barnyards and gardens as well as stores and warehouses. The culprits included town citizens, Confederate soldiers, slaves, and free blacks. Police came under considerable attack for not being more vigilant in preventing such crimes.[44] One citizen complained that "scarcely a day passes without our hearing of some chicken coop, pig pen or larder being robbed."[45]

Cities and towns under Union siege suffered mightily from bombardment. Public buildings, stores, shops, hotels, and houses were pulverized to mere shells, and many residents found themselves without homes and shelter. During the siege of Vicksburg, the inhabitants were reduced to living in caves, frequently trembling and praying as Union shells rained above them. Fire too was always a threat in an urban setting, where flames could spread easily from building to building along streets crowded with wooden structures. Many fires broke out in Richmond, and its authorities often suspected incendiaries. The Tredegar Iron Works, the Crenshaw Mills, the Shot and Shell Works, and several warehouses were completely or partially burned. Someone even attempted to set fire to the executive mansion. In Charleston in December 1861, a raging blaze, presumably ignited from a campfire started by slaves, swept through the seaport, destroying public buildings, schools, churches, and houses. When the conflagration ended, over 540 acres, 575 private dwellings, five churches, and numerous other structures had been destroyed. Many people were left homeless. The cost of the damage was estimated at between $5 million and $8 million. Near the end of the war, large sections of Atlanta and Columbia—with their stockpiles and warehouses filled with cotton, provisions, munitions, and other supplies—were destroyed by fires set by retreating Confederate troops and Sherman's advancing army.[46] Because of their constant dread of fire, urban dwellers resisted efforts by the Confederate government to conscript municipal firemen into the army. When the military drafted Mobile's firemen in 1864, the city howled in protest. Despite the opposition, however, all firemen under the age of forty-five were conscripted and sent to Montgomery, where they joined army companies as soldiers. But one fireman, John Burns, defied the draft and was arrested by district military authorities and jailed. He was soon released on a writ of habeas corpus and tried in a civil court, which ruled that "the military had no authority to arrest and imprison a fireman for an alleged offence." The court, however, was ultimately defied when Burns, after being discharged by the tribunal, was immediately drafted and sent to Montgomery anyway.[47]

Life for most Southerners who remained at home during the war was a rural existence. Nine out of ten Southerners lived in rural areas when the war began.[48] To a large extent, the cities and towns of the antebellum South were, as Emory M. Thomas has written, "reflections of the countryside rather than entities in themselves." They served as supply centers where planters and farmers sold their produce for export and bought imported manufactured goods and equipment. But the war "revolutionized" urban areas. Cities grew significantly in size, activities, and population, and some towns actually became cities. For example, "By 1863 Selma, Alabama, employed 3,000 civilians in an arsenal which did not exist in 1860. Over 10,000 people worked in Selma's war industries. Mobile grew from just over 29,000 people in 1860 to 41,000 in 1865. Most Atlantans date the origins of their city's boom to Confederate wartime. New Orleans grew tremendously in the two years before its capture in the spring of 1862. Richmond's wartime population swelled to two and a half times the 1860 figure." In addition to becoming industrial centers for the Confederacy, urban sites held the major headquarters for the military and all the auxiliary offices, hospitals, personnel, and other trappings of a military-industrial complex. Refugees and other new arrivals found work in the fledgling industries and bureaus. Despite an ever-tightening blockade and Federal sieges, merchants, brokers, speculators, hotels, restaurants, and theaters flourished amid this unprecedented surge of urban activity.[49] Some commercial interests in Southern cities such as New Orleans, Memphis, and Nashville actually profited economically from early Union occupation. U.S. military governments also inaugurated a number of public works that improved sanitation, streets, law enforcement, and health in cities.[50]

As a result of such changes, a significant segment of the home-front population experienced a previously unimaginable life in urban settings. Not all cities and towns in the Confederacy had the same importance or could claim the same level of sophistication as Richmond, New Orleans, Charleston, Mobile, or Nashville. Nor did all the residents in urban areas experience city life to the same degree. But those people who inhabited or took refuge in cities and towns generally had broader and more varied wartime experiences than those who remained in the countryside. They witnessed and participated in the industrial process. They were closer to the machinations of government and privy to the day-to-day dealings of commercial and financial institutions. They had certain cultural advantages usually denied to rural folk. They knew the psychological comfort of being in a large group rather than alone in a time of peril. But perhaps just as frequently—because the major urban sites in the South were objectives of the Union military—they felt unnerved and unsettled by the threat and reality of attack. They also had to endure the crime, violence, and vice that tended to flourish in urban settings. Thus not everyone on the Confederate home front lived in the same environment and had to cope with the same wartime circumstances. It is safe to say, however, that no one in town or countryside completely escaped the pain and suffering brought by the winds of war.

SEVEN

⸜⸝

RELIGION, EDUCATION, AND CULTURAL LIFE

Religion operated as a powerful force in the Confederacy. A significant number of ordained clergymen became army chaplains and braved combat along with the soldiers. Churches everywhere established relief programs to aid the destitute families of soldiers, and some created homes for orphans and special funds for the education of children whose fathers were serving in the army.[1] According to one historian, "Churches in the Confederate South took on social consciousness to a degree unknown before 1860. Not only did churches open their doors to soldiers, they sent preachers and literature into the camps. Church buildings became sewing centers for ladies who made uniforms. They became hospitals and wayside homes for troops in transit. Indeed few social services of any kind were not connected with one or more churches."[2]

Religious leaders also played an important role in sustaining the war effort. They consistently supported and encouraged secession. Once the war began, ministers, priests, and rabbis throughout the South exhorted their congregations to continue fighting for a cause that they claimed had God's blessing. Some exceptions existed, however. Quakers, for example, opposed armed conflict, and some churchmen in the border states, Federal-occupied territory, and eastern Tennessee and western Virginia remained loyal to the United States. A few clergymen opposed the war out of conscience. But by and large, "there can be no doubt that religious leaders of all denominations gave the Confederacy their overwhelming support and that as a group they were undoubtedly the most powerful factor in the maintenance of a high degree of morale among the people of the South." In fact, "The church was the most powerful organization influencing the lives of men and women in the South in the days before and during the Confederacy."[3]

Before the war most Southern clergymen had supported slavery and its extension, claiming that the institution had God's blessing. They endorsed states' rights and condemned abolitionists as evil. The antebellum dispute over the righteousness of slavery resulted in the split of denominations into "northern" and "southern" churches, although—at least officially—the Lutherans, Episcopalians, and Roman Catholics remained undivided. The Methodists were the first to undergo a split over slavery. In 1844 that denomination's conference requested that Bishop James O. Andrew of Georgia relinquish his office until such time as he renounced any connection with slavery. Angered by that request, Southern delegates withdrew from the conference and established the Methodist Episcopal Church, South. During the war the Confederacy's religious leaders preached that Southerners were God's chosen people and that their new nation's struggle for independence was sanctioned by God. The South's cause was the Almighty's cause, they asserted, and the people who fought, suffered, and died in that cause were doing his work.[4]

Furthermore, the Southern rebellion was a sacred war, a holy crusade, to fulfill the divine purpose and prevent the triumph of the infidel. Rev. J. Jones of Rome, Georgia, proclaimed that "if the rescue of the holy sepulcher from the infidel Moslem, induced three millions of men to lay their bones in the East, shall we not willingly contend to snatch the word of God from the modern infidel?" In May 1861 the Baptist Special Committee on the State of the Country decreed that the Confederate government was "contributing to the transcendent Kingdom of our Lord Jesus Christ." The Southern Baptist Convention quickly pledged its support for the new government. Presbyterians in Georgia urged the folk of the South: "Up, quit you like men. Pour your treasures into the lap of your country; throw your stout arms around her; let her feel the tendrils of enduring affection around her heart; and if need be, let your blood flow like water." The Methodists added their voices in support of the cause. The Methodist Rio Grande Mission Conference resolved "that the government of the Confederate States of America is right; to it we owe allegiance, and its fortunes we share, invoking Almighty God to uphold it in equity and wisdom." One Methodist conference expelled five members for disloyalty, "a crime sufficient to exclude them from the kingdom of grace and glory."[5] The Episcopal Church even issued a "Southern" version of the *Book of Common Prayer* to make it easier to justify violence for Southern independence. The Episcopal bishop Leonidas Polk of Louisiana, who became a lieutenant general in the Confederate army, asserted that "I believe most solemnly, that it's for . . . liberty . . . our hearth-stones, and our altars that we strike."

All of the eleven Roman Catholic bishops in the Confederate states supported the war. The Catholic priest James B. Sheeran became famous as a devotee of the

Confederate cause. A native of Ireland who had lived in the South for only three years, he joined a Louisiana regiment as a chaplain. During battle he sometimes rounded up stragglers and led them into combat himself. He "detested the Yankee invader as hotly as any Confederate could," called Federals "bandits," and attempted to convert Northern prisoners "not only to his own religious faith but to a realization of the justice and rightness of the Confederate cause."[6] Jews, too, gave their support to the cause. When New York's Samuel M. Isaac, editor of the *Jewish Messenger*, called for Southern Jews to remain loyal to the Union, the Jewish community in Shreveport, Louisiana, rejected his advice, cancelled its subscriptions, and pledged to support the "Southern Confederacy with our lives, liberty and all that is dear to us." In a Montgomery, Alabama, synagogue, Rabbi James Gutheim prayed for divine "favor and benevolence [for] our beloved country, the Confederate States of America. May our young Republic increase in strength, prosperity and renown."[7]

Preachers and other churchmen used the power of the pulpit to denounce specula- tors and extortioners, who were making profits at the expense and from the suffering of others. "These men," declared the Synod of the Evangelical Lutheran Church, "are the active coadjutors of our enemies in enslaving our country, impoverishing our people and ruining our cause." The religious community also denounced those Southerners in occupied areas who took the oath of allegiance to the United States. Baptists, for example, found it almost inconceivable that anyone would "bring so foul a blot on his character."[8]

Churches actually became mouthpieces for Confederate propaganda in their at- tempts to sustain morale on the home front. An extensive religious press augmented the messages from the pulpit supporting the war. Among the patriotic religious pub- lications were the *Christian Observer*, the *Southern Presbyterian Review*, the *Christian Advocate*, the *Central Presbyterian*, the *Southern Lutheran*, the *Southern Episcopalian*, and the *Church Intelligencer*—all exponents of waging war until victory was achieved. The *Southern Presbyterian Review*, for example, cried: "[L]et all the people, every- where, old and young, bond and free, *take up the war-cry*, and say, each to his neighbor, 'Gather ye together, and come against them, and rise up to the battle.'"[9]

In their zeal for encouraging the people to embrace violence, endure loss and sadness, and shed their blood in defense of the holy cause of Southern independence, religious leaders eventually found themselves facing a conundrum that required a convoluted rationalization of theology and justification of God's purpose. When early in the war the Confederate army achieved a number of major battlefield victories— such as First Manassas, Fredericksburg, and Chancellorsville—clergymen found it easy to point out that God was in his heaven and favoring the Confederacy. In the summer of 1861, Rev. C. A. Davis assured the crowd gathered for a public sermon in the Odd Fellows Hall in Memphis that "God is for us; and in a tone of defiance, we may ask, 'Who be against us?'"[10] But as the conflict wore on, as battles were lost, as casualties mounted, as home-front suffering increased, and as Southern victory seemed more and more remote, it became harder to convince Southerners that God was on their side. After Gettysburg and Vicksburg especially, disillusionment swelled and continued to grow, along with Union successes, until the war ended.[11]

The religious argument, therefore, was at best a paradox, perhaps even "a trap for Confederate will." God controlled events, the theological argument went, "and victory was a sign of God's favor." What then when the South began to lose? Had it lost favor with God? Was the collapse of the Confederacy the will of the Almighty? Was it possible that the cause was not just after all?[12] After viewing the devastation of Columbia, South Carolina, the devout diarist Grace Brown Elmore asked: "For what was this permitted, why does God allow the wicked to stalk through the land desolating alike the righteous, and those who know not God, when will he say [to the enemy] thou hast accomplished thy work now perish. Oh God we are sorely tried, we are an afflicted people, year after year has our cry gone forth, how long oh Lord, how long?"[13]

The Southern clergy struggled to answer those questions and assuage doubts in a way that would reassure the people that God had not abandoned them and their cause. He was merely testing them, ran one common rationalization from the pulpit. Like the biblical Job, the people must suffer to have their faith tested and prove themselves worthy of God's benevolence. In the end, if they remained steadfast in their faith, out of their painful ordeal would come "strength and redemption." They would have proved themselves worthy of salvation and victory over their enemies.[14]

Some ministers preached that battle defeats were punishment for Southerners' sins. Among these unholy transgressions were "violation of the Sabbath, intemperance, demagoguery, corruption, luxury, impiety, murmuring, greed and avarice, lewdness, skepticism, 'Epicurean expediency,' private immorality, ill treatment of slaves, profanity, a proud and haughty spirit, speculation, bribery, boastfulness, and . . . covetousness." When such sins had been cleansed through piety and prayer, the Almighty would once again give the South victories. After the major defeats at Gettysburg and Vicksburg, "there came an avalanche of sermons stressing the sins of the Confederate people." As the war continued to worsen for the South, Christian sermons increasingly stressed that the folk of the Confederacy needed to return to the teachings of Christ in order to gain God's favor anew and be set on the path to victory and independence. Preachers also tended to "minimize defeat and exaggerate the importance of minor Confederate successes."[15]

Until the end of the conflict, clergymen preached that salvation of the Confederacy was possible at any time if only the people would have faith in God and the cause and purge themselves of evil thoughts and deeds. But in the final months, even the most pious and patriotic among Southerners found their faith sorely tested. "Faith in God has never been more severely tried than now," wrote Grace Brown Elmore in March 1865. "We see the wicked flourish, we see them spread themselves over the whole land, we see our homes devastated and our fair fields made barren, we see starvation where there was plenty, and a dead silence reigns instead of the busy hum of the city, we hear nothing but the cry of anguish and the tale of distress, a dead weight rests on every heart, and yet we must trust in God. We must look to him and bide the Lord's time. Oh when will it come, my whole heart is sick, I faint from my weariness."[16] In an attempt to ignite or revive religious fervor for the Confederate war effort, President Davis periodically proclaimed national days of fasting, prayer, and thanksgiving. Churches and the religious press endorsed his proclamations.[17]

Many inhabitants of the home front began to contemplate that perhaps, in denying them victories and prolonging their suffering, God was punishing them for the sin of slavery. A poor woman from Charlotte, North Carolina, was convinced that God was permitting the Confederacy to lose the war as punishment for keeping other human beings in bondage. She wrote to the governor that "I believe slavery is doomed to dy out that God is agoing to liberate niggars, and fighting any longer is fighting against God."[18]

Some historians have argued that a widespread guilt about slavery and God's retribution for the institution weakened Southerners' morale and thereby contributed to the defeat of the Confederacy. Others have challenged that conclusion, maintaining that slavery was such an accepted part of most Southerners' lives that few questioned its morality.[19] But whether or not pervasive remorse over the sin of slavery affected the morale of a large portion of the home-front population, that morale certainly did weaken, and by the end of the war it had plummeted irretrievably. That plunge occurred despite the best efforts of spiritual leaders to encourage their congregations to remain steadfast in support of the Confederate cause. As late as February 1865, a Dr. Porter of the Charleston Church of the Holy Communion was urging his flock to "fight! fight my friends, till the streets run blood!"[20] Ultimately, however, unfaltering morale and the belief in a righteous struggle were more characteristic of the Southern clergy than of the majority of common folk.

Like churches, educational institutions of all types became patriotic and nationalistic exponents of Confederate policies. The antebellum Southern states in general had given little support to public schools for primary and secondary education. But several legislatures had begun funding free schools, and some large cities had appropriated taxes for basic education. Until the end of the war, Mobile's public school system, with its classrooms in Barton Academy, managed to maintain operations and hold examinations and graduations with the public attending. With the exception of those in Tennessee and North Carolina, however, most public schools in the Confederate states were woefully inadequate and operated primarily for indigent children.

Private academies were the principal centers of instruction for Southern students. A majority of these institutions had to close when the war brought financial troubles and many male teachers went into the army. But a number of them managed to remain open. Georgia had several well-respected academies: Chatham Academy in Savannah, the Collegiate Institute at Athens, and the Augusta Select Academy for

Boys and Girls. In Mobile the Catholic College at Spring Hill continued its courses, and a military academy opened. Instruction in private schools varied. In most of them, instructors taught the classics and other advanced subjects. At the Stevensville Academy in Virginia, for example, one student's course of study included Virgil, Caesar, Horace, Latin and Greek grammar, and algebra. North Carolina's renowned Bingham School, operated by William Bingham in Orange County, concentrated on preparing students for college. In 1864 Bingham secured a special charter from the state legislature exempting students from conscription but specifying that they undergo military training at the school and requiring that they be mobilized in the event of a local emergency. Bingham was appointed an ex officio colonel in the state militia, and his instructors received militia commissions.[21]

The supply of teachers in both public and private schools became depleted when many of the male instructors volunteered for or were drafted into the army. Schools often ceased instruction because they had no teachers. Women partly filled the shortage and for the first time began to appear in Southern classrooms in significant numbers. In North Carolina, for instance, the percentage of female teachers rose from 7.5 to 40 in the state's common (public) schools. Just as financial difficulties during the war forced academies throughout the South to shut down, so too did public schools close when their state funds went for war purposes. North Carolina was more fortunate than some states because Governor Vance and Superintendent of Common Schools Calvin H. Wiley exerted considerable effort to keep that state's educational funds directed to the public schools.[22]

Before the war Southern nationalists and educators resented Northern influences on their students. They objected to Northern textbooks, which they considered biased against the South. They particularly found fault with the antislavery rhetoric in those publications. In the 1850s a number of commercial conventions convened in Southern cities to promote business and trade and to address the condition of education. They observed that textbooks and other materials used in the schools of the South were largely imported from the North. Critics complained that even if textbooks had Southern authors, most were published in the North and came under the direction of Northern editors, who influenced the final products. The New Orleans convention of 1855 requested that the Louisiana legislature designate annual funds to support the writing and publishing of Southern textbooks. A Savannah convention suggested the prohibition of all Northern newspapers in the South, and it formed a committee to encourage the production of Southern educational texts. In 1857 and 1859 respectively, conventions in Knoxville and Vicksburg demanded the creation of a Southern publisher.[23]

Such efforts continued after the outbreak of the war. At the urging of Calvin H. Wiley and the State Educational Association of North Carolina, which convened in July 1861, a convention of Southern educators met in Columbia, South Carolina, on April 28, 1863. The objectives of the convention—attended by seventy delegates from six states—were "to promote education, encourage the production of elementary southern texts, and form a permanent association of teachers." The attendees appointed committees to study and report on curriculums and the use of the Bible in classroom texts and lessons. The Columbia convention scheduled another meeting for Atlanta in September but did not gather again until the winter of 1864–1865. The strain of the war made it difficult to convene teachers and develop standardized texts and guidelines for elementary education. Nevertheless, a consistent Southern nationalism prevailed in textbooks published during the war.[24]

Even before the 1863 convention, publishers throughout the South had begun producing textbooks with a patriotic Confederate theme. The supply of Northern materials had been halted by the war and by Southern objections to their messages of U.S. nationalism and antislavery sentiment. The war and home-front necessity actually gave Southern publishers a market. A few Northern texts did continue to be used in Confederate schools, sometimes in modified form. The *Revised Elementary Spelling Book* (1863) and the *Dixie Speller* (1864), for example, were adapted from Noah Webster's *Elementary Spelling Book* (1857). From 1861 to 1865, publishers in at least eight Confederate states issued a variety of textbooks including volumes for spelling, reading, grammar, geography, and arithmetic. Louisiana printed one text; South Carolina produced three, Tennessee six, Alabama eight, Texas eight, Georgia twenty, Virginia twenty-seven, and North Carolina forty.

The major publishers were located in the cities of Richmond, Raleigh, Greensboro, Charleston, Augusta, Macon, Mobile, and Nashville (prior to its early capture). Probably the most prolific of the textbook companies was Sterling, Campbell, and Albright of Greensboro, North Carolina. That firm printed editions of one primary grammar in 1861; two primary grammars, one *Primer for the Children*, three readers, and one speller in 1862; three arithmetic volumes, two grammars, two versions of *Primer for the Children*, one reader, and two spellers in 1863; three readers, one speller, and one *Primer for the Children* in 1864; and one *Verbal Primer* in 1865.[25] Mobile, Alabama, was another of the Confederacy's chief textbook publication centers. Although handicapped by a lack of paper, manpower, and good ink, as well as by worn-out and irreplaceable machinery, that city's publishers carried on a significant business during the war. W. G. Clark and Company of Mobile was the largest educational publisher in Alabama. Along with other firms in the port city, the company supplied Alabama and Mississippi with textbooks.[26]

Regardless of who published them, all the textbooks were organs of Confederate propaganda as well as instructional volumes. They generally praised Confederate courage and purpose and defended the institution of slavery. *Johnson's Elementary Arithmetic* contained the following patriotic problem: "If one Confederate soldier can whip 7 Yankees, how many soldiers can whip 49 Yankees?"[27] Sterling, Campbell, and Albright's *Our Own Third Reader* (1864) justified slavery through quotations from the Bible, such as one from Leviticus 25:44–45 that sanctified the purchase and ownership of slaves, and others that said slaves should remain always subservient to their masters. In her *Primary Geography* (1864), M. B. Moore conceded that Northerners were "refined and intelligent on all subjects but that of Negro slavery; on this they are mad."

Textbooks exalted the Confederate cause as a struggle for independence and against tyranny. They idealized Southern soldiers and their leaders as heroes embarked on a holy crusade. Charles Winslow Smythe's *Our Own Elementary Grammar*, published by Sterling, Campbell, and Albright, extolled the virtue of Gen. Thomas J. (Stonewall) Jackson and martyred him. "The name of Jackson, the Christian soldier, the heroic and skillful general will live forever in the memory of his countrymen," proclaimed the grammar. "The great heart of the nation throbs heavily at the portals of his grave."[28]

The war severely hampered or closed many of the Confederacy's colleges and universities. The antebellum South had a substantial number of such institutions, although many colleges were actually little more than preparatory schools. Nevertheless, half of the 240 colleges in the United States in 1850 were located in the South, and the region could claim one college student for every 247 white residents in 1860, when the North had just one student for every 703 people. When the war began, South Carolina College (later the University of South Carolina) had 184 students enrolled in its classes. East Tennessee University (forerunner of the University of Tennessee) enrolled 110 students every year, though more than half of them were in a preparatory department. The University of Mississippi registered about a hundred pupils annually. On the eve of the sectional conflict, the University of Georgia reached an enrollment of 159 and could boast a reputable law school and a distinguished faculty. The University of North Carolina registered 461 students, half of whom came from other states. Private colleges such as Wake Forest in North Carolina and Wofford in South Carolina could claim expanding enrollments, facilities, endowments, and faculties. In general the colleges and universities of the South were respectable centers of intellectual growth with academically competent and even distinguished instructors.[29]

The war, however, changed that situation. Military conscription and volunteering depleted student bodies and faculties. The conscription laws did not exempt college students, and the act of February 1864 lowered the draft age to seventeen. Some university presidents, such as Landon C. Garland of the University of Alabama and David L. Swain of the University of North Carolina, managed to obtain temporary exemptions for juniors and seniors. But in the final months of the conflict, the War Department, in desperate need of troops, revoked those deferrals.

Most institutions of higher learning were forced to close their doors before the war ended. Shortly after East Tennessee University began its September session in 1861, it shut down because most of its students had volunteered for the army, and the Confederate military had taken over its buildings to house the wounded. Federal troops occupied the grounds in September 1863. The University of Georgia remained in operation until the fall of 1863, when, with the majority of its former students in the military, it closed. A Confederate hospital and then a refugee camp took over the facilities. Finally the site became a Union headquarters. The University of Mississippi, Emory University in Atlanta, the University of Alabama, the College of Charleston, and Wofford and Wake Forest had to close. Among the schools that managed to remain in operation were the University of Virginia, Mercer University in Georgia, and the University of North Carolina. But all of them suffered reduced enrollments, staff, funding, and facilities. The University of Alabama and East Tennessee University saw large parts of their campuses burned, otherwise destroyed, or damaged by Union soldiers. The aspiring University of the South in Sewanee, Tennessee, burned nearly to the ground during the war. It would require several years for the postwar South to rebuild and reestablish its major institutions of higher learning.[30]

Higher education remained largely the privilege of white males. But education was becoming a cultural advantage for many young women of the gentry. The antebellum belle Virginia Caroline Tunstall of Alabama, for example, had first the benefit of plantation tutors, then two years of formal schooling at a Tuscaloosa institution. She finished her education with a diploma from Nashville Female Academy.[31] The number of female colleges and academies in the South had been expanding when the war broke out. In the decade of the 1850s, the "South outpaced the North in the chartering of women's colleges." Most women's institutions had Protestant church affiliations and ministers as presidents or directors. The Methodists supported the largest number of such schools. Some women's institutions, such as Wesleyan College in Macon, Georgia, and Salem College in North Carolina, managed to remain open for most of the war. Others, including Georgia's Tuscumbia Female Academy, had to close. The military took over several of the schools. In Alabama, for example, Auburn Masonic Female College became a soldiers' hospital, and Montevallo Female Institute became barracks.

The curriculum in women's institutions usually placed a heavy emphasis on religious instruction. Other subjects included geography, mathematics, Latin, French, and fundamental science. In most schools, however, there was a strong tendency "to prepare students for their distinct roles as women." Politics—with a proslavery bias—might be discussed in classrooms, but faculties did not "encourage an interest in women's rights."[32] When James A. Long addressed the graduates of the Edgeworth Female Seminary in North Carolina in 1858, he cautioned them to avoid involvement in politics and not "to soil your garments with matters which do not pertain to your position in society."[33]

Although upper-class women were not expected or encouraged to put their learning to use outside the home, an education reflected their social status. "Are we radically different from other girls," wondered Grace Brown Elmore in January 1862, "or has education made us so?" Tutored by her mother and having attended one of the female academies in Charleston, Grace seemed to develop a restlessness and discontent with the feminine sphere to which society confined her. Perhaps, she thought, her schooling might be applied to purposes higher or more fulfilling than domestic ones. "Should I break through and follow the best of my spirit?" she asked. "Shall I throw aside those conventionalities that bind me and follow where thought has so often traveled? Many and many a time have I thought that perhaps I was being educated for times of hard trial, and great action, where everything but the one purpose was to be given up, when no ties on earth would be sufficient to deter from the accomplishment of that purpose. And when the Right and wrong alone would be considered, without regard to the prejudices and opinions of others." Suffering poverty and the loss of their home after the war, Grace and her sisters "truly said good bye to being ladies of leisure." Elmore taught school at Chester Female Academy in South Carolina and at Mecklenburg Female College in North Carolina. She then returned to South Carolina and bought the family home at auction. There she taught for the rest of her life at a boarding school established by her sister Ellen, ultimately having "learned to act for and rely upon myself alone."[34]

Before the war graduates of women's colleges and academies were not encouraged to become teachers, but after many male instructors went into the army, the number of female teachers grew. The presence of women teachers in the South would continue to swell in the postwar period, as public school systems revived and expanded and additional teachers were sought. The need for family income also led more women to resort to teaching in the hard times that followed the sectional conflict.[35]

With Federal military support, education for former slaves began in occupied areas during the war. As the invading U.S. forces seized territory in the Confederacy, commanders began to assign area superintendents or education boards to supervise education for slaves who sought refuge within the Union lines. When the Bureau of Refugees, Freedmen, and Abandoned Lands (the Freedmen's Bureau) was established in March 1865, it took over much of the supervision of schooling for newly liberated blacks. Initially Union soldiers provided some instruction for the runaway slaves. But the majority of the teachers came from Northern—primarily New England—religious organizations and benevolent societies. Most of them were young women who possessed a sincere and idealistic desire to improve the lives of the freedmen.

Shortly after Gen. Ambrose E. Burnside seized much of coastal North Carolina for the Union in early 1862, he appointed Vincent Colyer, formerly an agent with the Washington, D.C., YMCA, to the office of superintendent of the poor for the area. In addition to providing relief and employment for white and black refugees, Colyer established schools for both races at the Federal headquarters in New Bern. He engaged a young woman, a resident of that town, to instruct poor whites. For the escaped slaves, he launched two evening schools with a total of 800 pupils. Some soldiers in the occupying New England regiments, especially the Twenty-fifth Massachusetts—a number of whom were college graduates—volunteered as teachers.[36]

The former slaves readily embraced the opportunity for education. One Union soldier, James A. Emmerton of the Twenty-third Regiment Massachusetts Infantry, reported that a group of freedmen, then workers at a Federal sawmill, displayed a burning desire for schooling. Each of the workers had "his spelling book which was speedily whipped out and zealously studied at every break, however short, in their onerous task." Emmerton observed that in the schools established for former slaves, the ages of the students ranged from ten to fifty, and, although the ability of the students "was as various as their ages, . . . all were eager." On some occasions "they were waiting for school to open one and two hours before the appointed time."[37]

In early 1863 army chaplain Horace James became the official in charge of the welfare of the many fugitive slaves arriving daily into Union lines. As the head of the new office of superintendent of Negro affairs, James made education his highest priority. By May 1863 thirty-two soldiers were serving under James's supervision as teachers for 485 "scholars" in Sunday schools and 328 students in a day school in New Bern. James soon started two new schools for African Americans. They were taught by female instructors from two Northern benevolent societies, the American Missionary Association and the New England Freedmen's Aid Society. The schools opened in July 1863 in two black churches in New Bern. Shortly thereafter the National Freedmen's Relief Association established another school for blacks in the town, and all three held both day and night classes under James's watchful eye. By early 1864 James supervised forty-six Northern schoolteachers in the occupied region of the state. Those teachers staffed twenty-six schools. At the end of the year, the number of teachers had risen to sixty-eight, of whom fifty-six were female and twelve were male. The American Missionary Association supplied twenty-two of those teachers, the New England Freedmen's Aid Society twenty, and the National Freedmen's Relief Association twenty-four. Four instructors provided by the last organization were black: Richard Boyle, James Keating, Martha Culling, and Robert Morrow. The other two of James's teachers were self-supporting and not affiliated with a philanthropic organization.[38]

Typical of the schools in various freedmen's camps created by the Federal army was the one set up by the American Missionary Association and the Boston Educational Society at the Trent River Settlement near New Bern. In February 1864 Sarah Pearson, the teacher in charge of the school, reported an enrollment of 280 pupils, 200 of which constituted the largest number present for any one class session. The subjects taught included spelling, reading, writing, geography, arithmetic, and singing.[39] Miss Pearson also held evening classes for several black soldiers and other adults who worked during the day. Two teaching assistants helped her. Those whites who observed or taught the students were impressed with their burning desire for education, and they marveled at the children's steadfastness in the face of the cruelty of slavery and the dangers of their flight to freedom. "Their earnestness of manner together with their simple faith is touching to witness," noted one observer. Assistant teacher Susan A.

Hosmer was particularly moved by the plight of a young pupil when she saw "the marks of the lash upon her back. They were an inch wide."[40]

Teachers and pupils alike feared Confederate attack, and sickness sometimes suspended classes. In April 1864 Sarah Pearson reported that "the school has again been disturbed through fear of rebel invasion, something of a panic existed for a few days, and my whole number has been less than it was during the last month." In June Miss Hosmer wrote that "sickness" was "still prevalent in Camp, many have died, . . . our school room was taken for a hospital for a few days, one woman died in the Recitation room, a young boy after he was removed also died, it seems strange to enter these rooms & teach after death has been there."[41]

In occupied Louisiana Gen. Nathaniel P. Banks, commander of the Department of the Gulf, established a board of education. The group had the power to collect taxes for schools, hire teachers, and construct schoolhouses for former slaves. The *New Orleans Tribune* of October 23, 1864, described the results of the board's efforts.

> The members of the Board of Education have applied themselves industriously to their task. They have 78 colored schools, attended by 7,900 students, with 125 teachers. . . . Of the 15,340 colored children who are inside Union lines in Louisiana, more than half are already in these schools, and it is hoped that within three or four months from now half of those who remain will also receive instruction.
>
> Although the schools have been open only a short time, one can already find proof of the aptitude of the negro to receive the elements of civilization. The children who began the alphabet three or four months ago are reading now in the first *Readers*, and are doing easily the primary rules of arithmetic. . . .
>
> The schools of the city number fifteen, with 41 teachers and an average attendance of 1,900 students. . . . These children are aged 5 to 18 years. There are also some adults of both sexes, maids, workers, seamstresses, who arrange to take off two hours daily from their work to attend school. Half of these people did not know their letters in October. . . .
>
> In the organization of these schools there are numerous difficulties to surmount, including racial prejudice. It was thought that good teachers could not be secured without going to the North for them. However, the white women of noble heart in New Orleans put themselves swiftly to the task, and have continued courageously in the face of calumnies, mockeries, and social proscription. One hundred of the teachers were born and raised in the South, and 75 are from Louisiana. Honor to them![42]

During the year 1864, Northern benevolent societies operated three or four schools for freedmen at Davis Bend, Mississippi. Twelve missionary teachers gave instruction to between 700 and 1,000 pupils. When the schools first opened, Henry Rountree of the Cincinnati Contraband Relief Commission noted that a larger classroom and benches for the students were needed at one of the schools, where three teachers delivered instruction in reading, spelling, and arithmetic. For the pupils' use, he ordered primers, slates, pencils, and "McGuffie's Eclectic Speller and Reader." One teacher requested *Montieth's First Lessons in Geography*. But learning for a number of the former slaves was incomplete and short lived, because "many of those brought to the Bend fresh from slavery chose to leave or were sent as hands to other plantations or drifted to the cities. Often a promising pupil disappeared after a few weeks, perhaps to return several months later to begin again." Teachers sometimes had difficulties with U.S. Army chaplain Joseph Warren, whom the Federal government had appointed as superintendent of education for the Vicksburg district. Warren was devoted to bureaucratic detail. He demanded precise monthly reports from the teachers and frequently criticized them for incomplete or missing records and for not filling out the proper forms for supplies or following other procedures to the letter. At the Davis Bend schools, conflict and a lack of cooperation existed among instructors from different religious denominations and philanthropic societies. And sickness from malaria and other maladies also incapacitated or killed a number of teachers.[43]

As part of the Federal land and labor experiment on the occupied Sea Islands of South Carolina, Northern missionary and philanthropic societies established schools there. By the end of 1862, more than 1,700 blacks attended classes on St. Helena, Ladies, and Port Royal Islands. Another 500 received instruction on Hilton Head and Paris Islands.[44] As in other areas, the island teachers confronted a number of disadvantages and obstacles that they had not anticipated when they left New England and other points in the North.

One of the most notable teachers was the black abolitionist Charlotte Forten, daughter of Philadelphia abolitionist and social activist Robert Bridges Forten and his wife, Mary Woods Forten. Charlotte Forten moved in 1853 from Philadelphia to Salem, Massachusetts, where she received a normal-school education; she then taught at various institutions in the North. In October 1862, with the sponsorship of the Port Royal Relief Association, she sailed to the Sea Islands to teach former slaves. Forten entered upon her duties with enthusiasm but, as did other Northern teachers, quickly found the task more difficult than she had imagined. On November 5 she recorded in her journal that she "had my first regular teaching experience, and . . . will acknowledge that it was *not* a very pleasant one. Part of my scholars are very tiny—babies I call them—and it is hard to keep them quiet and interested while I am hearing the larger ones. They are too young even for the alphabet, it seems to me. I think I must write home and ask somebody to send me picture-books and toys to amuse them with." Still exasperated a few days later, she lamented: "Had a dreadfully wearing day in school, of which the less said the better."[45] Still later she remarked on the difficulty of maintaining a learning environment in an overcrowded classroom. "We find it rather hard," she wrote, "to keep their attention in school. It is not strange, as they have been so entirely unused to intellectual concentration. It is necessary to interest them every moment, in order to keep their thoughts from wandering. . . . [W]e had of course but one room in which to hear all the children;

and to make one's self heard, when there were often as many as a hundred and forty reciting at once, it was necessary to tax the lungs very severely."[46]

Laura Towne from Philadelphia, another fervid abolitionist participating in the Port Royal enterprise, also described the difficulty of trying to teach youths with a dialect different from her own and no formal learning experience. The pupils, she declared, "had no idea of sitting still, of giving attention or ceasing to talk aloud. They lay down and went to sleep, they scuffled and struck each other. They got up by the dozen, made their curtsies, and walked off to the neighboring field for blackberries, coming back to their seats with a curtsy when they were ready. They evidently did not understand me, and I could not understand them, and after two hours and a half of effort I was thoroughly exhausted."

Miss Forten recognized that much of the problem in conducting orderly and effective classes was that many parents who worked in the cotton fields of the Sea Islands were, in effect, using the schools as "day care centers" for preschool children and infants. "The little ones," she observed, "were brought to school because the older children—in whose care their parents leave them while at work—could not come without them."[47] One teacher on Edisto Island described the dilemma of Hector, a thirteen-year-old pupil who brought his younger brother and a baby to class with him. Unable to quiet the crying, disruptive baby, whom he treated "most maternally," and simultaneously apply himself to the lesson, Hector ultimately had to leave the class.[48]

Problems such as overcrowded and disruptive classes and shortages of materials, instructors, and facilities compelled many of the originally idealistic Northern teachers to return home after short and disillusioning sojourns in the Civil War South. But others stayed the course. Charlotte Forten managed to bring some "order...out of chaos" in her classroom and became impressed with the commitment and respect that many of the freed persons had for education. "I never before saw children so eager to learn, although I had had several years' experience in New-England schools," she wrote in 1864. "The older ones during the summer, work in the fields from early morning until eleven or twelve o'clock, and then come into school, after their hard toil in the hot sun, as bright and anxious to learn as ever." The level of accomplishment varied, but "the majority learn with wonderful rapidity. Many of the grown people are desirous of learning to read. It is wonderful how a people who have been so long crushed to the earth, so imbruted as these have been—and they are said to be among the most degraded negroes of the South—can have so great a desire for knowledge, and such a capability for attaining it."[49]

In May 1864 Charlotte Forten resigned as a teacher on St. Helena Island because of failing health and returned to her family's home in Philadelphia. She published an account of her career on the island, and in the postwar years she continued to write, teach, and work for the interests of African Americans, becoming a founding member of the National Association of Colored Women. In 1878 she married Rev. Francis

Grimké, minister of the Fifteenth Street Presbyterian Church in Washington, D.C. She died in that city in 1914 at the age of seventy-six.[50] Laura Towne, imbued with "the root-and-branch abolitionism of New England," remained on St. Helena for the rest of her life, teaching and working on behalf of Sea Island blacks. Historian Willie Lee Rose has written of her that "Laura Towne was by no means blind to the faults of the freedmen." But she continued to serve them "well after her fellows had begun to forget" their original enthusiasm for the betterment of the lives of former slaves. "The advantage she enjoyed," according to Rose, "was a true liking for schoolteaching."[51]

The emotional impact of the war led to a plethora of poetry written in the Confederacy. Much of it was bad verse, dripping with romanticism and sentimentality. The newspapers filled their columns with poems by amateur writers, most of whom patriotically defended the Confederate cause and the Southern way of life. In January 1862, for instance, the *Charleston Daily Courier* published nineteen poems. Among them were "South Carolina's Justification to the North," "McClellan's Soliloquy," and "The Devil's Visit to Old Abe." Sometimes the works printed by the newspapers were merely rhymes to bolster support for the war. George W. Bagby, editor of the *Southern Literary Messenger*, declared in July 1863 that "we are receiving too much trash in rhyme. What is called 'poetry' by its authors is not wanted." Still, newspapers and some magazines continued to publish patriotic rhyme and doggerel.[52]

Virtually all Confederate poetry—even of the better sort—celebrated heroism, the martial spirit, Southern white womanhood, and the virtue of noble sacrifice for the cause. The best poetry written during the conflict was that of Henry Timrod of Charleston. Before the war he had been one of the literary group that formed around the noted South Carolina writer William Gilmore Simms. Timrod worked as a plantation tutor and published a small volume of poetry. Although he opposed secession, Timrod joined the Confederate army as a private, but he was discharged because of frail health. He then worked as a newspaper correspondent and assistant editor. His "Ethnogenesis" exalted the birth of the Southern Confederacy as the beginning of a superior culture dominated by a superior race. "The Cotton Boll" proclaimed the primacy of the South's agricultural life. "Spring" lamented the devastation of war on the region, and "A Cry for Arms" and "Ode to the Confederate Dead" called for steadfastness against the enemy and affirmed the sacrifice of the Southern soldier.[53]

Paul Hamilton Haynes, another member of the South Carolina literati, also composed some pro-Confederate poetry of acknowledged merit. He is remembered for such poems as "The Battle of Charleston Harbor," "The Blockaders," "My Mother Land," and "Our Martyrs." In "Southern Lyre," published in the *Southern Illustrated News* in 1863, he praised Southern poets, who he claimed had been denied recognition in American literature by prejudiced Yankees. Although Haynes served in the Confederate army in defense of Charleston harbor, he, like Timrod, left the service because of failing health. After Federal bombardment destroyed his Charleston house and library, he moved to Greenville, South Carolina, and continued to write verse for Southern newspapers and magazines. By 1864 he was exhibiting considerable personal frustration and despondency about the fate of the Confederacy.

Less-renowned poets who applied their pens in praise of Southern life and independence included the army chaplain Father Abraham Joseph Ryan, who composed several works under the name "Moina." After the war Ryan's "The Conquered Banner" and "The Sword of Robert E. Lee" became the most popular poems in the South. Georgia's Francis Orray Ticknor idealized the Confederate soldier in "Virginians of the Valley" and "Little Giffen," a sentimental composition about a drummer boy from Tennessee. John Reuben Thompson's "Music in the Camp," George W. Bagby's "The Empty Sleeve," and John W. Palmer's "Stonewall Jackson's Way" also romanticized Confederate heroes and the noble sacrifice of the Southern soldier. In "Maryland, My Maryland," James Ryder Randall denounced the barbarism of the Northern invaders. After the war much of the Confederate war verse was compiled in William Gilmore Simms's anthology *War Poetry of the South*.[54]

Simms was the South's leading writer of fiction. He authored some patriotic verse and editorials in support of the Confederate war effort, but he did not produce a novel about or during the war. His only major work of fiction was the serial "Paddy McGann; or, The Demon of the Stump," published in the *Southern Illustrated News*. An ardent secessionist and Confederate nationalist, Simms owned and managed without an overseer the large South Carolina plantation Woodlands. The plantation mansion burned in 1862 and was rebuilt, only to be destroyed again when Sherman's troops torched it. That time Simms lost his library of 10,740 volumes. He also lost thousands of dollars in revenue with the demise of the prewar Northern market for his books. Apparently the strain of the war and the death of his wife and two children inhibited Simms's literary production. In a January 1863 letter, he told John Reuben Thompson that he had written little in the past two years. "I need leisure, repose, and my wonted conveniences, for composition," he despaired. "I need not say to you, also, how much a man of my excitable temperament may be kept from his tasks by the condition of his Country."[55]

Novelist Augusta Jane Evans of Mobile produced the Confederacy's most successful war novel. Titled *Macaria; or, Altars of Sacrifice*, the book told a story of frustrated love in which the hero died on the battlefield. The author idealized Southern political and social thought, and she called for the people of the South to imitate the Greek heroine Macaria and make sacrifices in the cause of Confederate patriotism. After the war Evans published her most acclaimed novel, *St. Elmo*. That work was a romance offering escape from the still-remembered ravages of the war. It became one of the most popular fiction books in the United States, and its popularity led to the adoption of its title as a name for "inns" and homes. Another popular novel was *The Raids and Romance of Morgan and His Men*, which glorified the exploits of the Confederate cavalryman John Hunt Morgan and was written by Sallie Rochester Ford of Louisville, Kentucky.[56]

The home-front writing that would have the greatest impact on postwar generations—especially historians studying the conflict—consisted of the diaries and memoirs written by women of the Confederacy. Perhaps the most famous of such published works is Mary Boykin Chesnut's *A Diary from Dixie*. Of the many other journals and recollections compiled by Southern women, some of the most observant and insightful came from Catherine Ann Devereux Edmondston, Grace Brown Elmore, Sarah Katherine Stone, Sarah Morgan Dawson, Phebe Yates Pember, and Kate Cumming. Among men's diaries and memoirs, *A Rebel War Clerk's Diary* by John Beauchamp Jones of the War Department particularly stands out for its observations about the plight of civilians in the Confederacy.

British and European literature that enjoyed a readership among educated folk in the Confederacy included the works of Dickens, Thackeray, George Eliot, Wilkie Collins, Bulwer-Lytton, Scott, Hugo, Dumas, Shakespeare, Tennyson, the Brownings, and Byron. The young women of the Confederacy developed a taste for the sentimental and melodramatic novels of English writer Mary Elizabeth Braddon. The most popular historical accounts were those by Macaulay, Carlyle, and Gibbon. Books about the American Revolution held a special allure for readers of history, many of whom sought to draw parallels between the struggles for American and Southern independence. Soldiers and their relatives at home raised their spirits with the amusing writings of a few humorists. Among them were letters published in newspapers by the Confederacy's chief comic writer, Charles Henry Smith of Rome, Georgia. He adopted the byline "Bill Arp," an imaginary, illiterate country bumpkin. Many of Arp's letters and sketches were published in books after the war. The Virginia humorist George W. Bagby also wrote comic columns for newspapers and reprinted many of them in a book in 1863.[57]

The physical and psychological pain of the war cast a pall over social life in the South. But early in the conflict, when Southern patriotism and spirits ran high and deprivation had not taken hold, dances, balls, and parties were well attended, especially among the planter class and wealthy urbanites. Not surprisingly the upper classes, including such prominent people as Confederate officer James Chesnut Jr. and his wife, Mary Boykin Chesnut, of South Carolina, enjoyed the best of food, drink, and socializing. In May 1862 Mary Chestnut observed that "here in Columbia the family dinners are the specialty. You call or they pick you up and drive home with you. 'Oh stay to dinner.' And you stay gladly. They send for your husband. And he comes willingly. Then comes, apparently, a perfect dinner. You do not see how it could be improved. And they have not had time to alter things or add because of additional guests. They have everything of the best. Silver, glass, china, table linen—damask—&c &c. And then planters live 'within themselves,' as they call it. From the plantations come mutton, beef, poultry, cream, butter, eggs, fruits, and vegetables. It is easy to live here—with a cook who has been sent to the best eating house in Charleston to be trained."[58] As the capital of the Confederacy filled with prominent persons, Richmond set the social scene and had the most frequent and lavish parties and dinners. One observer in January 1864 noted that there were "parties every night in Richmond, suppers costing ten & twenty thousand dollars."[59] Of course the majority of the home-front population did not share such sumptuous pleasures. The poor especially endured a much more difficult four years than their social betters. But everyone—rich or poor, prominent or ordinary—sought the solace of each other's company amid the uncertainty and sadness of the war.

Charity bazaars served as social events as well as fairs for the sale of various items to raise funds for soldiers and their families. Grace Brown Elmore and her family spent much time working at bazaars in Columbia for the relief of soldiers. On February 7, 1865, she described how a charity bazaar gave its participants pleasure that temporarily relieved the anxiety of Sherman's approach. "If an entire stranger to all our circumstances had stepped into those halls," she wrote, "how little would he have guessed of the state of our country. On each side of the hall he could have seen booths, draped in the gayest colors red and white or blue, garlanded with evergreens, and filled with all sorts of nick nacks. . . . He would look upon the gay crowd in utter amazement. . . . Everybody left bad spirits and anxiety at the door, if Sherman was mentioned 'twas in a most casual way, nobody had time for blues, they jostled each other, laughed, and made fun, and forgot for the hour that the battle for home and fireside was soon to commence." She and other ladies enjoyed a flirtation with the paroled Confederate soldier Jessie Malachi (Mally) Howell, who had been interned at the Federal prison at Point Lookout, Maryland. "Mally Howell was very gay the last two nights at the bazaar," she recalled, "both tongue and pocket were unloosed, and he spent a fortune in treating us to ice cream and sherbet." Because of his experience, however, Howell must have expressed some despondent views about the war and the fate of the Confederate states, for Grace Elmore found it necessary to upbraid him for being "so gloomy." But "since then he has been most cheerful, and we don't hear much of his gloomy ideas about the Confederacy."[60]

Charitable, social, and civic organizations held balls, concerts, and amateur theatricals to raise funds for relief causes. In Mobile, for example, fund-raising productions were sponsored by the Young Men's Christian Association, the Samaritan Society, the Odd Fellows, ladies' aid societies, and various social clubs for young men. The public performers included the Mobile Amateur Minstrels and the Gulf City Harmonists. Widows of Confederate soldiers, the Catholic home for orphans, sick and wounded soldiers in local hospitals, and the poor received the proceeds from such events. Money collected at a number of sponsored balls went to the orphans and widows of thirty-seven Mobile firemen who had been killed in battle after being conscripted into the Confederate army.[61]

For social interaction and entertainment, families, friends, and neighbors often gathered at public dances and impromptu dances at home. "Starvation parties," where refreshments were sparse, provided opportunities for socializing if not feasting. Because of food shortages, picnics frequently became outings rather than meals. Southerners attempted to maintain normalcy by observing holidays and special events such as Christmas, birthdays, and marriages. Household games, including charades and fortune telling, were favorites, as were games of cards, checkers, and chess. Some households purchased and viewed stereopticon images. Children played traditional childhood games and enjoyed storytelling. For the literate with access to books, newspapers, and magazines, reading proved to be a favorite pastime. Thoroughbred racing and lavish parties continued on some plantations. In a few places, the antebellum practice of holding a grand tournament, followed by a coronation ball, went on during the war. On those occasions men dressed as medieval knights and riding fast on horseback attempted to spear a ring with a lance. In the evening a ball convened, a queen was crowned, and ladies awarded favors to the "knights."[62] Women found conversation, diversion, and companionship in clubs for sewing, knitting, and making bandages for Confederate soldiers and hospitals. Mary Waring of Mobile noted that at one meeting of the Soldiers' Hope Society, many of the town's ladies "arranged ourselves in groups of three's and four's all around the room, each one busily engaged in picking lint for our poor wounded soldiers, our tongues keeping time to our fingers."[63]

Music provided temporary relief for both soldiers in the field and the folk at home. Classical music had a following, especially among the educated populace. The poet Sidney Lanier, for example, enjoyed playing classical selections on his flute. Some female academies attempted to instruct their students in the classical repertoire. Catherine Hopley, from England, struggled to teach her students at a Baptist academy near Warrenton, Virginia, about classical music. But Hopley's pupils, like most Southerners, preferred popular tunes. Among these were "Dixie" (which became the "anthem" of the Confederacy), "The Bonnie Blue Flag," "Maryland, My Maryland," "Beauregard's March," "The Yellow Rose of Texas," and the sad and sentimental "Somebody's Darling," "Lorena," and "When This Cruel War Is Over." Group sings in homes that had a piano or other musical instrument made for frequent diversions. Sometimes group sings became public events. Spirits could revive at professional or amateur concerts, presented mainly in urban areas. Louis Moreau Gottschalk of New Orleans was the Confederacy's only piano virtuoso, and his compositions "Serenade," "The Last Hope," and "The Dying Poet" enjoyed wide appeal. Such was the people's appetite for music that publishers in the South produced more than 648 pieces of sheet music during the war.

Theaters remained open in the major towns and actually drew larger audiences than they had in peacetime. Richmond, Charleston, Nashville, Columbia, Augusta, Savannah, Atlanta, Mobile, Montgomery, and Jackson all had active theaters where major traveling companies appeared. Richmond boasted the most theaters, performances, and theatergoers. Large audiences filled the Richmond Theater (which burned) and its successor, the New Richmond, as well as the Varieties and Metropolitan theaters.[64] The Charleston Theater in South Carolina burned in December 1861, but the Hibernian Hall was shortly remodeled to accommodate productions and continued hosting performances until the end of the war. In Nashville in 1861, a newspaper editor supported keeping the theater open to provide entertainment for the many soldiers and civilians congregating in the town. A traveler observed that in Augusta "there is a very good theatre where they play every night."[65] The best-known theater troupe was the W. H. Crisp Company, whose male members were all soldiers discharged from the army. The most famous and admired actresses in the Confederacy were Jennie Powell, Mary Partington, Ida Vernon, and Ella Wren, the "accomplished trajedienne and Prima Donna," also known as "the Mockingbird of the Southern theatre." The South's favorite actors were E. R. Dalton, Walter Keeble, R. D'Orsay Ogden, Harry Macarthy, W. H. Crisp, and Charles Morton, billed as the "most versatile and popular Comedian and Vocalist in the Confederacy."[66]

Theaters were patronized primarily by the many soldiers, refugees, and working-class people who crowded the cities and towns. The upper classes and permanent residents generally shunned the performances, which they considered vulgar. Stage productions ranged from light comedy and musical numbers to the plays of Shakespeare. In the final weeks of the war, the people in Mobile attended productions of *Othello, Macbeth, King Lear*, and *Richard III*, as well as less weighty offerings. But the taste of the majority of Southerners leaned toward lighthearted, humorous, and sentimental plays and bawdy minstrel shows. Audiences sought to be amused and entertained as relief—however temporary—from the strain and horrors of the war.[67]

The comedian and singer Harry Macarthy did not often perform serious drama, although he was said to be "equally at home" in "high or low comedy, fine drama, songs, comic or sentimental." One Richmond critic preferred not to listen to him "tune his throat and stamp his feet in the rendition of vulgar songs and vulgar dances and vulgar jokes, to small audiences of questionable character." A newspaper editor in the Confederate capital cried that the city would remain a moral cesspool "until short skirts, and *nigger* dancing, ribaldry, blasphemous mock-piety, gross buffoonery, and other 'piquant' and profane attractions for the carnal-minded and illiterate, are excluded from the stage."[68]

A large number of the plays romanticized Southern civilization and war heroes and helped maintain Confederate patriotism among the home-front masses. These works included *The Roll of the Drum, The Battle of Manassas, The Virginia Cavalier*, and *The Guerrillas*. Farces such as *The Sergeant's Stratagem* and *Getting Promoted* made light of the soldier's experience. Others lampooned and satirized Abraham Lincoln, among them William Russell Smith's *The Royal Ape* and John Hill Hewitt's *King Linkum, the First*. Probably the two most popular plays were *Black-Eyed Susan* and

East Lynne. The latter entered the Confederacy when the English actress Ida Vernon ran the blockade and began performing in Southern theaters. Some theatergoers had the unique pleasure of viewing a mechanical device of Lee Mallory that employed moving miniature figures to depict scenes of war, nature, and pyrotechnics. Also for the excitement of theater audiences, "Burton's Southern Moving Dioramic" portrayed battle images on a large moving canvas.[69]

The arts of painting and sculpture also embraced Confederate patriotism. Painters' favorite subjects were war scenes and Confederate generals. One of the best-known paintings of the war was William D. Washington's *The Burial of Latané*, which depicted the interment of Capt. William Latané, one of Gen. J. E. B. Stuart's cavalrymen and reportedly the only soldier killed during Stuart's famed ride around McClellan's army during the Peninsula Campaign in 1862. John A. Elder, a Virginian, painted war landscapes, battle scenes, and a portrait of Robert E. Lee. Both Washington and Elder had studied with the painter Emanuel Leutze at his renowned studio in Germany. Baltimore's Adalbert J. Volck depicted the home front in his etchings entitled *Making Clothes for the Boys in the Army* and *Offering of Bells to Be Cast into Cannon*. Louis M. Montgomery, a member of the Washington Artillery of New Orleans, created 180 watercolors of camp life, fortifications, battles, and other wartime subjects. An oil painting of Stonewall Jackson by an unnamed artist sold for $320 in Richmond in late 1863.

Sculptors proved equally supportive of the Confederate cause. The most accomplished sculptor was William R. Barbee, who had studied in Italy. He fashioned a bust of Jackson, and plaster casts of that work sold for $10.00 each in Richmond in 1863. He also carved a bust of Jefferson Davis, of which 500 copies went on sale in England to raise funds for aid to Confederate prisoners of war. Even while the battles raged, patriotic groups called for monuments and statues to honor Confederate heroism and sacrifice. Usually, however, financial and other rigors of wartime prevented their completion during the conflict. For example, a statue of Stonewall Jackson planned during the war did not appear on Capitol Square in Richmond until 1875. It was in the decades following the war that statues and monuments glorifying the "lost cause" proliferated all over the South, promoted and erected by such neo-Confederate organizations as the United Daughters of the Confederacy.[70]

The war had a profound impact on the religious, educational, and cultural life of a large portion of the Confederacy's home-front population. Except for the circumstances of those African Americans who ran away and began a new existence under Federal protection, little changed in the social and cultural life of enslaved field hands and house servants. But in white society, religion, education, literature, theater, the visual arts, and public events all became swept up in the fervor of Confederate nationalism and helped in the government's struggle to sustain home-front morale and promote the war effort.

EIGHT

❧⚬❧

COURTSHIP, MARRIAGE, AND FAMILY LIFE

The disruption and dislocation caused by the war naturally limited the time and effort available for the rituals of courtship that had characterized antebellum life in the South. Distances between men in the army and women at home often affected the nuances of social custom and romance. For many couples the war sped up the process of courtship and marriage, and some relationships were entered into with haste and later regretted. But as nearly as possible, wartime Southerners adhered to the traditional practices of courtship. Men were expected to be pursuers—to woo and win women. The triumph of securing a bride was a major goal in nearly every man's life. Women, on the other hand, were to accept the passive role of the pursued. "Women, by the inalienable delicacy of their natures," opined the *Southern Literary Messenger* just before the war, "do not act the part of wooers. But as to men, if they deserve the name, they can in a great measure control their own destiny. . . . Among other things which they can do, they can marry." It was, in fact, every bachelor's duty and a sign of manhood to go after and win a marriage partner. Women who did not marry were not at fault, declared the *Messenger*. "Let them alone, since God has so willed it." Old maids were a "chirping and vivacious class of women who, from mere accident and the force of circumstances over which they have no control, bloom solitary in the desert."[1]

Most females of marriageable age hoped to be courted and wed. Not all, however, saw romance and marriage as essential elements in their lives. In 1862 Grace Brown Elmore proclaimed:

I shocked one of my sisters very much once, by saying that married or not I hoped and trusted I would one day have my own establishment independent of every one else. Marriage has precious little share in my plans for the future, in the first place because no one has ever asked me yet, and in all probability a man whom I would marry never will, and in the second, marriage to me would hardly be a happy state. I am not trusting enough, to let myself be guided by a human creature, nor do I believe any more in my power to retain than in power to gain love. I am exacting & dreadfully proud, so that I could scarcely be happy with any man. But I do not consider this the only means of happiness, if one consists, many people marry for the one interest to which they wish to devote their life, but my desire and will is to find an interest without the appendage of a husband.[2]

The Civil War resulted in a shortage of marriageable men on the home front in most of the rural South. Refugees also found it difficult to establish relationships that might lead to nuptials. Resentment and jealously frequently developed between local belles and refugee women in competition for the attention of available beaus. But in urban areas, where large numbers of troops and government workers were deployed, the dearth of marriage-age men was not as severe as in the countryside. A good many wartime marriages took place in the cities. In Savannah in 1861, George Anderson Mercer, a young lawyer and graduate of Princeton, observed a plethora of marriages in the city and commented that he too would soon become engaged to "a gentle creature."[3] In Richmond a virtual "marriage frenzy" occurred. "There seems to be a real marrying mania afloat here," remarked one Richmond woman in November 1864. Another reported that she "knew of 52 weddings to take place this fall & winter."[4] Indeed, a surplus of marriageable white men prevailed in the Confederate capital. According to historian E. Susan Barber's sample of 222 white marriages between April 1861 and April 1865, "nearly 40 percent involved grooms who identified their occupations as soldier or sailor, or men who worked in a war-related occupation that was exempt from field duty—contract surgeons, civilian hospital workers, government gunsmiths and munitions workers, machinists, blacksmiths, clerks, telegraphers, or ironworkers." That surplus of single white men would decline after the war, when women began to outnumber the eligible males in Richmond. Most white women who married in the city from 1861 to 1865 were between the ages of twenty-one and twenty-two, which was slightly older than during the antebellum era. The ages of the majority of white men who married in Richmond during those years were twenty-five to twenty-eight.

Young women in the Confederate capital did not suffer a shortage of suitors. Within three weeks in March 1862, one woman enjoyed six visits from Confederate officers, who came calling in pairs. She also accepted three invitations to visit a nearby army encampment to view drills and dress parades, listen to band concerts, and tour an officer's quarters. The female workers in government offices had ample opportunity to meet "admirers—and potential husbands—among their co-workers." Mattie Pierce, a clerk in the Ordnance Bureau, carried on two office romances simultaneously in June 1864. Lettie Jones, a Maryland refugee and clerk in the Treasury Office, met and subsequently married a Confederate soldier from New Orleans. Jefferson Davis's aide Burton Harrison became engaged to Constance Cary while they both worked for the government. They were married after the war and remained so for thirty years. Government employees Parke Chamberlayne and George W. Bagby courted in 1861–1862 and were married in St. Paul's Church in February 1863. After a honeymoon at "Uncle Fatback's" farm in Lynchburg, they returned to Richmond and went back to work, living in a boardinghouse. They stayed married until George died in 1883.

Not all wartime courtships, engagements, and marriages turned out to be happy or enduring, however. As Barber points out about Richmond, "Wartime flirtations occasionally drew naive young women into ill-advised or illicit relationships." Lettie Jones's older sister Ella entered into an affair with a Confederate officer who had a wife and children in Missouri. As a result of that relationship, Ella apparently underwent an abortion in a Richmond boardinghouse. Emily Pitts nursed Richmond soldier James Jeter Phillips back to health and married him. After the war he shot her in the head and strangled her to death. Phillips was executed for the murder. Although that case was extreme, wartime circumstances often ended relationships and inflicted tensions on marriages. Wives and children frequently found themselves separated from husbands and fathers. Loneliness and worry about the safety of loved ones imposed considerable strain on all members of a family. Divorce was possible in some states but often difficult to secure through the courts, and it carried a heavy social stigma.[5]

Marriage for persons of privileged circumstances could, of course, have advantages denied to the lower classes. The so-called Southern belle was not as common before or during the Civil War as has been portrayed in legend, film, and romance novels. "Nevertheless," write historians Carol K. Bleser and Frederick M. Heath, "authentic belles did exist in the nineteenth-century South, and they were sought after by men, both young and old, who expected them to be pretty, unmarried, affluent, charming, fashionable, and flirtatious."[6] Most nineteenth-century women in America of all classes married, at least ostensibly, for love and with a partner of their own choice.[7] Southern belles also "believed that marriage would provide them with social rank, material benefits, freedom, and companionship, and thus was far more desirable than remaining single." The hard realities of domestic responsibilities, however, often dashed such idealized hopes. But certain upper-class females, such as the childless Mary Boykin Chesnut and Virginia Tunstall Clay, actually used wartime circumstances to their advantage and continued to play the role of the flirtatious belle even after marriage.[8]

Born of prominent and wealthy parents in South Carolina in 1823, Mary Boykin had all the advantages of a privileged background. At age seventeen she married James

Chesnut Jr., a Princeton graduate and Charleston lawyer who was the son of one of South Carolina's wealthiest planters. A states'-rights Democrat, Chesnut helped lead the secession movement in his state and sat in the Confederate Congress. He served as an aide to Gen. P. G. T. Beauregard and to President Davis and then commanded the South Carolina reserves as a brigadier general. Mary Boykin Chesnut traveled with her husband during his wartime career, spending considerable time in such places as Montgomery, Richmond, and Columbia. She reveled in the social activities of the city and did not care for the isolation of plantation life. She was horrified by the devastation, pain, and death caused by the relentless fighting. But overall she seemed to enjoy the war, and her marriage to a prominent Confederate official made that experience possible.[9]

Mary took particular pleasure in Richmond's many parties, balls, church services, and other social gatherings. She often found herself the center of attention and especially attractive to the many military officers and government officials congregated in the Confederate capital. In her diary she boasted of her flirtations and declared that "I can make anybody love me if I choose." James and Mary Chesnut sometimes expressed jealously over each other's attentions to members of the opposite sex. Once James accused his wife of being too flirtatious with former governor John Manning of South Carolina, whom Mary regarded as "the handsomest man alive." She chastised James when "a very handsome woman" rushed up to him and began enquiring why he "had not been to see me &c &c." When he explained that he "never saw the woman in my life," Mary responded: "What a credulous fool you must take me to be." The most frequent cause of quarreling between James Chesnut and his wife was "her love of partying and his contrary attitude which ranged from reluctant assent to vigorous opposition."[10]

Virginia Tunstall Clay of Alabama also enjoyed the whirlwind of social activities that her standing in Confederate society and freedom from childcare permitted her. She had all the charm and allure of the stereotypical belle, and men found it easy to fall in love with her. Virginia Tunstall was born in 1825 in North Carolina, but after her mother's early death, she went to live with wealthy relatives in Tuscaloosa. While attending parties at the opening of the Alabama legislature in December 1842, she met twenty-six-year-old Clement Claiborne Clay, a new member of the legislature and the son of a wealthy planter and lawyer. Despite her many beaus, Virginia accepted his marriage proposal. Clement Clay never found a fulfilling career and depended largely on his father for financial support. He suffered from various illnesses, had difficulty achieving self-reliance, and endured depression and low self-esteem. In the 1850s Clay served in the U.S. Senate as a Democrat, during which time Virginia enjoyed Washington's many parties and receptions. After the war broke out, he served in the Confederate Senate, and his wife again reveled in the social whirl of a government capital. She found it extremely dull to remain at home in Alabama.

At the end of the war, Clement surrendered to Federal authorities and was imprisoned for nearly eleven months, during which he suffered from illness and depression. Poor health, debt, alcoholism, and self-doubt plagued him thereafter. But Virginia did not allow her husband's depression and sense of failure to inhibit her own behavior and pleasure. She always played the flirtatious belle. At one point Clement reminded her that as a married woman, "yr. future is made—you are not beau-catching." She spent money extravagantly, even after the pair had financial difficulties, and did not feel guilty or curb her spending in response to her husband's complaints. Unlike some women of her class, such as Mary Chesnut, Virginia declined to do hospital or charity work or to knit socks or roll bandages for the soldiers. The Clays' marriage had moments of pleasure and happiness as well as discontent and despair. Throughout their years together, the two continued to express their affection and concern for each other. But Clement's failure to maintain prominence in political and social circles and Virginia's inability to mature beyond the stage of spoiled Southern belle strained their relationship.[11]

As with the Chesnuts and Clays, flirting and jealously were common among men and women. Flirtation between the sexes did not end with marriage, and it frequently added tensions and worries about fidelity to the already substantial stress caused by wartime separations. North Carolina's Col. William Dorsey Pender (subsequently a general), who referred to himself as "quite a lion," took a perverse pleasure in writing to his wife, Fanny, about his encounters with attractive young women in Virginia in the spring of 1861. "There are lots of beautiful girls here," he wrote her, "so when I have nothing else to do, I can look at something beautiful or fine." He boasted to his wife of dining "with the most beautiful girl in Suffolk" and claimed that at least one female "intimated once or twice that she had fallen in love with me." On one occasion he "had a nice time dancing and flirting with a very nice girl. I am trying to get her to knit you a sac for the hair, but she said that she is not going to work for my wife, but will do anything for me."

Burdened with the responsibilities of managing their household and two children, one a newborn, Fanny Pender did not appreciate her husband's carrying on with other women, even if only to "make me jealous, or to make me appreciate your love still more." Appropriately chastised and apologetic, Pender begged Fanny to come visit him at camp. "Honey . . . I have been on thorns fearing you will not come," he implored. Apparently she did visit him that summer for several weeks, and briefly on subsequent occasions. Pender died of wounds shortly after the Battle of Gettysburg in July 1863; their third child was born four months later.[12]

Like Pender, soldiers of all social classes seeking the physical and emotional comforts of their homes and domestic partners wrote asking their spouses to join them at their stations or while the army was encamped and not on the move. Many wives, anxious to see their husbands, made the journeys. Not all women, however, were enthusiastic about leaving the relative quiet and security of home, family, and friends to join their mates. Others felt that their overwhelming responsibilities at home prevented them from visiting their husbands. Victoria Clayton of Alabama, for example, found that the supervision of their plantation prevented her from agreeing to the requests of her husband, Henry, to join him at camp. At first she complied with his wishes. But by 1863 she was emphasizing her growing home-front duties as a reason for not answering his repeated calls that she come to him. Victoria did join him at Christmas of that year to nurse him from a wound sustained at the Battle of Chickamauga. She became pregnant then and never visited her husband again in camp.[13]

Many wives, already stressed by having to manage homes, farms or plantations, children, and elderly relatives, did not want to add to their problems with unwanted pregnancy. It was not unusual throughout the wartime South for women to make considerable effort to avoid this condition through the use of birth control devices and procedures.[14] Lizzie Neblett of Texas, who had given birth to her fifth—an unplanned—child just before her husband left for the war, informed him that she did not intend to risk "for your sake" another "certain event happening." Therefore, "If you cant comply with my orders . . . about the preventatives to come in your pocket home—you . . . must submit to my laws after reaching home." Those laws, she assured him, would be "strict enough to ensure my safety."[15] Although abortion was not publicly approved, it was attempted and performed, usually by means of some primitive physical procedure or by drinking often ineffectual herbal concoctions such as cotton root.[16]

Needless to say, the spouses of common soldiers who attempted to spend time with their encamped husbands did not enjoy the same accommodations as did the women who had husbands of high rank. Yeoman wives who visited their husbands sometimes even suffered the stigma of being labeled "camp followers." Martha Futch of North Carolina longed to see her husband, John, and vowed to travel to Virginia to visit him. "I shal come to see you if you aint back by April," she wrote him on February 19, 1863. But he cautioned her not to make the trip because a military camp was no proper place for a respectable woman.[17]

Feeling abandoned and lonely, many women wrote to their men in the army describing the unhappiness and sense of emptiness that wartime separation had inflicted upon them. Mary Ann Angle of Virginia constantly worried about and longed to see her husband, Joel, of the Thirty-sixth Regiment. She wrote to him that "I sit and study ten thousand things to make me miserable and unhappy and when I sleep I see you in my sleep sometimes sick and sometimes wounded. Sometimes I see you comeing home and wake myself jumping up to meet you but when I wake you are gone and I lay down to cry myself to sleep again."[18]

Despite—or perhaps even because of—the hardship and separation, some women gained strength and self-reliance during the war. One such woman was Victoria

Hunter, the daughter of a prominent Alabama planter. After her mother died, she helped her father operate the family plantation. Victoria married Henry D. Clayton, the son of a large land and slave owner and prominent politician. Henry practiced law, and initially Victoria's role was typical for a plantation wife. She managed day-to-day domestic life, including that of the slaves. When Henry was away on business, supervision of the entire plantation fell to her. In contrast to Clement and Virginia Clay, Henry and Victoria Clayton shared strong interests. They became partners in active support of Confederate nationalism and incorporated considerable political activism into their relationship. Henry had long supported the South's position on slavery, and his wife enthusiastically embraced his views. The pair led a group of more than one hundred Southern settlers to the Kansas territory to bolster the number of proslavery voters there in the hope of bringing Kansas into the Union as a slave state. During that expedition Victoria was three months pregnant and "had to sleep on the ground, eat from tin trays, bathe when she could, and do without her usual comforts." At one point "she armed herself with a pistol and protected the women and children of the expedition while her husband joined a proslavery militia that threatened the Free-Soil town of Lawrence."

Back in Alabama the Claytons strongly advocated secession. After the state joined the Confederacy, Henry received a military commission, rose to the rank of major general, and commanded Alabama troops in Florida, Kentucky, Tennessee, Georgia, and North Carolina. He suffered wounds, lost troops in battle, and experienced growing anxiety about the war and his own survival. Separation from Victoria evidently made his condition more difficult to bear. He sought her emotional comfort and frequently beseeched her to join him in camp. Victoria, however, considered it important that she stay on the plantation to ensure its safety and proper operation. She protected her autonomy and rebuffed her father-in-law's efforts to take over her affairs. She ran the plantation efficiently, and Henry acknowledged her as a capable and equal partner in their business affairs.[19] By all appearances the marriage of Henry Clayton and Victoria Hunter was a success. It evidently was a union of affection, mutual respect, and shared interests. Yet, as it did all Southerners of the era, the Civil War changed both of them. Henry suffered physical and psychological wounds. For Victoria the war brought the opportunity to obtain a new sense of power and self-reliance.

Indeed, women, of all classes, rich or poor, young or old, married or single, gained greater self-reliance than they had ever known before. For some, such a change resulted from necessity as the war placed upon them new and greater burdens and responsibilities. Others found a chance to step voluntarily outside the traditional sphere for women. One such person was Delia Jones of Clayton, North Carolina, who wrote to Gov. Zebulon B. Vance in January 1863: "Thinking that the number of young men called to military service must necessarily diminish the number of secretaries, copyists, &c required in public & private affairs, I write to enquire if any such office as a woman could fill is now vacant. I would like to engage in something of the kind, being a swift penman & accustomed to writing a good deal." Unfortunately for the ambitious Miss Jones, the governor had "nothing at present which she could do."[20] A growing number of women sought work outside the home as the war continued, out of necessity, personal preference, or both.

Not surprisingly, the war inflicted the greatest burden on the working-class women of the South. More than anyone else, they had reason to be discontent and disillusioned with the progress of the Confederate war effort. Their husbands, fathers, and sons were away in the army, and the sole responsibility for running farms and small businesses frequently fell to the women left behind. They bore the weight of feeding and clothing their children, their aged relatives, and themselves with little or no assistance as resources grew ever more scarce.

Because of a shortage of male workers, who had been claimed by the army, a significant number of women found employment in the Confederate bureaucracy that grew to meet the needs of a burgeoning nation struggling to wage war. The majority of women who worked for the Confederate government were employed in the Treasury Department, where they performed the task of signing and numbering Confederate notes.[21] One woman with children to support and a husband in the army wrote to Secretary of the Treasury Christopher Memminger asking for such employment. "My object in getting employment," she informed him, "is to support myself and three children, all under eleven years of age, while my husband is in the army: and I wish to make a permanent arrangement for a year. I have no means of support and no near relation living, having lost my only brother in one of the battles before Richmond."[22] Other women filled clerical positions in the War Department, Commissary General, and Quartermaster Department. The relatively high salaries made the government jobs particularly attractive. In 1863, for example, a female clerk earned $65.00 per month, but a private in the army received only $11.00.[23]

With many male teachers serving in the army, a number of women with some level of education began to make inroads into the teaching profession, usually at lower salaries than men. The *Augusta Daily Constitutionalist* in Georgia observed that because the war had "swallowed up" young male teachers, "we are left with no resources then but to have female teachers." The newspaper concluded that such a change might be a beneficial one, as women were better "fitted, naturally and morally, for teachers of the young."

Despite the availability of paying jobs in government and teaching, upper-class women tended to shun even salaried work as demeaning to their position in society. But as time went on and economic circumstances worsened, women of all classes were forced to seek employment. Their working outside the home affected traditional domestic life in the Confederacy. It meant that women took on greater responsibility for the financial support of their families and had less time for household duties and the care of children.[24]

Along with their parents, children keenly felt the disruption and anxiety that the war inflicted on families. In many ways children were the war's most pathetic victims. Unfortunately, adults of all eras have not recorded many truthful accounts of the thoughts, emotions, and fears of their offspring, preferring to portray them in an idealized childhood in which they reflect well on their parents by remaining obedient, cheerful, accomplished, and quiet.[25] Nevertheless, some conclusions about children in the Confederacy can be reached. Post–Civil War psychoanalysts have theorized that one of the greatest fears of children is that their parents will abandon them.[26] That was true of the youngsters in the Confederacy, who despaired over their fathers' deaths in battle or long absences and lived in dread that their mothers might abandon them also. The mother of the little boy Blair Lee, for instance, noticed his uneasiness about his father and observed that he "seems to fear that I'll go away too."[27]

At times married couples in the Confederacy relieved their own wartime anxieties by eliciting desired behavior from their children. Written instructions and admonitions in the letters of adults—particularly fathers away at the front—reveal how parents used the tried-and-true devices of guilt and shame to draw "perfect" behavior from their offspring.[28] "Oh my dear daughter," wrote one father to his fourteen-year-old Emma, "your father may be lying dead in the field of battle and you may not know it. . . . O, Emma, Emma! How can you have the heart to go to dancing parties, against your kind mother's wishes and advice and your own conscience and judgment? How can you add to my grief and trouble by such a course?" A South Carolina father in the army wrote to his son to be always "obedient and grateful." A Georgia soldier reminded his children that he was "undergoing these hardships and dangers that you might remain at home and be comfortable as you are." Historian James Marten has written that Civil War "children must have understood how their behavior mattered to their parents. Perhaps they even understood that the war, while it did not change these expectations, sparked an urgency that might not have existed before."[29]

Children displaced by the war suffered especially from anxiety about instability and lack of permanence. As Union troops invaded the South, many families abandoned their homes and sought refuge away from the enemy's advance. Such flight disrupted schooling, pleasures, and routines of childhood and placed adult responsibilities on children. Daughters assumed many domestic duties, even becoming surrogate mothers when their own mothers became ill or distraught by the news of battlefield deaths or succumbed to other strains of a society at war. Sons sometimes had to serve as substitute husbands and fathers. A refugee mother had the heavy burden of moving her children out of harm's way, ensuring their safety in flight, and finding a new home where she could protect them. Mothers felt constantly anxious about the impact that deprivation and displacement were having on their families. Depression could suddenly seize those women who received word of the death, wounding, imprisonment, or sickness of a husband, father, son, or other relative.[30]

Those sons and daughters who remained at home frequently had to put aside childhood and undertake adult tasks on farms or work to earn extra income in urban jobs and factories. Some children were actually killed in the fighting that adhered to no battlefield boundaries but raged throughout the South, in countryside and town. Lida Lord Reed observed during the Union attack on Vicksburg that "a family living on the Jackson road were sitting together in the house when a shell came through the roof, and, bursting, killed the mother and one child, not even a fragment of the child being found." Under bombardment in the town, "another mother had her baby killed on her breast." Children adjusted their behavior quickly to the circumstances of war. Reed remarked that while Vicksburg was under siege, "it was curious to see how well trained the little ones were. At night when the bombs began to fly like pigeons over our heads, they would be waked out of sleep, would slip on their shoes, and run, without a word, like rabbits to the burrows. In the daytime they climbed the trees, gathered pawpaws, and sometimes went blackberrying up the road, but never far, the first sound of cannonading sent them scampering home."[31]

The war did not affect all Southern children in the same way. But most—from all classes—shared some behavioral characteristics shaped by the conflict. They early developed the political values of their parents. Their games and stories revolved around violence, competition, and reenactments of battles. Their ability to cope with anxiety caused by the war depended upon how well their parents, especially their mothers, managed their own apprehensions. Children often became rebellious and experienced nightmares and bed-wetting. But despite the psychological burdens that the war placed on Southern youngsters, they coped fairly well with stress and maintained stability in their lives by means of games, books, friendships, and other interests customarily associated with childhood. They found comfort in well-known stories and activities and repeated them time and again.[32] They possessed few new books or toys, especially if they had to flee their homes and could carry only limited baggage. But familiar toys helped boys and girls maintain a sense of "normalcy." When Grace King, a future author, fled New Orleans at the age of ten, she was permitted to take only one toy. She chose a rag doll, which she clung to tenaciously and continued to play with even as it came apart.[33] Nevertheless, children were never blind or immune to the trauma surrounding them. In the words of one Civil War child, Herman DeLong, many years after the sectional conflict ended, "One need not be grown-up to imbibe the peculiar feeling than hangs over everything in war."[34]

The war also had a profound impact on the domestic life of African American families. Federal invasion and the general disruption of relationships between white masters and black forced laborers made it possible for enslaved individuals and families to escape from bondage. As more bolted for the protection of the U.S. Army in occupied areas of the South, they seized opportunities that would help them establish, maintain, and protect a stable domestic life, which had often been denied them under a system that tended to separate couples and families. The Federal government and its relief programs, which consolidated into the Freedmen's Bureau in March 1865, gave blacks who found refuge within Union lines greater chances for successful family life than they had known before emancipation.

True, families could be separated when individuals, usually men, fled alone from the plantations and farms for Union lines, generally to work as laborers for the army or to serve in the newly formed black regiments. But just as often family groups escaped to freedom together, and the U.S. "government . . . generally attempted to keep black families together, while also employing black men as laborers [or soldiers] and encouraging self-support among their families."[35] Husbands, fathers, and sons who worked as laborers or joined the army frequently left their families alone and unprotected while they served elsewhere. Their absences, injuries, wounds, or deaths inflicted financial and emotional hardships on their families. However, former slave women left on their own generally coped well in providing themselves and their children with basic necessities, even when government aid was sparse. Those families in freedmen's camps or on Federal-operated plantations received some degree of government support, such as rations and clothing, in addition to their menfolk's army pay, small as it was (less than that of white soldiers). As noted earlier, a number of freedwomen found employment with the government as laundresses, cooks, seamstresses, and servants. Even under slavery women had gained experience in supporting their families with limited male assistance. For long stretches of time, they might have been forced to live apart from their husbands, who could belong to a master on another plantation or be taken far away to work. During the absences of husbands, the welfare of slave families frequently fell to wives. As a result "they may have adapted more easily to the hardships produced by [wartime] separation than their white counterparts whose menfolk were off fighting for the Confederacy, leaving them to run farms and support families, often for the first time."[36]

Still, whether they remained on the plantations or sought Federal protection, most slave couples made every effort to stay together. They took advantage of wartime circumstances and the presence of Federal troops to reunite with loved ones and strengthen marriage and familial relationships. Before the war Betty Johnson, a free woman of Fairfax County, Virginia, had married Benjamin Johnson, a slave in nearby Prince William County. Because of his status, they had to live mostly apart. When Confederate troops in the vicinity withdrew, however, Benjamin escaped from his master and united with his wife permanently. Soon after Mary Hughes married a member of the Thirty-eighth Infantry U.S. Colored Troops, she followed his regiment to Deep Bottom, Virginia, where she worked as a cook for the unit's commanding officer. When her husband, March, was wounded in battle, she nursed him in the army hospital.[37]

In December 1863 Rufus Wright, a former slave from North Carolina who had enlisted in the First U.S. Colored Infantry in July, married Elizabeth Turner, an ex-slave from Virginia. Presiding over the wedding was Henry M. Turner, an African

American minister of the African Methodist Episcopal Church and chaplain of the regiment. Wright and his wife corresponded frequently when he was away, and the couple visited whenever possible. On April 22, 1864, he wrote the following to her:

> My Dear wife I thake this opportunity to inform you that I am well and Hoping when thoes few Lines Reaches you thay my find you Enjoying Good Heath as it now fines me at Prisent Give my Love to all my friend I Received you Last letter and was verry Glad to Hear fome you you must Excuse you [me] fore not Riting Before this times the times I Recive you Letter I was order on a march and I had not times to Rite to you I met witch a Bad Michfochens I Ben [S]ad of I Lost my money I think I will com Down to See you this weeck I thought you Hear that I was hear and you wood com to see me Git a Pass and com to see me and if you cant git Pass Let me know it Give my Love to mother and Molley Give my Love to all inquiring fried
>   NO more to Say Still remain you Husband untall Death
>
>   Rufus Wright

Any further happiness that the couple shared was short lived, for Rufus Wright died of battle wounds on June 21, 1864.[38]

The war provided many such slave couples with the opportunity to secure legal marriages. Under slavery men and women usually lived in monogamous relationships and were joined together in some type of marriage ceremony. But their marriages had no legitimacy in law or permanent standing in Southern white religious dogma, and slave masters could dissolve them and break up families with impunity. Black men and women who reached Union-held territory, on the other hand, could obtain legitimate and solemnized marriages, and they eagerly sought such ties.[39] As historians Ira Berlin, Steven Miller, and Leslie S. Rowland have written, "Ex-slaves held firm convictions about what freedom should mean. At the very least, the integrity of their families should no longer depend upon the goodwill and fortunes of others. They therefore welcomed opportunities to place their personal relationships upon legal footing. Even before the end of the Civil War, thousands of husbands and wives reaffirmed unions established during slavery, often registering them in volumes provided by military superintendents of freedmen."[40] Army chaplains and missionary ministers performed numerous ceremonies, many of which were mass weddings. In large-scale ceremonies in Virginia in September 1861, Rev. L. C. Lockwood married eleven couples at Fort Monroe and twenty-one couples at Hampton. In July 1864 Northern missionary Lucy Chase observed one mass wedding that included forty African American couples and another that involved eighty couples.[41]

In the restrictive and dehumanizing environment of slavery, courtships were difficult. "Niggers didn't have time to do much courting in them days," recalled one ex-slave. "White folks would let them have suppers 'round Christmas time, then after that it was all over and no more gatherings till the next summer; then they would let them set out under the shade trees on Sunday evening, and all like that."[42] Nevertheless, most slaves endeavored to carry on traditional courtships. Men and women met and socialized in the evenings, on Sundays, during holidays, at weddings and parties and dances, or on any other special occasions that their masters allowed them to celebrate. They spoke of wanting to marry for love, and they sought as much time, romance, privacy, and dignity for their courting rituals and marriages as possible under the demeaning and frustrating circumstances of their existence. Slave families lived in crowded conditions, which inhibited privacy and intimacy. The typical slave cabin was a small, dark, dirty dwelling with a dirt floor and a mud-and-stick chimney. The average family occupying the usually sixteen-by-eighteen-foot room numbered five to six persons. The cabin could be even more crowded if the family took in orphans, the elderly, or friends.[43]

Slaves who remained on the plantations or ran away to freedom within Union lines married at around the same age as did whites. Among the more than 9,000 ex-slaves who registered their marriages under Federal occupation at Davis Bend, Natchez, and Vicksburg, Mississippi, in 1864–1865, fewer than 1 percent of males and fewer than 10 percent of females were between the ages of fifteen and twenty. Thirty-eight percent of males and 47 percent of females wed between the ages of twenty and twenty-nine. The rest were older. Fully 19 percent of the men and 8 percent of the women married over the age of fifty.[44]

Although under slavery marriages and families were frequently broken up by masters' selling their slaves to different locales, husbands and wives tried to stay together and with their children. They clung to first-time marriages; and when they ran away to Federal lines, they actively sought to be reunited with partners from whom they had been separated. Thomas Calaban, who commanded African American troops in Mississippi, observed that black couples had "an almost universal anxiety . . . to abide by first connections. Many, both men and women with whom I am acquainted, whose wives and husbands the rebels have driven off, firmly refuse to form new connections, and declare their purpose to keep faith with absent ones." Of course, not all ex-slave marriages entered into under Federal auspices were wise or lasting. John Eaton, a Federal chaplain and commander of black troops, noted, "It is not pretended that all marriages that have taken place were well advised, or will be happy, or faithfully observed. When marriages among whites shall all prove so, without exception, it will be time to look for such a happy state among the blacks."[45]

Like their young white counterparts, slave children felt the impact of war directly. They too suffered from shortages and fear. But they were forced to endure lives considerably more hardened and dehumanized that those of most white youths. Slave children were always subject to being sold away from their families. They often had the responsibility of caring for younger siblings while their parents worked in the fields or the plantation house. Slave children were forced to join the labor force at an early age and at times witnessed harsh punishment or demeaning treatment of their fathers and mothers by masters or overseers. Their world was constantly defined by the restraints and hardships of enforced servitude. Despite such conditions, slave children made friends, engaged in a variety of games and diversions, and displayed the typical characteristics of childhood development.

For many slave children, the war proved a liberating experience even while the fighting raged. Those who joined the flight to Federal-occupied areas experienced the exhilaration of being free. They received food and clothing and the rudiments of education under the largess of the U.S. military and missionary societies. Some had the misfortune to fall victim to disease in the unsanitary conditions in the freedmen's camps. Others were orphaned when their parents died or abandoned them. But those who found themselves alone and uncared for were usually quickly taken in by other black families.[46]

Sexual relations between whites and African Americans were common in the slavery system. They usually involved white men and single black girls and "varied from seduction to rape." According to historian Eugene D. Genovese, "Married black women and their men did not take white sexual aggression lightly and resisted effectively enough to hold it to a minimum." Nonetheless, miscegenation had a significant impact on Southern society and resulted in a large number of mulattoes, who lived in the greatest concentrations in cities and towns.[47] The practice was common enough to draw comment from Mary Boykin Chesnut, who marveled at the naivete and self-delusion of white planters' wives. "Like the patriarchs of old our men live in one house with their wives and concubines, and the mulattoes one sees in every family exactly resemble the white children—and every lady tells you who is the father of all the mulatto children in everybody's household, but those in her own she seems to think drop from the clouds, or pretends so to think."[48]

Sexual activity played a role in emotional attachments between men and women, whether the couples were white or black, single or married. The Confederate South was very much a part of the nineteenth century's Victorian world, which generally has been considered prudish or repressed with regard to physical relations between the sexes. "The truth though," notes historian Stephen W. Berry II, "is that Victorians were only starched about sexual expression in public; so long as private matters were kept private, men and women were allowed to practice a sexuality that was open-tempered, passionate, and playful."[49]

Because sex was a subject to be kept private, little information has survived about the intimate lives of Southern folk. But in the minds of most people of the Confederacy, ideally—if not always in reality—sexual relations were reserved for marriage. Homosexuality, although undoubtedly practiced, was seldom mentioned. "Sodomy" and "buggery," the customary terms in the mid-nineteenth century, were unlawful and socially condemned. But, according to one historian, there is "no record of a Civil War soldier having been disciplined for either offense, although there are records of three pairs of U.S. Navy sailors who were court-martialed for such activity."[50] Soldiers on both sides committed rape on civilian women, although it is not known how many women were so violated. Victims were most often African American.[51]

Generally, Confederate society allowed men a certain leeway in having sexual feelings and did not regard male desires as sinful. Nevertheless, it expected men to control themselves and overcome premarital passions. Women, on the other hand, were not considered to have strong sexual urges. Their desires, the argument went, remained weaker than those of men, and their morally superior natures made it easier for them to suppress lust. A man's promiscuity might be partly excused on the basis that he was, after all, a man. But a woman's "instinct for chastity" was "an intrinsic piece of her equipment, bequeathed to her by God. The loss of that instinct, regardless of fault or circumstance, could fairly be regarded as unfeminine, ungodly, and unnatural, and the faintest whisper of scandal could destroy a woman's good name forever."[52] Married women had some degree of freedom in having and expressing affection for their husbands and enjoying the physical pleasures of their connubial relationship. Clement Clay lamented that Virginia was not always in his bed. She responded that she missed him especially at night and declared on one evening when she was alone that she would like to "be with my old rooster."[53]

Whites often tried to portray blacks as less modest and more sexually promiscuous than themselves. But contrary to these unjust images, slave couples regarded their romantic feelings and contacts as special and private, and they were no more promiscuous than whites. Moreover, venereal diseases "may well have struck southern whites more often than blacks."[54]

The Civil War devastated and dislocated numerous families and ended many intimate relationships. Husbands, wives, children, and sweethearts frequently saw the ties that bound them weaken and even break. For freed slaves, however, the invasion of the Northern army brought positive alterations in their marriage and family arrangements. They could sustain legal marriages and, in most instances, cohesive families under Federal protection. Some white women also experienced positive changes. As the Confederate war effort made new demands upon them and altered their traditional domestic situations, they gained a new degree of self-reliance and independence. Amid the upheaval precipitated by the war, all Southerners tried to preserve or improve their personal relationships, including courtship, marriage, and family life. But in the end, no aspect of life on the Confederate home front was left untouched by the strains of war.

EPILOGUE

During the Civil War, the people of the Confederate States of America struggled to cope with a crisis that spared no one, military or civilian. Although no single experience was common to all Southerners, a great many suffered poverty, dislocation, and heartbreak. The military draft, heavy taxes, and restrictions on personal freedoms led to widespread dissatisfaction and cries for peace. The Confederacy became a region of divided loyalties, where pro-Union and pro-Confederate neighbors sometimes clashed violently. For African Americans, however, the war brought liberation from slavery and the promise of a new life. White women, too, saw their lives transformed as wartime challenges gave them new responsibilities and experiences.

The question of why the South lost the Civil War will always be a subject of debate. Some historians have stressed the lack of military strength and battlefield successes as the reason. Theirs is a viable argument. Without sufficient military prowess and resources, no nation—or aspiring nation—stands a reasonable chance of achieving lasting victory in war.

Other scholars have attributed the defeat to different causes: inferior political and military leadership, the failure of foreign diplomacy, an overemphasis on states' rights and individual liberties, financial instability, and a largely agricultural economy. Still others contend that the Confederacy failed to triumph simply because its people did not possess the will to win.

All these points of view have validity, and all those factors played some part in the Confederate defeat. But in considering the home-front population, perhaps the last point is the most perplexing and generates the most debate. Did the Confederate war effort fail in large measure because the folk of the South failed to support it? One could reasonably argue that just as a national government must have a strong military force to win a war, it must also have the blessing and support of its population, especially if that war is prolonged.

Some scholars have theorized that from the very beginning of secession, the people of the South lacked—that is, never had—sufficient will to see the war through to the end. Other historians challenge that conclusion and maintain that the loss of will developed over a period of time as the war continued and hardships grew, with no victory in sight.[1] The question of whether or when the folk of the Confederacy lost their will can never be answered to everyone's satisfaction. The population of the South—rich and poor, male and female, slaveholders and non-slaveholders, white, black, and foreign—was simply too diverse for anyone to reach a definite conclusion about something as abstract as the "will of the people."

Nevertheless, the evidence suggests that at the time their states seceded from the Union, white Southerners generally accepted, or at least acquiesced in, their leaders' decision to wage war. Public morale and patriotism began to fade only when the war went on too long, when battles were lost and casualties mounted, when deprivation and hardships at home became painful, and when the central government enacted restrictive laws and called for greater sacrifices despite little sign of pending victory. The year 1863 marked the beginning of the end for the Confederate States of America and also the point at which white Southerners' support for the war began to collapse.

By 1863 Federal invasion had inflicted the devastation and cruelty of war directly upon civilians in the South. The blockade of ports had become effective, and shortages were a part of day-to-day life. The conscription act had been expanded, opposition to forced military service had grown, and desertion was on the rise. The Confederate government had imposed demoralizing martial law and suspended habeas corpus in some areas. The tax-in-kind and impressment laws added to the growing disaffection. The Emancipation Proclamation of January 1 instilled disillusionment and weakened war support among the common people by reinforcing the idea that the war was being fought not for independence or states' rights but for the preservation of slavery. The proclamation and the subsequent enlistment of former slaves into the Union army also created—among slaveholders and non-slaveholders alike—a widespread and chilling fear that slaves would be incited to rise up and murder whites. Any hopes for foreign intervention on behalf of the Confederate cause had been dashed by the impact of the Emancipation Proclamation in Britain and Europe, as well as the failure of the Southern armies to win a decisive battle. Then came the devastating defeats at Gettysburg and Vicksburg in July. Talk of peace negotiations and an end to the war began to spread. Many Southerners started to embrace the view of one farmer who wrote to his governor on December 30 that "there seems to be no escape for us from these sore troubles but to make peace with the North on the best terms we can."[2]

How the government of President Jefferson Davis managed for almost another year and a half to keep the people at home embroiled in a horrible fight for a lost cause is a conundrum that requires further inquiry. But even those historians who cannot accept 1863 as the onset of the collapse of public morale and the inevitability of Confederate defeat will have to consider seriously the autumn of 1864, when Sherman had captured Atlanta, the Army of Northern Virginia was besieged at Petersburg, and Lincoln's reelection had signaled the willingness of Northern voters to see the war through to the end.

Regardless of when the people of the Confederacy might have abandoned their will to persevere in the Civil War, it can be said with certainty that by the time the struggle ended in the spring of 1865, no such will still existed. Southern folk were exhausted and no longer wanted to continue the fight. They had grown weary of a war from which they and their leaders could find no refuge short of surrender.

NOTES

INTRODUCTION

1. Charles H. Wesley, *The Collapse of the Confederacy*, with a new introduction by John David Smith (Columbia: University of South Carolina Press, 2nd ed., 2005), xxxviii.

2. More than two decades after Ramsdell's book appeared, Mary Elizabeth Massey summarized the historiography of the home front and called for still more studies. More recently James L. Roark has discussed the state of scholarship on the subject. Mary Elizabeth Massey, "The Confederate States of America: The Home Front," in Arthur S. Link and Rembert W. Patrick, eds., *Writing Southern History: Essays in Historiography in Honor of Fletcher M. Green* (Baton Rouge: Louisiana State University Press, 1965), 249–272; James L. Roark, "Behind the Lines: Confederate Economy and Society," in James M. McPherson and William J. Cooper, eds., *Writing the Civil War: The Quest to Understand* (Columbia: University of South Carolina Press, 1998), 201–227.

CHAPTER 1

1. Bell Irvin Wiley, *The Life of Johnny Reb: The Common Soldier of the Confederacy* (Baton Rouge: Louisiana State University Press, reprint, 1978), 75.

2. James I. Robertson Jr., *Soldiers Blue and Gray* (Columbia: University of South Carolina Press, 1998), 162.

3. Robertson, *Soldiers Blue and Gray*, 103.

4. Wiley, *Life of Johnny Reb*, 208.

5. Mark Mayo Boatner III, *The Civil War Dictionary* (New York: David McKay Co., 1959), 169, 602–603; Patricia L. Faust et al., eds., *Historical Times Illustrated Encyclopedia of the Civil War* (New York: HarperCollins, 1986), 25, 448; Clement Eaton, *A History of the Southern Confederacy* (New York: Free Press, reprint, 1965), 100.

6. William Core to Zebulon B. Vance, January 12, 1863, Vance, Governors Papers, State Archives, North Carolina Office of Archives and History, Raleigh.

7. David A. Norris, "'For the Benefit of Our Gallant Volunteers': North Carolina's State Medical Department and Civilian Volunteer Efforts, 1861–1862," *North Carolina Historical Review* 75 (July 1998): 304; Richard C. Wade, *Slavery in the Cities: The South, 1820–1860* (New York: Oxford University Press, 1964), 138–141.

8. Emory M. Thomas, *The Confederate State of Richmond: A Biography of the Capital* (Baton Rouge: Louisiana State University Press, 2nd ed., 1998), 110.

9. *Memphis Daily Appeal*, August 2, 1861.

10. Norris, "'For the Benefit of Our Gallant Volunteers,'" 304; Thomas J. Farnham and Francis P. King, "'The March of the Destroyer': The New Bern Yellow Fever Epidemic of 1864," *North Carolina Historical Review* 73 (October 1996): 471; Judkin Browning and Michael Thomas Smith, eds., *Letters from a North Carolina Unionist: John A. Hedrick to Benjamin S. Hedrick* (Raleigh: North Carolina Office of Archives and History, 2001), 261.

11. James I. Robertson Jr., *Civil War Virginia: Battleground for a Nation* (Charlottesville: University Press of Virginia, 1991), 92–96; Norris, "'For the Benefit of Our Gallant Volunteers,'" 297–319; Eaton, *History of the Southern Confederacy*, 103.

12. Norris, "'For the Benefit of Our Gallant Volunteers,'" 297–319; Eaton, *History of the Southern Confederacy*, 103–104.

13. James M. McPherson, *Battle Cry of Freedom: The Civil War Era* (New York: Oxford University Press, 1988), 478–479.

14. Eaton, *History of the Southern Confederacy*, 103.

15. McPherson, *Battle Cry of Freedom*, 479.

16. C. Vann Woodward, ed., *Mary Chesnut's Civil War* (New Haven, CT: Yale University Press, 1981), 641.

17. Sue M. Chancellor, "Personal Recollections of the Battle of Chancellorsville," in Charles G. Waugh and Martin H. Greenburg, eds., *The Women's War in the South: Recollections of the American Civil War* (Nashville, TN: Cumberland House, 1999), 72–73.

18. Joe A. Mobley, "The American Civil War: 'Our Most Tremendous Experience,'" *Carolina Comments* 39 (July 1991): 130.

19. Bell Irvin Wiley, *Confederate Women: Beyond the Petticoat* (New York: Barnes and Noble, reprint, 1975), 154.

20. William J. Cooper Jr., *Jefferson Davis, American* (New York: Vintage Books, 2001), 515–516.

21. Woodward, *Mary Chesnut's Civil War*, 372.

22. Mary Elizabeth Massey, *Refugee Life in the Confederacy*, with a new introduction by George C. Rable (Baton Rouge: Louisiana State University Press, 2nd ed., 2001), 115, 126–129.

23. Mark E. Neely Jr., *Southern Rights: Political Prisoners and the Myth of Confederate Constitutionalism* (Charlottesville: University Press of Virginia, 1999), 41; Mary Elizabeth

Massey, *Ersatz in the Confederacy: Shortages and Substitutes on the Southern Homefront*, with a new introduction by Barbara L. Bellows (Baton Rouge: Louisiana State University Press, 2nd ed., 1993), 40, 44–46; Eaton, *History of the Southern Confederacy*, 232–233; E. Merton Coulter, *The Confederate States of America, 1861–1865* (Baton Rouge: Louisiana State University Press, 1950), 248.

24. Eaton, *History of the Southern Confederacy*, 141, 232; Neely, *Southern Rights*, 37.

25. Coulter, *Confederate States of America*, 414.

26. Thomas, *Confederate State of Richmond*, 81–82, 107.

27. *Advertiser and Register* (Mobile), January 1, 1865.

28. *Advertiser and Register*, February 7, 21, 1865.

29. *Advertiser and Register*, February 10, 1865.

30. *The War of the Rebellion: A Compilation of the Official Records of the Union and Confederate Armies*, series 1, vol. 49, pt. 1:105.

31. Mobley, "American Civil War," 131.

32. W. Buck Yearns and John G. Barrett, eds., *North Carolina Civil War Documentary* (Chapel Hill: University of North Carolina Press, 1980), 76–78.

33. Farnham and King, "'March of the Destroyer,'" 440–441, 471.

34. Farnham and King, "'March of the Destroyer,'" 440, 459–461.

35. Paul E. Steiner, *Disease in the Civil War: National Biological Warfare in 1861–1865* (Springfield, IL: Charles C. Thomas Publisher, 1968), 20–21.

36. H. H. Cunningham, *Doctors in Gray: The Confederate Medical Service* (Baton Rouge: Louisiana State University Press, 1958), 190–194; Farnham and King, "'March of the Destroyer,'" 449–450.

37. Massey, *Ersatz in the Confederacy*, 115.

38. Massey, *Ersatz in the Confederacy*, 115–117.

39. Massey, *Ersatz in the Confederacy*, 115–122; John Hammond Moore, comp., *The Confederate Housewife: Receipts and Remedies, Together with Sundry Suggestions for Garden, Farm, and Plantation* (Columbia, S.C.: Summerhouse Press, 1997), 146.

40. Massey, *Ersatz in the Confederacy*, 122–123; Thomas P. Lowry, *The Story the Soldiers Wouldn't Tell: Sex in the Civil War* (Mechanicsville, PA: Stackpole Books, 1994), 100.

41. Massey, *Ersatz in the Confederacy*, 123; Myrtle C. King, ed. and comp., *Anna Long Thomas Fuller's Journal, 1856–1890: A Civil War Diary* (Alpharetta, GA: Priority Publishing, 1999), 33.

42. Charles W. Allison, comp., *James Wyche Family History* (Charlotte, N.C.: Charles W. Allison, 1955), 127–130; Account Book of Dr. Cyril Granville Wyche, 1861–1864, in the possession of Elizabeth Calder Wyche, Whiteville, N.C., [3, 4, 7, 8, 11, 12, 13, 34, 38–40].

43. Cunningham, *Doctors in Gray*, 35–36; Albert B. Moore, *Conscription and Conflict in the Confederacy* (Columbia: University of South Carolina Press, reprint, 1996), 68.

44. Steiner, *Disease in the Civil War*, 4–5, 15.

45. Browning and Smith, *Letters from a North Carolina Unionist*, 172, 176, 178, 258, 261.

46. Jim Downs, "The Other Side of Freedom: Destitution, Disease, and Dependency among Freedwomen and Their Children during and after the War," in Catherine Clinton and Nina Silber, eds., *Battle Scars: Gender and Sexuality in the American Civil War* (New York: Oxford University Press, 2006), 90.

47. Thomas, *Confederate State of Richmond*, 114; Steiner, *Disease in the Civil War*, 43.

48. Steiner, *Disease in the Civil War*, 15, 22–23; Cunningham, *Doctors in Gray*, 194–195.

49. Steiner, *Disease in the Civil War*, 16.

50. Cunningham, *Doctors in Gray*, 202–204.

51. Lowry, *Story the Soldiers Wouldn't Tell*, 69–72.

52. Thomas, *Confederate State of Richmond*, 68–69.

53. Lowry, *Story the Soldiers Wouldn't Tell*, 79, 83–87.

54. *Advertiser and Register*, September 22, 1865.

55. Lowry, *Story the Soldiers Wouldn't Tell*, 108; Robertson, *Soldiers Blue and Gray*, 120; James I. Robertson Jr., *General A. P. Hill: The Story of a Confederate Warrior* (New York: Random House, 1987), 11–12 (quotation).

56. Steiner, *Disease in the Civil War*, 16.

57. Lowry, *Story the Soldiers Wouldn't Tell*, 108.

58. Cunningham, *Doctors in Gray*, 184–190, 201–202, 205–208; Steiner, *Disease in the Civil War*, 1–2, 12–13, 16–20, 38–42, 69, 72, 110, 111, 172–173; Coulter, *Confederate States of America*, 429.

CHAPTER 2

1. *Charleston Mercury*, February 2, 1861.

2. Paul W. Gates, *Agriculture and the Civil War* (New York: Alfred A. Knopf, 1965), 3–126; John Solomon Otto, *Southern Agriculture during the Civil War Era, 1860–1880* (Westport, CN: Greenwood Press, 1994), 19–45.

3. Gates, *Agriculture and the Civil War*, 13–20; Frank L. Owsley, *King Cotton Diplomacy: Foreign Relations of the Confederate States of America* (Chicago: University of Chicago Press, 1935), 49–50; Richard C. Todd, *Confederate Finance* (Athens: University of Georgia Press, 1954), 35–45, 127–129.

4. Otto, *Southern Agriculture during the Civil War*, 7–15.

5. Coulter, *Confederate States of America*, 239–241; Charles W. Ramsdell, *Behind the Lines in the Southern Confederacy* (Baton Rouge: Louisiana State University Press, reprint, 1997), 34–36; James L. Roark, *Masters without Slaves: Southern Planters in the Civil War and Reconstruction* (New York: W. W. Norton and Co., 1977), 38–45.

6. Stanley Lebergott, "Why the South Lost: Commercial Purpose in the Confederacy, 1861–1865," *Journal of American History* 70 (June 1983): 58–74; Lebergott, "Through the Blockade: The Profitability and Extent of Cotton Smuggling, 1861–1865," *Journal of Economic History* 41 (December 1981): 867–888; Roark, *Masters without Slaves*, 45.

7. Georgia Lee Tatum, *Disloyalty in the Confederacy*, with a new introduction by David Williams (Lincoln: University of Nebraska Press, 2nd ed., 2000), 19.

8. Ramsdell, *Behind the Lines*, 34–36; Coulter, *Confederate States of America*, 286; Walter L. Fleming, *Civil War and Reconstruction in Alabama* (New York: Macmillan Co., 1905), 181; *Official Records of the Union and Confederate Armies*, series 1, vol. 49, pt. 1: 906–907.

9. Roark, *Masters without Slaves*, 42–43.

10. Coulter, *Confederate States of America*, 239–242.

11. Charles P. Roland, *The Confederacy* (Chicago: University of Chicago Press, 1960), 69; Coulter, *Confederate States of America*, 245; Eaton, *History of the Southern Confederacy*, 233.

12. Gates, *Agriculture and the Civil War*, 68; Otto, *Southern Agriculture during the Civil War*, 16.

13. Coulter, *Confederate States of America*, 246–247.

14. Leon F. Litwack, *Been in the Storm So Long: The Aftermath of Slavery* (New York: Alfred A. Knopf, 1979), 36–38, 52–59, 135–139, 144–145; Roark, *Masters without Slaves*, 74–85.

15. Eugene D. Genovese, *Roll Jordan Roll: The World the Slaves Made* (New York: Vintage Books, 1974), 151.

16. Emory M. Thomas, *The Confederacy as a Revolutionary Experience* (Englewood Cliffs, N.J.: Prentice Hall, 1971), 87.

17. Coulter, *Confederate States of America*, 207–208; Faust et al., *Encyclopedia of the Civil War*, 761–762; Thomas, *Confederate State of Richmond*, 112; Thomas, *Confederacy as a Revolutionary Experience*, 88–90.

18. Coulter, *Confederate States of America*, 203–204, 210.

19. Thomas, *Confederacy as a Revolutionary Experience*, 88–89.

20. Coulter, *Confederate States of America*, 214–217; Eaton, *History of the Southern Confederacy*, 241–243; Massey, *Ersatz in the Confederacy*, 160–161 (quotations).

21. Coulter, *Confederate States of America*, 212; Roland, *Confederacy*, 68; Thomas, *Confederate State of Richmond*, 112.

22. Massey, *Ersatz in the Confederacy*, 160.

23. Catherine Clinton, "'Public Women' and Sexual Politics during the Civil War," in Clinton and Silber, *Battle Scars*, 70–73 (quotation on 71).

24. David Williams, *A People's History of the Civil War: Struggles for the Meaning of Freedom* (New York: New Press, 2005), 96–97.

25. Coulter, *Confederate States of America*, 236–237; Williams, *People's History of the Civil War*, 97–98; Eaton, *History of the Southern Confederacy*, 243.

26. Coulter, *Confederate States of America*, 236–238.

27. Massey, *Ersatz in the Confederacy*, 159.

28. Massey, *Ersatz in the Confederacy*, 161–162.

29. James A. Huston, "Roads," in Richard N. Current et al., eds., *Encyclopedia of the Confederacy* (New York: Simon and Schuster, 4 vols., 1993), 3:1338–1340.

30. Otto, *Southern Agriculture during the Civil War*, 27.

31. Robert C. Black III, *The Railroads of the Confederacy* (Chapel Hill: University of North Carolina Press, 2nd ed., 1998), 5 (quotation), chart following xxi.

32. Black, *Railroads of the Confederacy*, 3.

33. Black, *Railroads of the Confederacy*, 4–5, 7: Charles S. Davis, *The Cotton Kingdom in Alabama* (Montgomery: Alabama State Department of Archives and History, 1939), 129.

34. Black, *Railroads of the Confederacy*, 9–10, 21–25, 124–130.

CHAPTER 3

1. *Charleston Mercury*, June 15, 1861.

2. King, *Anna Long Thomas Fuller's Journal*, 32.

3. Massey, *Ersatz in the Confederacy*, 55; Ella Lonn, *Salt as a Factor in the Confederacy* (Tuscaloosa: University of Alabama Press, reprint, 1965).

4. Massey, *Ersatz in the Confederacy*, 79–80; Ramsdell, *Behind the Lines*, 43; Coulter, *Confederate States of America*, 210.

5. Robertson, *Civil War Virginia*, 108.

6. Soldiers' Wives to Zebulon B. Vance, March 21, 1863, Vance, Governors Papers.

7. Katherine M. Jones, ed., *Heroines of Dixie: Confederate Women Tell Their Story of the War* (New York: Bobbs-Merrill Co., 1955), 276–277.

8. William A. Graham to Zebulon B. Vance, February 21, 1863, Vance, Governors Papers.

9. Massey, *Ersatz in the Confederacy*, 99, 105–113, 157; Coulter, *Confederate States of America*, 210–218; Eaton, *History of the Southern Confederacy*, 241–243.

10. Massey, *Ersatz in the Confederacy*, 87.

11. Massey, *Ersatz in the Confederacy*, 61.

12. Woodward, *Mary Chesnut's Civil War*, 584.

13. *Advertiser and Register*, January 12, 16, February 5, 1865.

14. Massey, *Ersatz in the Confederacy*, 61–69, 72–76.

15. Massey, *Ersatz in the Confederacy*, 87–89.

16. Massey, *Ersatz in the Confederacy*, 81, 90–91, 97.

17. Massey, *Ersatz in the Confederacy*, 99–113, 139–157.

18. Todd, *Confederate Finance*, 35–45; Ramsdell, *Behind the Lines*, 12, 23; *Advertiser and Register*, January 8, 1865.

19. Robertson, *Civil War Virginia*, 109.

20. Ramsdell, *Behind the Lines*, 75; Walter J. Fraser Jr., *Charleston! Charleston! The History of a Southern City* (Columbia: University of South Carolina Press, 1989), 265.

21. King, *Anna Long Thomas Fuller's Journal*, 32.

22. Lida Lord Reed, "A Woman's Experience during the Siege of Vicksburg," in Waugh and Greenburg, *Women's War in the South*, 84.

23. Reed, "Woman's Experience during the Siege of Vicksburg," 89–90, 91.

24. Woodward, *Mary Chesnut's Civil War*, 747.

25. Thomas, *Confederate State of Richmond*, 119–122; Emory M. Thomas, "The Richmond Bread Riot of 1863," *Virginia Cavalcade* 18 (summer 1968): 41–47; Michael B. Chesson, "Harlots or Heroines? A New Look at the Richmond Bread Riot," *Virginia Magazine of History and Biography* 92 (April 1984): 131–175; Cooper, *Jefferson Davis*, 482.

26. Frank Moore, ed., *The Rebellion Record: A Diary of American Events, with Documents, Narratives, Illustrative Incidents, Poetry, Etc.* (New York: G. P. Putnam, 11 vols., 1868), 7:98.

27. Williams, *People's History of the Civil War*, 174–175.

28. John G. Barrett, *The Civil War in North Carolina* (Chapel Hill: University of North Carolina Press, 1963), 188; *Carolina Watchman* (Salisbury), March 23, 1863.

29. Soldiers' Wives to Zebulon B. Vance, March 21, 1863, Vance, Governors Papers.

30. Yearns and Barrett, *North Carolina Civil War Documentary*, 220–221.

31. Williams, *People's History of the Civil War*, 175–176.

32. *Memphis Daily Appeal*, June 15, 1861.

33. Bell Irvin Wiley, *Plain People of the Confederacy* (Baton Rouge: Louisiana State University Press, 1944), 42; Ramsdell, *Behind the Lines*, 61–82, 89–91; Paul D. Escott, "Poverty and

Governmental Aid for the Poor in Confederate North Carolina," *North Carolina Historical Review* 61 (October 1984): 462–480; T. Conn Bryan, *Confederate Georgia* (Athens: University of Georgia Press, 1953), 71–73, 102; Joe A. Mobley, *"War Governor of the South": North Carolina's Zeb Vance in the Confederacy* (Gainesville: University Press of Florida, 2005), 158–161, 163.

34. Paul D. Escott, "'The Cry of the Sufferers': The Problem of Welfare in the Confederacy," *Civil War History* 23 (September 1977): 228–240.

35. Ramsdell, *Behind the Lines*, 61.

36. Louise B. Hill, *State Socialism in the Confederate States of America* (Charlottesville, VA: Historical Publishing Co., 1936), 3.

37. Massey, *Ersatz in the Confederacy*, 33.

38. Massey, *Ersatz in the Confederacy*, 6.

39. Ramsdell, *Behind the Lines*, 21–23; Coulter, *Confederate States of America*, 223–232.

40. *Picayune* (New Orleans), January 29, February 15, 1865.

41. Williams, *People's History of the Civil War*, 182.

42. Regulators to Zebulon B. Vance, February 18, 1863, Vance, Governors Papers.

43. F. N. Boney, "Virginia," in W. Buck Yearns, ed., *The Confederate Governors* (Athens: University of Georgia Press, 1985), 223.

44. Massey, *Ersatz in the Confederacy*, 17–21.

45. McPherson, *Battle Cry of Freedom*, 616–617; Coulter, *Confederate States of America*, 249–254; Faust et al., *Encyclopedia of the Civil War*, 379; Tatum, *Disloyalty in the Confederacy*, 18; Bryan, *Confederate Georgia*, 92.

46. Zebulon B. Vance to James A. Seddon, December 21, 1863, Vance, Governors Papers.

47. Tatum, *Disloyalty in the Confederacy*, 22–23; Mark Grimsley, *The Hard Hand of War: Union Military Policy toward Southern Civilians* (Cambridge: Cambridge University Press, 1995); John G. Barrett, *Sherman's March through the Carolinas* (Chapel Hill: University of North Carolina Press, 1956).

48. Jacqueline Glass Campbell, *When Sherman Marched North from the Sea: Resistance on the Confederate Home Front* (Chapel Hill: University of North Carolina Press, 2003), 53.

49. Robertson, *Civil War Virginia*, 108.

50. Todd, *Confederate Finance*, 144–148; Emory M. Thomas, *The Confederate Nation, 1861–1865* (New York: Harper and Row, 1979), 197–199; Coulter, *Confederate States of America*, 177–182.

CHAPTER 4

1. Marli F. Weiner, ed., *Heritage of Woe: The Civil War Diary of Grace Brown Elmore, 1861–1868* (Athens: University of Georgia Press, 1997), 22.

2. Randall C. Jimerson, *The Private Civil War: Popular Thought during the Sectional Conflict* (Baton Rouge: Louisiana State University Press, 1980), 213.

3. Moore, *Conscription and Conflict*, 1–26, 114.

4. Moore, *Conscription and Conflict*, 52–54.

5. John Q. Anderson, ed., *Brokenburn: The Journal of Kate Stone, 1861–1868* (Baton Rouge: Louisiana State University Press, 1955), 103.

6. Woodward, *Mary Chesnut's Civil War*, 340.

7. Robertson, *Soldiers Blue and Gray*, 37–38.

8. Moore, *Conscription and Conflict*, 12–19; George C. Rable, *The Confederate Republic: A Revolution against Politics* (Chapel Hill: University of North Carolina Press, 1994), 199–200; Paul D. Escott, *After Secession: Jefferson Davis and the Failure of Confederate Nationalism* (Baton Rouge: Louisiana State University Press, 1978), 80–93 (quotation on 81).

9. Moore, *Conscription and Conflict*, 44–45.

10. Martha Coltrane to Zebulon B. Vance, November 18, 1862, in Frontis W. Johnston and Joe A. Mobley, eds., *The Papers of Zebulon Baird Vance* (Raleigh: North Carolina Office of Archives and History, 2 vols. to date, 1963–), 1:374–375.

11. Moore, *Conscription and Conflict*, 49, 67–68 (quotation on 67–68); Robertson, *Soldiers Blue and Gray*, 38.

12. L. K. Walker to Zebulon B. Vance, January 16, 1863, Vance, Governors Papers.

13. Moore, *Conscription and Conflict*, 73–74; William C. Davis, *Look Away! A History of the Confederate States of America* (New York: Free Press, 2002), 235–236.

14. Carl H. Moneyhon, *The Impact of the Civil War and Reconstruction on Arkansas: Persistence in the Midst of Ruin* (Baton Rouge: Louisiana State University Press, 1994), 112–113.

15. Moore, *Conscription and Conflict*, 308.

16. Robertson, *Soldiers Blue and Gray*, 39–40 (quotation); Escott, *After Secession*, 125–126.

17. Ella Lonn, *Desertion during the Civil War* (New York: Century Company, 1928), 28; Escott, *After Secession*, 126–127.

18. Coulter, *Confederate States of America*, 463–464.

19. John Futch to Martha Futch, August 3, 1863, Futch Letters, Private Collections, State Archives, North Carolina Office of Archives and History, Raleigh.

20. John Futch to Martha Futch, August 6, 1863, Futch Letters; Louis H. Manarin and Weymouth T. Jordan Jr., comps., *North Carolina Troops: A Roster* (Raleigh: North Carolina Office of Archives and History, 15 vols. to date, 1966–), 3:593.

21. Jones, *Heroines of Dixie*, 348.

22. Eaton, *History of the Southern Confederacy*, 261; Robertson, *Soldiers Blue and Gray*, 79–80, 132–136 (quotation on 79).

23. Robert D. Graham to William A. Graham, August 20, 1863, in J. G. de Roulhac Hamilton, Max R. Williams, and Mary Reynolds Peacock, eds., *The Papers of William Alexander Graham* (Raleigh: North Carolina Office of Archives and History, 8 vols., 1957–1992), 5:520–522.

24. J. G. de Roulhac Hamilton, "North Carolina Courts and the Confederacy," *North Carolina Historical Review* 4 (October 1927): 366–371.

25. Zebulon B. Vance to Jefferson Davis, May 13, 1863, Vance, Governors Letter Books, State Archives, North Carolina Office of Archives and History, Raleigh.

26. Lonn, *Desertion during the Civil War*, 25–27; Richard E. Beringer, Herman Hattaway, Archer Jones, and William N. Still Jr., *Why the South Lost the Civil War* (Athens: University of Georgia Press, 1986), 434–435; Robertson, *Soldiers Blue and Gray*, 135.

27. Lonn, *Desertion during the Civil War*, 226, 231; Escott, *After Secession*, 127.

28. Escott, *After Secession*, 128.

29. Lonn, *Desertion during the Civil War*, 62–91; William T. Auman, "Neighbor against Neighbor: The Inner Civil War in the Randolph County Area of Confederate North Carolina," *North Carolina Historical Review* 61 (January 1984): 59–92.

30. Daniel W. Crofts, *Reluctant Confederates: Upper South Unionists in the Secession Crisis* (Chapel Hill: University of North Carolina Press, 1989); Thomas, *Confederate Nation*, 234; John C. Inscoe and Gordon B. McKinney, *The Heart of Confederate Appalachia: Western North Carolina in the Civil War* (Chapel Hill: University of North Carolina Press, 2000), 105–138.

31. Phillip Shaw Paludan, *Victims: A True Story of the Civil War* (Knoxville: University of Tennessee Press, 1981).

32. William H. Nulty, *Confederate Florida: The Road to Olustee* (Tuscaloosa: University of Alabama Press, 1990), 31, 38–39.

33. Thomas, *Confederacy as a Revolutionary Experience*, 104–105.

34. Coulter, *Confederate States of America*, 87–88.

35. Bryan, *Confederate Georgia*, 137–139.

36. John B. Robbins, "The Confederacy and the Writ of Habeas Corpus," *Georgia Historical Quarterly* 55 (spring 1971): 83–101; William B. Robinson Jr., *Justice in Gray: A History of the Judicial System of the Confederate States of America* (Cambridge, Mass.: Harvard University Press, 1941); Neely, *Southern Rights*, 11–28, 162 (quotation on 162); Thomas, *Confederate State of Richmond*, 81–84; Thomas, *Confederacy as a Revolutionary Experience*, 63–64.

37. Moneyhon, *Impact of the Civil War and Reconstruction on Arkansas*, 110–111.

38. Neely, *Southern Rights*, 51–54.

39. Moore, *Conscription and Conflict*, 44–45.

40. Memory F. Mitchell, *Legal Aspects of Conscription and Exemption in North Carolina* (Chapel Hill: University of North Carolina Press, 1965), 3–60; Hamilton, "North Carolina Courts and the Confederacy," 366–371.

41. Richard E. Yates, "Governor Vance and the Peace Movement," Part 2, *North Carolina Historical Review* 17 (April 1940): 92–93.

42. Cooper, *Jefferson Davis*, 510–511; Escott, *After Secession*, 201–202.

43. Roland, *Confederacy*, 130.

44. J. G. Randall and David Donald, *The Civil War and Reconstruction* (Lexington, Mass.: D. C. Heath and Co., 2nd ed., 1969), 363–364, 506; McPherson, *Battle Cry of Freedom*, 556–558, 664–665.

45. Roland, *Confederacy*, 126–127.

46. Roland, *Confederacy*, 144–145.

47. Tatum, *Disloyalty in the Confederacy*, 24–35; William T. Auman and David D. Scarboro, "The Heroes of America in North Carolina," *North Carolina Historical Review* 58 (October 1981): 327–363; Auman, "Neighbor against Neighbor," 59–92.

48. Mobley, *"War Governor of the South,"* 113–126; William C. Harris, *William Woods Holden: Firebrand of North Carolina Politics* (Baton Rouge: Louisiana State University Press, 1987), 127–155.

49. McPherson, *Battle Cry of Freedom*, 693–694.

50. Roland, *Confederacy*, 127.

51. *North Carolina Standard* (Raleigh), November 17, 1863; W. Buck Yearns Jr., "North Carolina and the Confederate Congress," *North Carolina Historical Review* 27 (July 1952):

359–378; John L. Cheney Jr., ed., *North Carolina Government, 1585–1979: A Narrative and Statistical History* (Raleigh: North Carolina Department of Secretary of State, 1981), 388–389.

52. *Dictionary of North Carolina Biography*, s.v. "Leach, James Thomas."

53. Roland, *Confederacy*, 61–62, 77–78, 98–99; Robert E. Corlew, "Henry S. Foote," in Current et al., *Encyclopedia of the Confederacy*, 2:597–600; Coulter, *Confederate States of America*, 550.

54. McPherson, *Battle Cry of Freedom*, 822–824; David Donald, *Lincoln* (New York: Simon and Schuster, 1995), 556–561.

CHAPTER 5

1. John Hope Franklin and Alfred A. Moss Jr., *From Slavery to Freedom: A History of African Americans* (New York: Alfred A. Knopf, 8th ed., 2000), 220–244; Litwack, *Been in the Storm So Long*, 3–63, 133–139.

2. Horace James, *Annual Report of the Superintendent of Negro Affairs in North Carolina, 1864: With an Appendix Containing the History and Management of the Freedmen in This Department up to June 1st 1865* (Boston: W. P. Brown Printers, n.d.), 43–44.

3. Woodward, *Mary Chesnut's Civil War*, 464.

4. Mary Stark, "Living with the Enemy: The Jefferson Davis Family and Their Servants," *American History* 41 (April 2006): 57–62, 73 (quotations on 61, 62).

5. David M. Potter, *The Impending Crisis, 1848–1861* (New York: Harper and Row, 1976), 371–384; Franklin and Moss, *From Slavery to Freedom*, 70, 101–102, 158–166; James M. McPherson, *The Struggle for Equality: Abolitionists and the Negro in the Civil War and Reconstruction* (Princeton: Princeton University Press, 1964); Stephen B. Oates, *The Fires of Jubilee* (New York: Harper and Row, 1975).

6. Franklin and Moss, *From Slavery to Freedom*, 233.

7. Anderson, *Brokenburn*, 33, 37.

8. Franklin and Moss, *From Slavery to Freedom*, 233.

9. Bell Irvin Wiley, *Southern Negroes, 1861–1865* (New Haven, CT: Yale University Press, 1938), 5.

10. James M. McPherson, *The Negro's Civil War: How Negroes Felt and Acted during the War for the Union* (New York: Vintage Books, 1965), 56–57.

11. George P. Rawick, ed., *The American Slave: A Composite Autobiography* (Westport, CN: Greenwood Press, 19 vols., 1972–1977), 14, pt. 2:227–228.

12. Litwack, *Been in the Storm So Long*, 52.

13. Wiley, *Southern Negroes*, 206; Patricia Click, *Time Full of Trial: The Roanoke Island Freedmen's Colony, 1862–1867* (Chapel Hill: University of North Carolina Press, 2001), 1–17; Joe A. Mobley, *James City: A Black Community in North Carolina, 1863–1900* (Raleigh: North Carolina Office of Archives and History, 1981), 22–25.

14. Willie Lee Rose, *Rehearsal for Reconstruction: The Port Royal Experiment* (New York: Bobbs-Merrill Co., 1964).

15. Janet Sharp Hermann, *The Pursuit of a Dream* (New York: Oxford University Press, 1981), 37–60 (quotations on 60).

16. Ira Berlin et al., eds., *The Wartime Genesis of Free Labor: The Lower South*, series 1, vol. 3 of *Freedom: A Documentary History of Emancipation, 1861–1867* (Cambridge: Cambridge University Press, 1990), 621–627; James, *Annual Report of the Superintendent of Negro Affairs*, 8.

17. Wiley, *Southern Negroes*, 175–177, 195–196; Randall and Donald, *Civil War and Reconstruction*, 371–372; Allen C. Guelzo, *Lincoln's Emancipation Proclamation: The End of Slavery* (New York: Simon and Schuster, 2004), 5–6, 37–54, 63–65, 73–75.

18. Joseph T. Glatthaar, *Forged in Battle: The Civil War Alliance of Black Soldiers and White Officers* (New York: Free Press, 1990), 6–10; Wiley, *Southern Negroes*, 295–344; Dudley Taylor Cornish, *The Sable Arm: Negro Troops in the Union Army* (New York: Longmans, Green, and Co., 1956), x–xii, 56–57, 129–130; Guelzo, *Lincoln's Emancipation Proclamation*, 217–218; John David Smith, ed., *Black Soldiers in Blue: African American Troops in the Civil War Era* (Chapel Hill: University of North Carolina Press, 2002).

19. George F. Winston to a friend or neighbor, February 15, 1863, New Bern Occupation Papers, Southern Historical Collection, University of North Carolina Library, Chapel Hill.

20. King, *Anna Long Thomas Fuller's Journal*, 46.

21. Wiley, *Plain People of the Confederacy*, 84.

22. Coulter, *Confederate States of America*, 265–266; Mobley, *"War Governor of the South,"* 76–98; Cooper, *Jefferson Davis*, 439–440.

23. John Cimprich and Robert C. Mainfort Jr., "The Fort Pillow Massacre: A Statistical Note," *Journal of American History* 76 (December 1989): 830–837; Andrew Ward, *River Run Red: The Fort Pillow Massacre in the American Civil War* (New York: Viking Penguin, 2005); Weymouth T. Jordan Jr. and Gerald W. Thomas, "Massacre at Plymouth: April 20, 1864," *North Carolina Historical Review* 72 (April 1995): 125–193.

24. Coulter, *Confederate States of America*, 258–259; Harrison A. Trexler, "The Opposition of Planters to the Employment of Slaves as Laborers in the Confederacy," *Mississippi Valley Historical Review* 27 (June 1941): 220.

25. Zebulon B. Vance to James A. Seddon, February 12, 1863, Vance, Governors Letter Books.

26. Zebulon B. Vance to William H. C. Whiting, May 21, 1863, Vance, Governors Letter Books.

27. Robert F. Durden, *The Gray and the Black: The Confederate Debate on Emancipation* (Baton Rouge: Louisiana State University Press, 1972), 24, 30, 35, 79, 121, 124; McPherson, *Battle Cry of Freedom*, 832–834; Mark L. Bradley, "'This Monstrous Proposition': North Carolina and the Confederate Debate on Arming the Slaves," *North Carolina Historical Review* 80 (April 2003): 159–163, 166.

28. Bradley, "'This Monstrous Proposition,'" 173–174.

29. McPherson, *Battle Cry of Freedom*, 836.

30. Beth G. Crabtree and James W. Patton, eds., *"Journal of a Secesh Lady": The Diary of Catherine Ann Devereux Edmondston, 1860–1866* (Raleigh: North Carolina Office of Archives and History, reprint, 1995), 651.

31. Eaton, *History of the Southern Confederacy*, 265.

32. *Milton Chronicle*, November 4, 1864.

33. Escott, *After Secession*, 253.

34. Thomas, *Confederate Nation*, 296–297; Eaton, *History of the Southern Confederacy*, 265; McPherson, *Battle Cry of Freedom*, 837.

35. Bruce Levine, *Confederate Emancipation: Southern Plans to Free and Arm Slaves during the Civil War* (New York: Oxford University Press, 2006), 153.

36. Ervin L. Jordan Jr., "Free Blacks," in Current et al., *Encyclopedia of the Confederacy*, 2:642; Ira Berlin, *Slaves without Masters: The Free Negro in the Antebellum South* (New York: Pantheon Books, 1974), 108, 176, 278–279.

37. Jordan, "Free Blacks," 642; Berlin, *Slaves without Masters*, 223–226; Thomas, *Confederate State of Richmond*, 29; William L. Barney, *The Secessionist Impulse: Alabama and Mississippi in 1860* (Princeton, N.J.: Princeton University Press, 1974), 216; James Benson Sellers, *Slavery in Alabama* (Tuscaloosa: University of Alabama Press, 1964), 232.

38. Yearns and Barrett, *North Carolina Civil War Documentary*, 250.

39. Wade, *Slavery in the Cities*, 248–249; Carter G. Woodson, ed., *Free Negro Owners of Slaves in the United States in 1830* (Washington, D.C.: Association for the Study of Negro Life and History, 1924), 1; Loren Schweninger, "John Carruthers Stanly and the Anomaly of Black Slaveholding," *North Carolina Historical Review* 67 (April 1990): 159–192.

40. Jordan, "Free Blacks," 643; Caryn Cosse Bell, "Free Creoles of Color," in Current et al., *Encyclopedia of the Confederacy*, 2:645 (quotation); McPherson, *Negro's Civil War*, 24.

41. *Advertiser and Register*, March 24, 1865.

42. R. L. Gibson to D. H. Maury, April 8, 1865, "The Negro in the Military Service of the United States, 1639–1886," Records of the Adjutant General of the United States, Record Group 94, Microcopy 858, National Archives, Washington, D.C.

43. *Memphis Daily Appeal*, May 14, 1861.

44. Wiley, *Southern Negroes*, 160–162; Berlin, *Slaves without Masters*, 89–107 (quotation on 89); Jordan, "Free Blacks," 643.

45. Ella Lonn, *Foreigners in the Confederacy* (Chapel Hill: University of North Carolina Press, 1940), 1, 30.

46. Lonn, *Foreigners in the Confederacy*, 29–31.

47. Lonn, *Foreigners in the Confederacy*, 3, 481; Coulter, *Confederate States of America*, 409; Herbert Weaver, "Foreigners in Ante-bellum Towns of the Lower South," *Journal of Southern History* 13 (February 1947): 65–66; U.S. Bureau of the Census, *Eighth Census of the United States, 1860: Population Schedule*, 228.

48. Weaver, "Foreigners in Ante-bellum Towns," 65–69.

49. Lonn, *Foreigners in the Confederacy*, 338–339.

50. Lonn, *Foreigners in the Confederacy*, 132–139, 318–342; Jason H. Silverman, "Foreigners," in Current et al., *Encyclopedia of the Confederacy*, 2:602–604.

51. Louis E. Schmier, "Jews," in Current et al., *Encyclopedia of the Confederacy*, 2:845–846; Eaton, *History of the Southern Confederacy*, 150; Eli N. Evans, *Judah P. Benjamin: The Jewish Confederate* (New York: Free Press, 1988), 47–48, 306; Lonn, *Foreigners in the Confederacy*, 336.

52. Peter F. Walker, *Vicksburg: A People at War, 1860–1865* (Chapel Hill: University of North Carolina Press, 1960), 77–78.

53. Lonn, *Foreigners in the Confederacy*, 2, 335–336.

54. Lonn, *Foreigners in the Confederacy*, 337.

55. Massey, *Refugee Life in the Confederacy*, 81.

56. Coulter, *Confederate States of America*, 223.

57. Lonn, *Foreigners in the Confederacy*, 13–18; Jason H. Silverman, "Germans," in Current et al., *Encyclopedia of the Confederacy*, 2:675–676.

CHAPTER 6

1. George C. Rable, "Refugeeing," in Current et al., *Encyclopedia of the Confederacy*, 3:1318.

2. Massey, *Refugee Life in the Confederacy*, 68, 114.

3. Massey, *Refugee Life in the Confederacy*, 5, 28–29.

4. Crabtree and Patton, *"Journal of a Secesh Lady,"* 117, 119.

5. Massey, *Refugee Life in the Confederacy*, 68.

6. Massey, *Refugee Life in the Confederacy*, 48–49, 71–74, 93.

7. Walker, *Vicksburg*, 77.

8. Massey, *Refugee Life in the Confederacy*, 78–80.

9. Crabtree and Patton, *"Journal of a Secesh Lady,"* 176.

10. Massey, *Refugee Life in the Confederacy*, 80–81.

11. Barrett, *Civil War in North Carolina*, 350–366.

12. Massey, *Refugee Life in the Confederacy*, 81–83.

13. Woodward, *Mary Chesnut's Civil War*, 716, 718–719.

14. Massey, *Refugee Life in the Confederacy*, 83–85; Edward M. Shoemaker, "Savannah," in Current et al., *Encyclopedia of the Confederacy*, 3:1366; Bryan, *Confederate Georgia*, 71–73, 102.

15. Massey, *Refugee Life in the Confederacy*, 86.

16. Massey, *Refugee Life in the Confederacy*, 86–87, 256; Walter Lord, ed., *The Fremantle Diary: Being the Journal of Lieutenant Colonel Arthur James Lyon Fremantle, Coldstream Guards, on His Three Months in the Southern States* (Boston: Little, Brown, and Co., 1954), 105.

17. Massey, *Refugee Life in the Confederacy*, 88–90; William C. Harris, *With Charity for All: Lincoln and the Restoration of the Union* (Lexington: University Press of Kentucky, 1997), 23–32.

18. Massey, *Refugee Life in the Confederacy*, 90–92.

19. Anderson, *Brokenburn*, 191.

20. Massey, *Refugee Life in the Confederacy*, 92–93; *Eighth Census of the United States, 1860: Population Schedule*, 228; Clement Eaton, *The Growth of Southern Civilization, 1790–1860* (New York: Harper and Row, 1961), 248–249; Coulter, *Confederate States of America*, 409.

21. Thomas, *Confederate State of Richmond*, 16, 21–24, 29–30; Michael B. Chesson, "Richmond, Virginia," in Current et al., *Encyclopedia of the Confederacy*, 3:1329–1333.

22. Robertson, *Civil War Virginia*, 9, 15, 43, 114; Robert M. Browning Jr., *From Cape Charles to Cape Fear: The North Atlantic Blockading Squadron during the Civil War* (Tuscaloosa: University of Alabama Press, 1993), 41, 52, 160; McPherson, *Battle Cry of Freedom*, 423–427.

23. Eaton, *Growth of Southern Civilization*, 53, 143–147, 241; Stephen R. Wise, *Lifeline of the Confederacy: Blockade Running during the Civil War* (Columbia: University of South Carolina Press, 1988), 21–23, 74–89; Harris, *With Charity for All*, 171–196.

24. Edward L. Ullman, "Mobile: Industrial Seaport and Trade Center" (Ph.D. diss., University of Chicago, 1943), 17; Peter J. Hamilton, *Mobile of the Five Flags* (Mobile, AL: Gill Printing Co., 1913), 269–270; Davis, *Cotton Kingdom in Alabama*, 129, 140; Weymouth T. Jordan, "Antebellum Mobile: Alabama's Agricultural Emporium," *Alabama Review* 1 (July 1948): 200.

25. Eaton, *Growth of South Civilization*, 249; Wise, *Lifeline of the Confederacy*, 17–18 (quotation on 18); Bryan, *Confederate Georgia*, 58, 71–73, 102, 172, 223.

26. Campbell, *When Sherman Marched North from the Sea*, 19.

27. Fraser, *Charleston! Charleston!*, 198–199, 261–270; William W. Freehling, *Prelude to Civil War: The Nullification Controversy in South Carolina, 1816–1836* (New York: Harper and Row, 1965), 39–42.

28. Wise, *Lifeline of the Confederacy*, 23–24, 86–89, 168.

29. Alan D. Watson, *Wilmington, North Carolina, to 1861* (Jefferson, N.C.: McFarland and Co., 2003), 215–226, 245–247; Barrett, *Civil War in North Carolina*, 244–247; Hugh Talmage Lefler and Albert Ray Newsome, *North Carolina: The History of a Southern State* (Chapel Hill: University of North Carolina Press, 1973), 363–364, 380, 458–459; Catherine W. Bishir and Michael T. Southern, *A Guide to the Historic Architecture of Eastern North Carolina* (Chapel Hill: University of North Carolina Press, 1996), 240, 247, 248.

30. Barrett, *Civil War in North Carolina*, 262–284; Rod Gragg, *Confederate Goliath: The Battle of Fort Fisher* (New York: HarperCollins, 1991).

31. Walter T. Durham, "Nashville, Tennessee," in Current et al., *Encyclopedia of the Confederacy*, 3:1107–1108.

32. Charles F. Bryan Jr., "Chattanooga, Tennessee," in Current et al., *Encyclopedia of the Confederacy*, 1:291–293.

33. McPherson, *Battle Cry of Freedom*, 414–418; Walter T. Durham, "Memphis, Tennessee," in Current et al., *Encyclopedia of the Confederacy*, 3:1028–1030.

34. Bryan, *Confederate Georgia*, 110–111, 164, 165; Ralph B. Singer Jr., "Atlanta, Georgia," in Current et al., *Encyclopedia of the Confederacy*, 1:108–111.

35. Bryan, *Confederate Georgia*, 12, 28, 29, 58, 103; Faust et al., *Encyclopedia of the Civil War*, 30–31.

36. Coulter, *Confederate States of America*, 410.

37. Thomas, *Confederate State of Richmond*, 39, 65, 67.

38. Lowry, *Story the Soldiers Wouldn't Tell*, 77.

39. Wiley, *Life of Johnny Reb*, 53.

40. Lowry, *Story the Soldiers Wouldn't Tell*, 70–71.

41. Thomas, *Confederate State of Richmond*, 68–70, 81–84, 105–107; Coulter, *Confederate States of America*, 411.

42. Fraser, *Charleston! Charleston!*, 256–257.

43. Barrett, *Civil War in North Carolina*, 257.

44. Thad Holt Jr., ed., *Miss Waring's Journal, 1863–1865: Being the Diary of Miss Mary Waring, during the Final Days of the War between the States* (Mobile, AL: Graphics Inc., 1964), 15; *Advertiser and Register*, January 1, 15, 16, February 21, 1865.

45. *Advertiser and Register*, January 24, 1865.

46. Mary Ann Webster Loughborough, *My Cave Life in Vicksburg: With Letters of Trial and Travel: By a Lady* (New York: D. Appleton and Co., 1864); Coulter, *Confederate States of*

America, 412; A. A. Hoehling, *Last Train from Atlanta* (New York: Thomas Yoseloff, 1958); Marion Brunson Lucas, *Sherman and the Burning of Columbia* (Columbia: University of South Carolina Press, reprint, 2000); Campbell, *When Sherman Marched North from the Sea*, 6, 59; Grimsley, *Hard Hand of War*, 142–143, 169, 191.

47. *Advertiser and Register*, July 24, 1864.

48. Roark, "Behind the Lines," 223–224.

49. Thomas, *Confederacy as a Revolutionary Experience*, 93–99.

50. David R. Goldfield, *Cotton Fields and Skyscrapers: Southern City and Region, 1607–1980* (Baton Rouge: Louisiana State University Press, 1982), 81–82.

CHAPTER 7

1. Beringer et al., *Why the South Lost the Civil War*, 95; James W. Silver, *Confederate Morale and Church Propaganda* (New York: W. W. Norton and Co., reprint, 1967), 78–80, 93.

2. Thomas, *Confederacy as a Revolutionary Experience*, 117.

3. Beringer et al., *Why the South Lost the Civil War*, 85–86, 496–497n; Silver, *Confederate Morale and Church Propaganda*, 16–22, 93–94 (quotation on 93–94).

4. Beringer et al., *Why the South Lost the Civil War*, 84, 85; Silver, *Confederate Morale and Church Propaganda*, 16, 23, 25, 52; Charles S. Sydnor, *The Development of Southern Sectionalism, 1819–1848* (Baton Rouge: Louisiana State University Press, 1948), 297–299.

5. Silver, *Confederate Morale and Church Propaganda*, 26, 28, 60, 61, 75.

6. Beringer et al., *Why the South Lost the Civil War*, 85, 86, 90–100.

7. Schmier, "Jews," 845.

8. Silver, *Confederate Morale and Church Propaganda*, 72, 73.

9. Silver, *Confederate Morale and Church Propaganda*, 42–63 (quotation on 51).

10. *Memphis Daily Appeal*, August 4, 1861.

11. Silver, *Confederate Morale and Church Propaganda*, 32, 36.

12. Beringer et al., *Why the South Lost the Civil War*, 98.

13. Weiner, *Heritage of Woe*, 108.

14. Roark, "Behind the Lines," 219–220.

15. Silver, *Confederate Morale and Church Propaganda*, 31, 36, 53.

16. Weiner, *Heritage of Woe*, 106.

17. Harry S. Stout, *Upon the Altar of the Nation: A Moral History of the American Civil War* (New York: Viking, 2006), 85–90.

18. Poor Woman and Children to Zebulon B. Vance, January 10, 1865, Vance, Governors Papers.

19. Beringer et al., *Why the South Lost the Civil War*, 354–367.

20. Silver, *Confederate Morale and Church Propaganda*, 55.

21. Clement Eaton, *The Waning of the Old South Civilization, 1860–1880's* (Athens: University of Georgia Press, 1968), 104–105; *Dictionary of North Carolina Biography*, s.v. "Bingham, William"; Fleming, *Civil War and Reconstruction in Alabama*, 214–216.

22. Eaton, *Waning of the Old South Civilization*, 106.

23. Karen C. Carroll, "Sterling, Campbell, and Albright: Textbook Publishers, 1861–1865," *North Carolina Historical Review* 63 (April 1986): 170–172.

24. Carroll, "Sterling, Campbell, and Albright," 173–174.

25. Carroll, "Sterling, Campbell, and Albright," 178–180, 198; Coulter, *Confederate States of America*, 518–519.

26. Massey, *Ersatz in the Confederacy*, 143; Coulter, *Confederate States of America*, 517–518; Fleming, *Civil War and Reconstruction in Alabama*, 217.

27. Roland, *Confederacy*, 162.

28. Carroll, "Sterling, Campbell, and Albright," 196–197.

29. Joseph M. Stetar, "Higher Education," in Current et al., *Encyclopedia of the Confederacy*, 2:517.

30. Eaton, *Waning of the Old South Civilization*, 106–108; Stetar, "Higher Education," 517–518; Roland, *Confederacy*, 163; Coulter, *Confederate States of America*, 519–520.

31. Wiley, *Confederate Women*, 40.

32. Elizabeth Fox-Genovese, "Women's Education," in Current et al., *Encyclopedia of the Confederacy*, 2:520.

33. Victoria E. Bynum, *Unruly Women: The Politics of Social and Sexual Control in the Old South* (Chapel Hill: University of North Carolina Press, 1992), 56.

34. Weiner, *Heritage of Woe*, xxxv–xxxvi, 14, 31.

35. Fox-Genovese, "Women's Education," 520–521.

36. Vincent Colyer, *Report of the Services Rendered by the Freed People to the United States Army, in North Carolina, in the Spring of 1862, after the Battle of New Bern* (New York: Vincent Colyer, 1864), 43–44.

37. James A. Emmerton, *A Record of the Twenty-third Regiment Mass. Vol. Infantry in the War of the Rebellion, 1861–1865* (Boston: William Ware and Co., 1886), 96–97.

38. James, *Annual Report of the Superintendent of Negro Affairs*, 11–12, 39, 41–42; Nancy Smith Linthicum, "The American Missionary Association and North Carolina Freedmen, 1863–1868" (master's thesis, North Carolina State University, 1977), 94–96; January–June entries, 1863, Samuel A. Walker Diary, 1862–1863, Private Collections, State Archives, North Carolina Office of Archives and History, Raleigh.

39. "Monthly Report of a Colored School Taught by Sarah M. Pearson, in New Berne, for the Month of February, 1864," North Carolina Letters, American Missionary Association Archives (microfilm), Amistad Research Center, Tulane University, New Orleans.

40. Susan A. Hosmer to George Whipple, September 11, 1863, North Carolina Letters, American Missionary Association Archives.

41. "Monthly Report of a Colored School Taught by Sarah M. Pearson for the Month of April, 1864," and Susan A. Hosmer to George Whipple, June 10, 1864, North Carolina Letters, American Missionary Association Archives.

42. McPherson, *Negro's Civil War*, 130–131.

43. Hermann, *Pursuit of a Dream*, 54–56.

44. Rose, *Rehearsal for Reconstruction*, 85–89, 229–235.

45. Brenda Stevenson, ed., *The Journal of Charlotte Forten Grimké* (New York: Oxford University Press, 1988), xxxiii, xxxvi, 3–55, 394, 399.

46. McPherson, *Negro's Civil War*, 117.

47. McPherson, *Negro's Civil War*, 116, 119.

48. Rose, *Rehearsal for Reconstruction*, 231–232.

49. McPherson, *Negro's Civil War*, 116–117.

50. Stevenson, *Journal of Charlotte Forten Grimké*, xxxvi–xl, 49–55.

51. Rose, *Rehearsal for Reconstruction*, 78, 372.

52. Eaton, *Waning of the Old South Civilization*, 96–97.

53. Roland, *Confederacy*, 155; Eaton, *Waning of the Old South Civilization*, 98.

54. Roland, *Confederacy*, 155–156; Eaton, *Waning of the Old South Civilization*, 97–99.

55. Eaton, *Waning of the Old South Civilization*, 94–96.

56. Roland, *Confederacy*, 156; E. Merton Coulter, *The South during Reconstruction* (Baton Rouge: Louisiana State University Press, 1950), 235–237; Russel Blaine Nye, *Society and Culture in America, 1830–1860* (New York: Harper and Row, 1974), 99; Eaton, *Waning of the Old South Civilization*, 92.

57. Eaton, *Waning of the Old South Civilization*, 91–94; Roland, *Confederacy*, 157–158; Eaton, *History of the Southern Confederacy*, 216–217.

58. Woodward, *Mary Chesnut's Civil War*, 347.

59. Massey, *Refugee Life in the Confederacy*, 184.

60. Weiner, *Heritage of Woe*, 93–94.

61. *Advertiser and Register*, January 8, 25, 26, February 8, March 8, 1865.

62. Massey, *Refugee Life in the Confederacy*, 186, 191, 194, 200; Roland, *Confederacy*, 164; Coulter, *Confederate States of America*, 490; Eaton, *Waning of the Old South Civilization*, 100.

63. Holt, *Miss Waring's Journal*, 10–11.

64. Roland, *Confederacy*, 158; Eaton, *Waning of the Old South Civilization*, 100–102; Massey, *Refugee Life in the Confederacy*, 201–202; Coulter, *Confederate States of America*, 486–488.

65. Eaton, *Waning of the Old South Civilization*, 84–85.

66. Coulter, *Confederate States of America*, 486; Eaton, *Waning of the Old South Civilization*, 87.

67. Eaton, *Waning of the Old South Civilization*, 86–87; *Advertiser and Register*, February 12, 16, 24, 28, 1865.

68. Coulter, *Confederate States of America*, 487–489.

69. Eaton, *Waning of the Old South Civilization*, 87; Coulter, *Confederate States of America*, 489–490.

70. Coulter, *Confederate States of America*, 490–493; Eaton, *Waning of the Old South Civilization*, 102–103; Karen L. Cox, *Dixie's Daughters: The United Daughters of the Confederacy and the Preservation of Confederate Culture* (Gainesville: University Press of Florida, 2003).

CHAPTER 8

1. Stephen W. Berry II, *All That Makes a Man: Love and Ambition in the Civil War South* (New York: Oxford University Press, 2003), 86–88.

2. Weiner, *Heritage of Woe*, 40.

3. Eaton, *Waning of the Old South Civilization*, 82.

4. E. Susan Barber, "'The White Wings of Eros': Courtship and Marriage in Richmond," in Catherine Clinton, ed., *Southern Families at War: Loyalty and Conflict in the Civil War South* (New York: Oxford University Press, 2000), 119.

5. Barber, "Courtship and Marriage in Richmond," 120–126 (quotations on 122, 124); Carl N. Degler, *At Odds: Women and the Family in America from the Revolution to the Present* (New York: Oxford University Press, 1980), 165–167.

6. Carol K. Bleser and Frederick M. Heath, "The Impact of the Civil War on a Southern Marriage: Clement and Virginia Tunstall Clay of Alabama," in Waugh and Greenburg, *Women's War in the South*, 72.

7. Degler, *At Odds*, 12–14.

8. Bleser and Heath, "Impact of the Civil War on a Southern Marriage," 72–73.

9. Wiley, *Confederate Women*, 7–10.

10. Wiley, *Confederate Women*, 11–14, 15–17, 19, 32–34 (quotations on 16, 19).

11. Bleser and Heath, "Impact of the Civil War on a Southern Marriage," 370–385 (quotation on 373).

12. Christian G. Samito, "'Patriot by Nature, Christian by Faith': Major General William Dorsey Pender, C.S.A.," *North Carolina Historical Review* 76 (April 1999): 173–174. See also *Dictionary of North Carolina Biography*, s.v. "Pender, William Dorsey," and William W. Kessler, ed., *The General and His Lady: The Civil War Letters of William Dorsey Pender to Fanny Pender* (Gettysburg, Pa.: Ron R. Van Sickle, 1988).

13. Henry Walker, "Power, Sex, and Gender Roles: The Transformation of an Alabama Planter Family during the Civil War," in Clinton, *Southern Families at War*, 184.

14. Lowry, *Story the Soldiers Wouldn't Tell*, 93–94.

15. Drew Gilpin Faust, *Mothers of Invention: Women of the Slaveholding South in the American Civil War* (Chapel Hill: University of North Carolina Press, 1996), 124.

16. Lowry, *Story the Soldiers Wouldn't Tell*, 96–98.

17. Martha Futch to John Futch, February 19, 1863, Futch Letters.

18. Robertson, *Soldiers Blue and Gray*, 103.

19. Walker, "Power, Sex, and Gender Roles," 178–180 (quotation on 179).

20. Delia Jones to Zebulon B. Vance, January 6, 1863, Vance, Governors Papers.

21. Faust, *Mothers of Invention*, 88–92.

22. Stout, *Upon the Altar of the Nation*, 107.

23. Williams, *People's History of the Civil War*, 146.

24. Williams, *People's History of the Civil War*, 144–147.

25. See Alice Miller, *The Drama of the Gifted Child: The Source of the True Self* [originally published as *The Prisoners of Childhood*] (New York: Basic Books, 1981).

26. Miller, *Drama of the Gifted Child*, 10–14, 79.

27. James Marten, *The Children's Civil War* (Chapel Hill: University of North Carolina Press, 1998), 78.

28. Marten, *Children's Civil War*, 87, 116.

29. Marten, *Children's Civil War*, 88, 94.

30. Massey, *Refugee Life in the Confederacy*, 30, 31, 129.

31. Reed, "Woman's Experience during the Siege of Vicksburg," 86, 88.

32. Marten, *Children's Civil War*, 112, 148–172.

33. Massey, *Refugee Life in the Confederacy*, 200–201.

34. Marten, *Children's Civil War*, 6.

35. Michelle A. Krowl, "For Better or Worse: Black Families and 'the State' in Civil War Virginia," in Clinton, *Southern Families at War*, 35–36.

36. Krowl, "For Better or Worse," 38.

37. Krowl, "For Better or Worse," 38–39, 42–43.

38. Ira Berlin, Steven F. Miller, and Leslie S. Rowland, "Afro-American Families in the Transition from Slavery to Freedom," in Donald G. Nieman, ed., *The African American Family in the South, 1861–1900* (New York: Garland Publishing, 1994), 93–94.

39. Genovese, *Roll Jordan Roll*, 458–482; Herbert G. Gutman, *The Black Family in Slavery and Freedom, 1750–1925* (New York: Vintage Books, 1976), 412–418; Donald R. Shaffer, "In the Shadow of the Old Constitution: Black Civil War Veterans and the Persistence of Slave Marriage Customs," in Clinton, *Southern Families at War*, 59–71.

40. Berlin, Miller, and Rowland, "Afro-American Families in the Transition from Slavery to Freedom," 92–93.

41. Krowl, "For Better or Worse," 44.

42. Genovese, *Roll Jordan Roll*, 469.

43. Genovese, *Roll Jordan Roll*, 468–469, 524–527.

44. Gutman, *Black Family in Slavery and Freedom*, 20.

45. Gutman, *Black Family in Slavery and Freedom*, 21.

46. Marten, *Children's Civil War*, 129–158; Krowl, "For Better or Worse," 46–47; Genovese, *Roll Jordan Roll*, 502–519.

47. Genovese, *Roll Jordan Roll*, 413–415.

48. Woodward, *Mary Chesnut's Civil War*, 29.

49. Berry, *All That Makes a Man*, 115.

50. Lowry, *Story the Soldiers Wouldn't Tell*, 109–110.

51. Lowry, *Story the Soldiers Wouldn't Tell*, 123–131; Grimsley, *Hard Hand of War*, 199, 220; Campbell, *When Sherman Marched North from the Sea*, 45–46, 120n; Joseph T. Glatthaar, *The March to the Sea and Beyond: Sherman's Troops in the Savannah and Carolinas Campaigns* (New York: New York University Press, 1985), 73–74.

52. Berry, *All That Makes a Man*, 117.

53. Bleser and Heath, "Impact of the Civil War on a Southern Marriage," 386.

54. Genovese, *Roll Jordan Roll*, 459.

EPILOGUE

1. One exponent of the latter view, James M. McPherson, differentiates between "lacked" and "lost." He insists that "There is a difference—a significant difference" between the two terms. According to him, "A people at war whose armies are destroyed or captured, whose railroads are wrecked, factories and cities are burned, ports seized, countryside occupied, and crops laid waste quite naturally lose their will to continue the fight because they have lost the means to do so." McPherson concludes that "military defeat caused loss of will, not vice versa." James M. McPherson, *Drawn with the Sword: Reflections on the American Civil War* (New York: Oxford University Press, 1996), 128–129.

2. Philip Hodnett to Zebulon B. Vance, July 30, 1863, Vance, Governors Papers.

BIBLIOGRAPHICAL ESSAY

From varying perspectives that have changed over time, generations of historians have addressed topics related to life on the Confederate home front. The following essay discusses my personal selections and recommendations from the many influential books related to conditions in the Civil War South.

Even before Charles H. Wesley and Charles W. Ramsdell, scholars had begun to write about internal aspects of the South's struggle to achieve a victory that would lead to an independent nation. In 1924 Albert B. Moore's *Conscription and Conflict in the Confederacy* effectively described the Confederate government's conscription policies and the demoralizing impact those policies had on many Southerners. The next year Frank L. Owsley's *State Rights in the Confederacy* argued that the Confederate cause crumbled because the central government and its citizens were more concerned with protecting the rights of the states than with supporting a strong national government that could effectively wage war. *Desertion during the Civil War* (1928), written by Ella Lonn, explored the extent of desertion from the Confederate army and how it reflected a growing dissatisfaction among the population with continuing the war. In 1934 Georgia Lee Tatum further revealed the nature of disaffection and a desire for peace in her *Disloyalty in the Confederacy.* Lonn demonstrated the impact that deprivation and shortages of necessities had on the home front in *Salt as a Factor in the Confederacy* (1933). The first scholarly study to treat the role of Southern women was *The Women of the Confederacy* (1936), by Francis B. Simkins and James W. Patton. Louise Bile Hill's *State Socialism in the Confederate States of America* (1936) maintained that the Confederacy's "socialistic" policy for blockade-running helped the aspiring nation survive for a time, but that the government's intervention in private enterprise was too limited and too late to avert defeat. Published in 1938, Bell Irvin Wiley's *Southern Negroes, 1861–1865* was subsequently criticized for its use of stereotypical terms in referring to blacks. Nevertheless, the book widened the serious exploration of African Americans in the Confederacy. Lonn's 1940 study *Foreigners in the Confederacy* introduced a new cast of wartime Southerners. In *Justice in Gray: A History of the Judicial System of the Confederate States of America* (1941), William B. Robinson Jr. examined the courts and laws of the wartime South.

Wesley's *The Collapse of the Confederacy* (1937) was the first work to portray collectively the various aspects of home-front life and to offer the opinion that the Confederacy collapsed because its citizens lacked the will to continue the war until victory was achieved. Ramsdell's 1937 lecture and his *Behind the Lines in the Southern Confederacy* (1944) echoed Wesley's theme and called for more studies about the home front.

A large number of historians answered that call in the next two decades. Mary Elizabeth Massey's singular *Ersatz in the Confederacy: Shortages and Substitutes on the Southern Homefront* (1952) described in detail how Southerners coped with deprivation during the war. Her excellent 1964 work *Refugee Life in the Confederacy* brought to light the plight of those folk who fled their homes to escape the onslaught of an invading army. Scholarly urban studies were introduced with the publication of A. A. Hoehling's *Last Train from Atlanta* (1958); Peter F. Walker's *Vicksburg: A People at War, 1860–1865* (1960); and Fleming Corley's *Confederate City: Augusta, Georgia, 1860–1865* (1960). Published in 1952, *The Railroads of the Confederacy*, by Robert C. Black III, remains the best work on rail transportation. *Agriculture and the Civil War* (1965), by Paul W. Gates, added new information on the nature and role of farms and plantations during the war. The subject of agriculture was further discussed in John Solomon Otto's *Southern Agriculture during the Civil War Era, 1860–1880* (1994). For the role of churches and religion, *Confederate Morale and Church Propaganda* (1957), by James W. Silver, is still the standard source. The best single work on cultural life—literature, art, music, theater—remains Clement Eaton's *The Waning of the Old South Civilization, 1860–1880's* (1968).

General studies from the 1950s and 1960s that are essential reading for today's students of the home front are E. Merton Coulter's *The Confederate States of America, 1861–1865* (1950); Clement Eaton's *A History of the Southern Confederacy* (1954); and Charles P. Roland's *The Confederacy* (1960). An excellent recent general discussion of the home front can be found in William C. Davis's *Look Away! A History of the Confederate States of America* (2002). The four-volume *Encyclopedia of the Confederacy* (1993), edited by Richard N. Current and others, contains much information compiled by Civil War scholars on a variety of topics related to conditions in the South during the sectional conflict.

Since the 1950s probably no subject has commanded more attention than antebellum slavery and the plight of African Americans in the South. Among the many works that provide useful information specifically about the war years are James M. McPherson's *The Negro's Civil War: How Negroes Felt and Acted during the War for the Union* (1965); McPherson's *The Struggle for Equality: Abolitionists and the Negro in the Civil War and Reconstruction* (1964); Willie Lee Rose's *Rehearsal for Reconstruction: The Port Royal Experiment* (1964); Eugene D. Genovese's *Roll Jordan Roll: The World the Slaves Made* (1974); Herbert G. Gutman's *The Black Family in Slavery and Freedom, 1750–1925* (1976); James L. Roark's *Masters without Slaves: Southern Planters in the Civil War and Reconstruction* (1977); Leon F. Litwack's *Been in the Storm So Long: The Aftermath of Slavery* (1979); Janet Sharp Hermann's *The Pursuit of a Dream* (1981); and Patricia Click's *Time Full of Trial: The Roanoke Island Freedmen's Colony, 1862–1867* (2001). Helpful for information about former slaves who joined the Union army are Joseph T. Glatthaar's *Forged in Battle: The Civil War Alliance of Black Soldiers and White Officers* (1990), and *Black Soldiers in Blue: African American Troops in the Civil War Era* (2002), edited by John David Smith. The immediate impact that the Emancipation Proclamation had in the Confederacy is best described in Allen C. Guelzo's *Lincoln's Emancipation Proclamation: The End of Slavery* (2004). The Confederacy's last-minute, desperate attempt to emancipate slaves and enlist them into the Confederate army is well covered in Robert F. Durden's *The Gray and the Black: The Confederate Debate on Emancipation* (1972) and Bruce Levine's *Confederate Emancipation: Southern Plans to Free and Arm Slaves during the Civil War* (2006). The topic of free blacks in the Confederacy deserves more attention from historians. But useful—even though it deals primarily with the antebellum era—is Ira Berlin's *Slaves without Masters: The Free Negro in the Antebellum South* (1974). An indispensable source for studying African Americans during the Civil War and Reconstruction is the ongoing multivolume series *Freedom: A Documentary History of Emancipation, 1861–1867*, compiled and edited by Ira Berlin, Leslie S. Rowland, and others.

With the exception of African American slaves, probably no group had their lives so changed by the Civil War as did the women of the South. For decades diaries and journals of upper-class women such as Mary Boykin Chesnut have been part of the history of the war. More recently, however, historians have expanded their investigations to include working-class women. Among the important studies of women in the Confederacy are *Civil Wars: Women and the Crisis of Southern Nationalism* (1989), by George C. Rable; *Mothers of Invention: Women of the Slaveholding South in the American Civil War* (1996), by Drew Gilpin Faust; *Unruly Women: The Politics of Social and Sexual Control in the Old South* (1992), by Victoria E. Bynum; *Divided Houses: Gender and the Civil War* (1992), edited by Catherine Clinton and Nina Silber; and *The Civil War as a Crisis in Gender: Augusta, Georgia, 1860–1890* (1995), by Lee Ann Whites.

Recently the topics of marriage, sexual relations, family, and children have received some attention. Significant contributions on these subjects include *All That Makes a Man: Love and Ambition in the Civil War South* (2003), by Stephen W. Berry II; *The*

Story the Soldiers Wouldn't Tell: Sex in the Civil War (1994), by Thomas P. Lowry; *Southern Families at War: Loyalty and Conflict in the Civil War South* (2000), edited by Catherine Clinton; *Battle Scars: Gender and Sexuality in the American Civil War* (2006), edited by Catherine Clinton and Nina Silber; and *The Children's Civil War* (1998), by James Marten.

Works that shed light on Confederate loyalty and wartime Unionism in the South include Daniel W. Crofts's *Reluctant Confederates: Upper South Unionists in the Secession Crisis* (1989); *The Heart of Confederate Appalachia: Western North Carolina in the Civil War* (2000), by John C. Inscoe and Gordon B. McKinney; and William W. Freehling's *The South vs. the South: How Anti-Confederate Southerners Shaped the Course of the Civil War* (2001). The depths of violence that resulted from divided loyalties are graphically illustrated in Phillip Shaw Paludan's *Victims: A True Story of the Civil War* (1981).

The nature of the hardship endured by the population as Northern troops invaded the South is well recounted in Joseph T. Glatthaar's *The March to the Sea and Beyond: Sherman's Troops in the Savannah and Carolinas Campaigns* (1985); Mark Grimsley's *The Hard Hand of War: Union Military Policy toward Southern Civilians* (1995); and Jacqueline Glass Campbell's *When Sherman Marched North from the Sea: Resistance on the Confederate Home Front* (2003). David Williams's *A People's History of the Civil War: Struggles for the Meaning of Freedom* (2005) gives a broad account of both the Northern and Southern home fronts and argues that the Civil War was a "rich man's war" inflicted on a reluctant working class. In *Upon the Altar of the Nation: A Moral History of the American Civil War* (2006), author Harry S. Stout examines the question of the morality of the war as considered by the populations in both the North and the South.

Perceptive discussions of Confederate politics and nationalism include Paul D. Escott's *After Secession: Jefferson Davis and the Failure of Confederate Nationalism* (1978); Emory M. Thomas's *The Confederate Nation, 1861–1865* (1979); Drew Gilpin Faust's *The Creation of Confederate Nationalism: Ideology and Identity in the Civil War South* (1988); William C. Davis's *"A Government of Our Own": The Making of the Confederacy* (1994); and George C. Rable's *The Confederate Republic: A Revolution against Politics* (1994). Thomas's *The Confederacy as a Revolutionary Experience* (1971) introduced the thought-provoking argument that the Confederate war effort produced a sweeping "revolution" in the political, economic, and social milieu of the South. Equally provocative was the influential *Why the South Lost the Civil War* (1986), by Richard E. Beringer, Herman Hattaway, Archer Jones, and William N. Still Jr. The book addressed such topics as Southern nationalism and the role of religion, and it rekindled the perennial debate over the people's "will to win."

INDEX

African Americans. *See* Free blacks;
    Freedmen; Slaves
Agriculture, 19–23. *See also specific
    products*
Alcoholic beverages, 7
Alcoholism, 7–9
Alcorn, James Lusk, 21–22
Allen, Henry W., 74
American Missionary Association, 113
Anderson, Joseph R., 24, 26
Andrew, James O., 104
Angle, Mary Ann, 130
Art, 123
Atlanta, 97
Atlanta Medical College, 97
Augusta, 97–98

Bagby, George W., 117, 118, 127
Banks, Nathaniel P., 114
Barbee, William R., 123
Barksdale, Ethelbert, 59
Bashong, Madam, 77
Beef, 22

Benjamin, Judah P., 81
Betsey (slave), 67
Blockade, Federal, 11, 20, 33, 45
Bolles, C. P., 9–10
Borcke, Heros von, 80
Boston Educational Society, 113
Boyle, Richard, 113
Bradford, Susan, 34
"Bread riots," 42–43
Brown, Joseph E.: appeals for less cotton
    production, 21; demands distilleries close,
    7; objects to conscription, 51; supports
    peace negotiations, 62; urges relief laws,
    44
Buchanan, Felix, 49–50
Bureau of Refugees, Freedmen, and
    Abandoned Lands, 112
Burnadoz, Rosieste, 77
Burnside, Ambrose E., 84
Butler, Benjamin S., 70

Calaban, Thomas, 137
Campbell, John A., 63

Cards, cotton, and wool, 36

Carlton, Mrs., 84

Cary, Constance, 127

Chamberlayne, Parke, 127

Chancellor, Sue, 5–6

Charities, 120

Charleston, 94

Charlottesville General Hospital, 3

Chattanooga, 96

Chesnut, James, 127–28

Chesnut, Mary Boykin: becomes refugee,
    87–88; comments on slave butler, 66;
    diary of, 119; marriage of, 127–28; as
    nurse, 5

Children: impact of war on, 133–34,
    137–38; as industrial workers, 27;
    mortality of, 6

Chimborazo Hospital, 3

Churches: denominations of, 104–5;
    establish relief programs, 103;
    publications of, 105; support Confederate
    war effort, 103–7

Cincinnati Contraband Relief Commission,
    114

Cities and towns: crime in, 98–100; fire in,
    100–101; populations of, 91; as refugee
    centers, 85–91; social ills in, 98–100;
    under Union siege, 41, 100; unique war
    experiences in, 101. *See also individual
    cities*

Civic organizations, 120

Clay, Clement Claiborne, 128–29

Clay, Virginia Tunstall, 128–29

Clayton, Henry D., 131

Clayton, Victoria Hunter, 130–31

Cleburne, Patrick, 74, 80

Cobb, Howell, 75

Colyer, Vincent, 112

Confederate States Laboratory, 27, 28

Conscription, Confederate, 50–52

Core, William, 2

Corn, 21, 22

Cornelius (slave), 67

Cornmeal, 22

Cotton, 20–22

"Cotton diplomacy," 20

Courtship: among slaves, 136–37; among
    whites, 125–27

Creoles, 77–78

Crime, in cities, 98–100

Crisp, W. H., 122

Cumming, Kate, 4, 119

Curry, G. W., 3

Dalton, E. R., 122

Davis, C. A., 105

Davis, Edward, 6

Davis, Jefferson: appeals for less cotton
    production, 21; asks Congress to purchase
    slaves, 74; commissions Sally Tompkins,
    4; confronts rioters, 42; death of son of, 6;
    declares martial law, 58–59; requests
    suspension of habeas corpus, 60; slaves of,
    66–67

Davis, Rebecca, 6

Davis, Varina, 66, 86

Davis Bend Plantation, 70, 114

Dawson, Sarah Morgan, 119

De Leon, David Camden, 80–81

DeLong, Herman, 134

Dentist, 13

Desertion, Confederate, 53–57

Diaries, 119

Dick (slave), 66, 67

Direct Trade and Cotton Spinners
    Convention of Georgia, 25

Disease, causes of, 14, 17. *See also specific
    diseases*

Distillation, of alcoholic beverages, 7

Divorce, 127

Douglass, Frederick, 23

Drugs, 11–13

Drunkenness, 7–9

Eaton, John, 137

Edmondston, Catherine Ann Devereux, 75,
    84, 86, 119

Education: colleges and universities, 110–11;
    female institutions, 111–12; freedmen
    schools, 112–17; supports Confederate

war effort, 107; textbooks for, 109–10; white public and private schools, 107–8

Elder, John A., 123

Elmore, Grace Brown, 106–7, 111–12, 119, 120, 125–26

Emancipation Proclamation, 61, 71–72, 142

Emmerton, James A., 113

Ersatz remedies, 36–40

Evans, Augusta Jane, 118

Family life: among slaves, 134–35; among whites, 132

Farragut, David G., 92–93

Fiction, 118

First North Carolina Hospital, 3

Flour, 22

Floyd, John B., 54

Floyd, Richard F., 57

Foodstuffs, imported, 22

Foote, Henry S., 63, 81

Ford, Sallie Rochester, 119

Foreigners: populations of, 78–79; prejudice against, 80; support Confederacy, 82. *See also specific nationalities*

Forten, Charlotte, 115–17

Forten, Mary Woods, 115

Forten, Robert Bridges, 115

Free blacks: as Confederate soldiers, 77–78; occupations of, 76; populations of, 75–76; restrictions against, 76–77; whites' fear of, 78

Freedmen, 69–70

Freedmen's Bureau, 112

Fremantle, Arthur James Lyon, 89

Fremont, John C., 70–71

Frenkel, Louis, 59–60

Fuller, Anna Long Thomas, 13, 33, 41, 72

Futch, Charley, 53–54

Futch, John, 53–54

Futch, Martha, 53–54

Gambling, 98, 99

Garland, Landon C., 110

Georgia Hospital and Relief Association, 98

Germans, 79, 80, 82

Gibson, Randall L., 78

Girardy, Camille, 25

Glenn, David Chalmers, 59–60

Gorgas, Josiah, 23

Gottschalk, Louis Moreau, 121

Gregg, William, 24

Grimké, Francis, 116–17

Gutheim, James, 105

Habeas corpus, 55, 59, 60

Hampton Roads Conference, 63

Hancock, William M., 59

Harby, Levy Myers, 81

Harmon Brothers, 81

Harris, Isham G., 89

Harrison, Burton, 127

Haynes, Paul Hamilton, 117–18

Hedrick, John A., 14

Hemp, 20

Henry (slave), 67

Henry, John, 27

Heroes of America, 61

Hewitt, John Hill, 122

Higginson, Thomas Wentworth, 71

Hindman, Thomas C., 59

Holden, William W., 62

Holmes, Theophilus, 59

Hooker, Joseph, 5

Hopley, Catherine, 121

Hospitals, 3–4

Howell, Jesse Malachi, 120

Humorists, 119

Hunger, 33–34, 41–43

Hunter, D., 2

Hunter, David S., 71

Hunter, Robert M. T., 63

Impressment, Confederate, 46–47, 73

Industry: cottage, 36; deterrents to, 26; development of, 25; labor strikes in, 27–28; products of, 24–25; revolution in, 23; working conditions in, 26–27

Inflation, 29, 40–41
Irish, 27, 79, 80

Jackson, William, 67
James, Horace, 66, 113
Jews, 46, 80–82
Jim (slave), 67
Johnson, Andrew, 89
Johnson, Benjamin, 135
Johnson, Betty, 135
Johnston, Joseph E., 67
Jones, Delia, 131–32
Jones, Ella, 127
Jones, J., 104
Jones, John Beauchamp, 119
Jones, Lettie, 127

Kate, 9
Keating, James, 113
Keeble, Walter, 122
King, Grace, 134

Lane, James H., 71
Lanier, Sidney, 121
Lazarus, Nathan, 81
Leach, James T., 63
Leary, Mr. and Mrs., 84
Lee, Robert E., 53, 74
Letcher, John, 42, 46
Levy, Lionel, 81
Lincoln, Abraham, 61, 63, 70–71
Literature, 117–19
Lockwood, L. C., 136
Long, James A., 111
Louisiana Exile Relief Committee, 89

Macarthy, Harry, 122
Magee, Warren, 2
Malaria, 11
Mallory, Lee, 123
Mangum, Nancy, 43
Manufacturing. *See* Industry
Manufacturing and Direct Trade Association
    of the Confederate States, 25

Marriage: among slaves, 135–37; among
    whites, 125–27
Martial law, Confederate, 7–8, 58–59, 99
Maury, D. H., 78
Mayo, Joseph, 42
McDaniel, Dr., 9
McDowell, Irvin, 67
Measles, 17
Medical College of South Carolina, 13
Medical College of Virginia, 13
Medicine, 11–13
Memminger, Christopher Gustavus, 80
Memphis, 96–97
Mercer, George Anderson, 126
Milton, John, 57–58
Missionaries, 62, 113
Mobile, 93
Montgomery, Louis M., 123
Moore, M. B., 110
Moore, Samuel Preston, 12, 15
Moore Hospital, 3
Morrow, Robert, 65–66, 113
Morton, Charles, 122
Mother's Home Association, 3
Mumps, 17
Music, 121
Myers, Abraham C., 81

Nashville, 95–96
National Association of Colored Women,
    116
National Freedmen's Relief Association, 113
Nativism, 80
Neblett, Lizzie, 130
New England Freedmen's Aid Society, 113
New Orleans, 92–93
Norfolk, 92
Nurses, 4

Odd Fellows, 120
Ogden, R. D'Orsay, 122

Painting, 123
Palmer, John W., 118

Partington, Mary, 122

Peace and Constitutional Society, Arkansas, 61

Peace movement, 61–63

Pearson, Richmond M., 55, 60

Pearson, Sarah, 113

Pember, Phebe Yates, 119

Pemberton, James, Jr., 67

Pender, Fanny, 129

Pender, William Dorsey, 129

Phelps, John W., 71

Phillips, James Jeter, 127

Physicians, 13–14

Pierce, Mattie, 127

Pitts, Emily, 127

Planters, 21

Planters Convention of the South, 25

Pneumonia, 15

Poetry, 117–18

Polignac, Camille A. J. M., 80

Pollard, Edward A., 82

Poor relief, 43–45

Porcher, Francis Peyre, 12

Pork, 22, 36–37

Porter, Dr., 107

Port Royal Relief Association, 115

Powell, Jennie, 122

Preston, John S., 6

Preston, Margaret, 34

Prostitution, 15–16, 98–99

Quaker Belt, North Carolina, 61

Railroads, 30–31

Ramsdell, Charles W., xii–xiii

Randall, James Ryder, 118

Reed, Lida Lord, 41–42, 134

Refugees: destinations of, 85, 91; living conditions among, 88; numbers of, 83, 85–86; poor among, 84; transportation difficulties of, 85, 90–91

Reid, Joseph, 51

Reilly, Martin, 27

Religion, 103–7

Rheumatism, 17

Rice, 20

Richmond, 42, 91–92

Richmond Typographical Society, 28

Roads, 29

Rountree, Henry, 114

Rutledge, Mrs. Ben, 87–88

Ryan, Abraham Joseph, 118

Salt, 33, 34, 37

Samaritan Society, 120

Savannah, 93

Scarlet fever, 17

Sculpture, 123

Scurvy, 17

Sea Islands, South Carolina, 70, 115

Seward, William H., 63

Sexual relations, 138–39

Sheeran, James B., 104–5

Shelton Laurel Massacre, 57

Sherman, William T., 26, 47

Shoes, 24

Shortages, of food and supplies, 28, 33–36, 40–41

Simms, William Gilmore, 117, 118

Skinner, Mrs., 84

Slade, Richard, 1–2

Slave patrols, 67

Slavery, guilt about, 107

Slaves: considered for Confederate army, 74–75; courtship and marriage among, 135–37; defy owners, 67–68; family life among, 134–35; impressed by Confederates, 73; insurrections by, 67; labor of, essential, 22–23, 65; living conditions among, 137; massacred as Union soldiers, 73; respond to Emancipation Proclamation, 71–72; serve as spies, 67; serve in Union army, 71, 135–36; work in industry, 26

Smallpox, 14–15

Smith, Charles Henry, 119

Smith, Edmund Kirby, 61

Smith, William, 74

Smith, William Russell, 122
Smuggling, by planters, 21–22
Smythe, Charles Winslow, 110
Social activities, 119–21
South Carolina Sea Islands, 70, 115
Southern Telegraphic Association, 28
Speculation, by merchants, 28–29, 45–46, 105
Stanly, John Carruthers, 77
State Educational Association of North Carolina, 108
Stephens, Alexander H., 62, 63
Sterling, Campbell, and Albright, 109
Stone, Sarah Katherine (Kate), 50–51, 67–68, 90–91, 119
Stoneman, George H., 87
Substitution, under conscription, 51
Sugar, 20, 34
Surgery, 13, 17
Swain, David L., 110

Tax-in-kind, 47–48
Taylor, Susie King, 68
Telegraph operators, 28
Ten Percent Plan, 61
Textbook publishing, 109
Textiles, 24–25
Theater, 121–23
Thompson, John Reuben, 118
Ticknor, Francis Orray, 118
Tift, Asa F., 27
Timrod, Henry, 117
Tobacco, 20–21
Tompkins, Sally, 4
Toombs, Robert, 21, 62
Towne, Laura, 116, 117
Transportation, 29–31
Tredegar Iron Works, 23–24, 26
Trent River Settlement, North Carolina, 69
Turner, Elizabeth, 135–36
Turner, Henry M., 135–36
Twenty-Negro Law, 52

Typhoid fever, 15
Typhus, 15

Unionism, in Confederacy, 57–58
U.S. Colored Troops, 71, 73

Vance, Zebulon B.: on court decision regarding desertion, 55; demands distilleries close, 7; in 1864 gubernatorial election, 62; refuses slave impressment, 73–74; urges relief laws, 44
Venereal disease, 15–17
Vernon, Ida, 122, 123
Vice, in cities, 98–100
Vicksburg, 41–42
"Vigilance committees," 58
Volck, Adalbert J., 123

Wailes, Benjamin L. C., 81
Waring, Mary, 121
Warren, Joseph, 115
Washington, William D., 123
Wesley, Charles H., xii–xiii
Wheat, 20, 22
Whiting, William H. C., 73–74
Wiley, Calvin H., 108
Williams, Alpheus, 47
Wilmington, 86, 94–95
Winder, John H., 8, 58–59, 99
Winder Hospital, 3
Winston, George F., 72
Women: and birth control, 130; as government workers, 132; as industrial workers, 26, 27–28; and marriage, 125–26; operate farms and plantations, 131, 132; slave, gain self-reliance, 135; as teachers, 132
Wren, Ella, 122
Wright, Rufus, 135–36
Wyche, Cyril Granville, 13

Yellow fever, 9–10
YMCA, 99, 112, 120
Yulee, David (Levy), 81

About the Author

JOE A. MOBLEY is a former historian and administrator with the North Carolina Office of Archives and History. He currently teaches in the Department of History at North Carolina State University, Raleigh. He is the author of a number of books, articles, and book reviews.

Recent Titles in
Reflections on the Civil War Era

Decision in the Heartland: The Civil War in the West
Steven E. Woodworth

True Sons of the Republic: European Immigrants in the Union Army
Martin W. Öfele